THE CHINESE ECONOMY IN THE EARLY TWENTIETH CENTURY

The Chinese Economy in the Early Twentieth Century

Recent Chinese Studies

Edited by

Tim Wright
Senior Lecturer in Chinese Studies
Murdoch University, Western Australia

St. Martin's Press

First published in Great Britain 1992 by
THE MACMILLAN PRESS LTD
Houndmills, Basingstoke, Hampshire RG21 2XS
and London
Companies and representatives
throughout the world

This book is published in Macmillan's *Studies on the Chinese Economy*
General Editors: Peter Nolan and Dong Fureng

A catalogue record for this book is available
from the British Library

ISBN 0–333–53383–6

Printed in Great Britain by
Billing and Sons Ltd
Worcester

First published in the United States of America 1992 by
Scholarly and Reference Division,
ST. MARTIN'S PRESS, INC.,
175 Fifth Avenue,
New York, N.Y. 10010

ISBN 0–312–07547–2

Library of Congress Cataloging-in-Publication Data
The Chinese economy in the early twentieth century : recent Chinese
studies / edited by Tim Wright.
p.   cm.
Includes index.
ISBN 0–312–07547–2
1. China—Economic conditions—1912–1949.   2. Capitalism—China–
–History—20th century.   I. Wright, Tim.
HC427.8.C4875   1992
330.951'04—dc20
                                                            91–34667
                                                                CIP

Contents

Contents

List of Tables

Acknowledgments

First and foremost I would like to thank all the Chinese historians who gave their time and knowledge to help me understand their field. Their contributions have been invaluable both in the selection of articles to be translated and in giving me ideas for the introduction. In this case more than usual, however, it must be stressed that overall responsibility for the interpretations in my introduction remains with myself: I am sure none of my Chinese colleagues would agree with all I say, and some might agree with very little. Colleagues at Murdoch also provided many useful ideas, especially when I presented the introductory chapter in the form of a seminar; I would like particularly to thank Beverley Hooper and Bruce Campbell. The original translation of the Chinese articles was done by Mr Ci Hongfei (first half of Chapter 13), Ms Ding Yaoxia and myself (Chapter 5), Mr Liu Yingsheng (Chapter 9), Professor Wang Dehua (Chapters 3 and 7), Professor Wang Yintong (Chapters 8, 10 and 11), Professor Wu Shimin (Chapters 2, 6, 12 and the second half of 13) and myself (Chapter 5). I am very grateful to them all. In all cases I have revised the original translation substantially to fit into the overall scheme of the book. Many thanks to Peter Nolan for first suggesting this book to me and to Tim Farmiloe and Tony Grahame for their editorial support. Finally thanks to Cathy Williams for typing the original translations into the word processor.

TIM WRIGHT

Notes on the Contributors

Ci Hongfei works at the Nankai Institute of Economics, Tianjin.

Ding Changqing is a senior member of the Nankai Institute of Economics, Tianjin.

Du Xuncheng is a researcher in the Institute of Economics, Shanghai Academy of Social Sciences.

Liu Foding is Professor and head of the economic history group at the Nankai Institute of Economics.

Ma Bohuang is Research Professor at the Institute of Economics, Shanghai Academy of Social Sciences.

Shen Zuwei is a researcher in the Institute of Economics, Shanghai Academy of Social Sciences.

Wang Yuru works at the Nankai Institute of Economics, Tianjin.

Xiong Xingmei is Professor and head of the Institute of International Economics, Nankai University.

Xu Dingxin is Research Professor at the Institute of Economics, Shanghai Academy of Social Sciences.

Xu Xinwu is Research Professor at the Institute of Economics, Shanghai Academy of Social Sciences.

Tim Wright is Senior Lecturer in Chinese Studies at Murdoch University, Western Australia.

Wu Chengming is Professor in the Institute of Economics, Chinese Academy of Social Sciences, Beijing.

Zhang Zhongli is Research Professor and President of the Shanghai Academy of Social Sciences.

1 Introduction: Modern Chinese Economic History in a Period of Change

Tim Wright

It is over twenty-five years since Albert Feuerwerker wrote his survey of modern Chinese economic history as it is studied in China.[1] For the first fifteen of those years, the only changes from the picture he painted were towards an even more deadening orthodoxy and an almost complete drying-up of publication. Since 1978, however, the writing of modern Chinese economic history has been transformed along with the rest of Chinese society. New concerns and issues have emerged to complement, though not entirely replace, those discussed by Feuerwerker; new methodologies are at least discussed and in general a much broader range of opinions allowed.[2]

The aim of this book is to present to Western readers some of the more important articles exemplifying these trends. In this introduction I analyse and put into context the major changes in economic historiography in China. After briefly outlining the institutional structure of the discipline and examining methodological developments, the bulk of the chapter then analyses major issues raised throughout the 1980s under four headings: capitalism and China's modernisation; agriculture and the traditional economy; foreign economic relations; and the role of the state.

Ever since 1949 the domination of state over society and the weakness, even to the point of non-existence, of civil society has meant that the history of economic historiography, like that of other disciplines, has been the history of the state. This was true from the first, conscious, attempt to establish the discipline on a Marxist basis by appointing Soviet and Chinese experts to train a cadre of historians at People's University in Beijing. It remained so throughout the vicissitudes of the next three decades and, despite all the changes since 1978 (and they have been real ones), the words with which Feuerwerker opened his article remain valid:

It will be evident to a reader of historical works produced in the People's
Republic of China that these writings, in the choice of subject-matter and
in its treatment, are decidedly influenced by the current domestic and
foreign political 'line' of the Communist Party and Government.'[3]

Just as before lessons are being drawn from the past to legitimise current policies, while the tendency identified by Feuerwerker towards an
evaluative approach remains a very important aspect of the new scholarship.

Similar conclusions can be drawn about all areas of academic scholarship
and cultural production in China. In a review of developments in the
social sciences in the early 1980s, Colin Mackerras wrote: 'in practice
contemporary Chinese scholarship remains tightly linked with politics.
It is a political line much broader and more interesting than that which
obtained during the Cultural Revolution, but it is politics none the less.'[4]
Similarly Perry Link, writing about the 'new realist literature', argues that,
despite the relaxation of controls on writers at the end of the 1970s, the
leadership's basic perception of the relationship between literature and
politics had not changed: 'It . . . is clear that social and moral purposes
(and more diffusely, political ones) remain the heart of the matter for the
Party leadership.'[5]

In economic history the domination of the state is manifested in a view
which locates the discipline mainly in the context of current political
needs and debates. This is not merely a matter of the state imposing its
priorities; it also reflects a long-held perception of China's writers and
scholars. In a general way, historians see China's current problems in an
historical context and believe that a correct historical understanding is a
precondition for their solution. Fu Zhufu (1902–85), one of China's most
eminent historians, argued that the central reason for the slow development
of China's industry was the many thousand year-old legacy of feudalism;
the common perception that imperialism was mainly to blame needed to be
corrected. Fu believed that study of these issues 'had a certain significance
in guiding the current reform of China's economic system'.[6] Similarly
one scholar argued that the dominant formulation of China's society as
'semi-colonial semi-feudal' had delayed and hindered the completion of
China's historic anti-feudal task and was the ideological origin of the
continued need even today to struggle against feudal remnants.[7]

More specifically the fundamental thrust of most of the new interpretations has been to support the reforms promoted by the post-Mao
Chinese leadership. Economic historians as well as economists are 'guiding
and legitimising the new development strategy'.[8] Thus Chinese scholars

explicitly use lessons from the past to provide models for contemporary economic managers. As one of the leading Chinese scholars said in his opening address to the Chinese Economic History Association in 1986:

> Economic history is especially important *in providing an historical basis for economic policy-making*, in terms of summing up the historical experience of economic development, distinguishing between right and wrong and seeking the correct road towards modernisation and construction.[9]

In addition, historical analogy is often used as a weapon in Chinese political discourse; the most famous example is, of course, from the 1960s when Wu Han's play about Hai Rui was read as an attack on Mao. The same happens in economic history as well, and ostensibly historical works sometimes have a second level of more immediate meaning; for instance an article on foreign trade in the nineteenth century might be read (and intended) as taking a position on current trade policy. Indeed, as we shall see, the contemporary resonances have made re-interpretation difficult on some issues.

Despite the continuing link between politics and scholarship the post-Mao line has allowed for far more pluralism than at any time since 1949. Scholars have been able to use the slogan 'Seek Truth from Facts' (for all its theoretical inadequacies) as the justification for a more 'objective' analysis of the historical record. The range of acceptable opinions is much wider than it was previously and genuine differences can be aired, for instance in the debate on the 'Central Theme of Modern Chinese Economic History' (Chapter 5), without becoming absolutised in terms of the socialist line versus the capitalist line. Not only have many specific aspects of the orthodoxy as outlined by Feuerwerker been challenged but also it would be much more difficult now to produce such a single summation of Chinese views of their modern economic history.

This pluralism is first and foremost a state-sponsored pluralism. It is the result less of declarations of independence by historians than of a decision by the leadership that the deadening orthodoxy of Maoism was dysfunctional to the system as a whole. State-sponsored pluralism and reform from above have therefore been the predominant theme of political reform in 1980s China.

Having said that, civil society, in this area as in others, is beginning very hesitantly to assert itself. Historians have been much less willing to follow every turn of party policy, and this process is likely to be hastened

rather than impeded by the massive popular disillusionment following 4
June 1989. The vast increase in the number of publications, some at least
semi-private, has reduced the effectiveness of government control, though
a number of the more daring were closed down in the aftermath of June.
The establishment of academic groups such as the Chinese Economic
History Association is another manifestation of civil society beginning
to claim limited autonomy from the state. Although, however, pluralism
is very gradually coming to acquire its own momentum and to transcend
the limits imposed by the state, it is important not to exaggerate the extent
of the process.

A further difference from the 1950s, and more particularly from the
1960s and 1970s, is that the *content* of the line, at least up to June 1989,
has been one with which economic historians are much more comfortable
and which they find much easier to support than they did earlier. The
emphasis on economic growth and a more modern urban society has wide
support among intellectuals, even granting scepticism as to the ability of
the Communist Party to achieve it. Thus the interpretations developed by
economic historians (while not necessarily more 'correct') have at least
been less forced than in the Maoist period.

INSTITUTIONAL STRUCTURE OF ECONOMIC HISTORY IN CHINA

Research into economic history in China is carried out in three types of
institution. First the various branches of the Academy of Social Sciences,
which are full-time research institutions, support the study of modern
economic history mainly in their Institutes of Economics (pre-modern
economic history is mostly the province of the Institutes of History).
Scholars at the Chinese Academy of Social Sciences in Beijing have
mostly concentrated on the nineteenth century, and so are little represented
here. But the work of Wu Chengming gives a focus for the study of
economic history throughout the country, and Wu and his colleagues are
also coordinating the compilation of *The History of Chinese Capitalism*, a
collaborative project by historians across China. Of all tertiary and research
institutions, the Academy is most closely tied in with government policy,
as is indicated by the fact that its senior positions are on the Central
Committee's *nomenklatura* list.[10]

The Shanghai Academy of Social Sciences, which in the late 1980s
was headed by economic historian Zhang Zhongli, has been much more
interested in the twentieth century, as one might expect given the predominance of Shanghai in China's modern economy. They have collected and

published archival materials from many of China's leading companies in the pre-1949 period.

Economic history is also taught widely in universities and colleges throughout China and many important articles are written by university teachers. Among the leading universities for research into economic history are Fudan in Shanghai and Xiamen in Fujian. Most important of all for modern economic history is the Nankai Institute of Economics in Tianjin, which is a full-time research institution. In the 1920s and 1930s the Institute was the leading organ for research into China's economy,[11] and it has continued that work in the post-1949 period. It is now engaged on a project to produce new textbooks on modern Chinese economic history, based not on the old dogmas but on careful quantitative analyses.

Finally, considerable historical research is done in organs of government economic administration, such as the People's Bank and the various administrative bureaux set up to run different industries in major cities. Several leading historians in the Academies served in the bureaux during the socialist transformation of industry in the 1950s. Many of the publications from these sources have concentrated on collections of materials, though this has also been a major focus of the work of academic institutions.

Financial stringency as well as Party control make the institutional structure of economic history fragile. Chinese universities and research institutions, like those of other countries, are suffering from financial cut-backs, while students are less willing to embark on an academic career, especially in economic history. It is difficult to recruit good graduate students in the field, as rewards elsewhere are so much more substantial. Those who are recruited often seek to study abroad.

That structure is also weakened by the compartmentalisation of the field. There is little horizontal cooperation except on major projects such as *The History of Chinese Capitalism*. Thus scholars everywhere are continually reinventing the wheel, and getting their re-invention published: large numbers of articles, sometimes using exactly the same material, make the same point in re-evaluating, for example, industrial management or the 1935 currency reform. Individual archives or library collections are sometimes seen as the property of the senior person in charge of them and too seldom as open to the whole scholarly community, whether Chinese or foreign. (Indeed Chinese scholars have sometimes complained that it is easier for foreigners to get access to these collections.)

Publications, as well as institutions, exhibit diversity. In the 1980s there has been a huge burgeoning in the number of publications. Of the 1392 articles published on modern Chinese economic history between 1949 and 1983 55 per cent were published between 1978 and 1983, and production has continued to grow:[12] by mid 1988 almost 2200 articles and 174 books had been published over the previous ten years.[13] Whereas in the late 1960s and early 1970s academic publication virtually came to a halt and Western scholars could almost work on China on the basis of the American translation series, now the proliferation of publications has exceeded the capacity of the translators and presents major problems of control. No Western, and very few Chinese, libraries can hope to subscribe to more than a limited portion of the periodicals. This situation is alleviated to some extent by the series published by the People's University,[14] which reprints major articles each month on economic history (and on a host of other topics).

The various publications have a clear ranking within China. The most prestigious are those published by the Academy, such as *Studies in Chinese Economic History, Historical Studies*, and *Studies in Modern History*. Just for that reason, however, they tend to be slightly conservative and are seen by younger scholars as being dominated by the '*lao touzi*' (old men). Both the Chinese and the Shanghai Academies, as well as the Nankai Institute, also publish more exploratory periodicals, which in theory are '*neibu*' (not for general circulation and especially not for sale to foreigners), though in practice it is quite easy to see these materials while in China, and some find their way abroad. A few other specialised journals, notably *Studies in Chinese Social and Economic History* (published in Xiamen), carry a lot of material on modern economic history. Beyond that, many articles are carried in the social science editions of the journals published by nearly every university and college in China. These sometimes put forward new views though they are obviously of very varying quality.

The publication of books still largely comprises collections of materials, of which a large number have been published which are central to the research of both Chinese and Western scholars, and general surveys with titles such as *Modern Economic History of China*. Monographs based on scholarly research are still not plentiful, though their number is increasing. One by-product of the economic reforms, however, is making publication much more difficult. The ending of state subsidies for publishing houses has forced them to pay their own way and, in China as elsewhere, academic books are not very profitable. Publishers are therefore often demanding subsidies before they will publish academic books. A leading Shanghai historian, responsible for editing a series on the city's industries, told me in 1988 that his book on silk (an industry of the first importance) had been ready for over two years but had not yet been published in the absence of a subsidy from an industrial company.

METHODOLOGY

The process of the disintegration of Marxism in China has gone less far in economic history than in economics. Whereas the latter is moving rapidly in the direction of Western-style positivist economics and away from political economy, with its stress on class relations and ownership,[15] most published works on modern economic history, including the articles translated here, remain within the broad framework of Marxism, thus dealing in part with concepts and questions unfamiliar to Western economic historians. Nevertheless, the editors of *Studies in Chinese Economic History* felt it necessary in 1990 to reaffirm the guiding role of Marxism in their field.[16]

Marxism is, however, defined in a different way from in the Maoist period: Wu Chengming characterises it not as a dogma but as a method, that of historical materialism, the basis of which comes down to three propositions,[17] each of which could be distinguished quite sharply from the orthodoxy under Mao. First, each sphere of society – culture, politics, economics – is relatively independent and requires separate study to discover its particular laws of motion. Second, the situation must be seen as a whole and economic history needs to take account of culture and politics; the Stalinist mechanistic definition of the relationship between base and superstructure is discarded in favour of a dialectical relationship whereby, although 'in the last instance' the economy decides, that is not necessarily so for any particular case or time. Third, the relationship between the forces and relations of production is also dialectical, while production and distribution each has its own rules of development.

As in the Maoist period, most Chinese historians still characterise the pre-1949 Chinese social formation as 'semi-colonial semi-feudal'. (This does not mean that half Chinese society was colonial, the other half feudal but that China was a society which was partly colonised and undergoing a transition from a feudal to a capitalist society.) Although few scholars discard it totally, the concept has increasingly come under challenge. In one of the most cogent critiques, a Guangdong scholar points out that it is a mixture of economic (semi-feudal) and political (semi-colonial) criteria, and encompasses two processes which are not logically or even temporally connected. How far, if at all, the two aspects were linked is a key point of difference between those questioning and those defending the traditional concept. This issue has very broad ramifications: one leading critic argues that the concept was used one-sidedly to elevate the peasants and the peasant movement and deny or devalue the historical role of the bourgeoisie; likewise it stressed violent revolution and opposed compromise or reform of any kind.[18] In the view of many critics, China's pre-war society essentially belonged to the category of capitalism, albeit of deformed or underdeveloped capitalism.[19]

One problem bedevilling the use of these concepts has been the vagueness of the term 'feudalism'. Wu Chengming has developed an alternative designation for 'semi-feudalism' in the idea of 'modern feudalism', the central characteristic of which was a high level of commercialisation, including foreign trade. Landlords were mostly of a new type, being deeply involved in other activities, especially commerce. This social formation, which existed in many other Third World countries, was much more flexible than 'ancient' feudalism and was not necessarily doomed to extinction, were it not for the revolution and land reform.[20]

Although Marxist concepts of social formation remain as the framework for research, economic history has not been immune from the same forces that have affected economics. With the switch from 'politics in command' to 'economics in command', economic historians have declared independence and are now increasingly putting economic construction and the more general process of modernisation in the forefront, whereas previously periodisation and framework were determined by Party-dominated political history.

One of the key specific changes in economics,[21] a switch in attention from the relations to the forces of production, has been parallelled in economic history. Historians now criticise earlier work as almost exclusively concerned with the relations of production and with class struggle.[22] The new emphasis gives more space to the development of the forces of production, that is to statistical measures and causes of the growth of output and of technical progress. Nevertheless, this change is far from universal and a recent textbook states clearly that 'the object of investigation of the economic history of a country is its relations of production'.[23] Even Wu Chengming criticises Western historians for their almost exclusive emphasis on the forces, while neglecting the relations, of production.

Wu also reviews methodological trends in the West, finding on the whole that they have limited relevance for China. In the case of the quantitative revolution and the new economic history, he argues that counterfactual methods have had poor results, in that hypothesis is different from history, while the limited availability of data will mean that only simple statistical tools such as regression analysis are likely to be useful.[24] Moreover, these methods are applicable only to quantitative not to qualitative change and thus cannot help the study of the relations of production.

Nevertheless, increased quantification is likely to be a growing and healthy trend in Chinese economic history. A number of articles have evaluated the quantitative data for pre-modern economic history[25] and, in the modern field, more attention to aggregate statistics will reduce the tendency to argue by (often tendentious) example. In this collection the articles on economic development by Wu Chengming and Wang Yuru (Chapters 2 and 4) and those on agriculture by Xu Xinwu and Ding Changqing (Chapters 8 and 9) all produce quantitative macroeconomic estimates through which they question many of the old assumptions about the failure of the Chinese economy.

Overall, however, few new statistical series have been produced since the pioneering work edited by Yan Zhongping in the 1950s,[26] which remains a key resource, though it is surely time to revise many of the series and to add new data and estimates. While the obstacles to such a project, in the form of lack of source materials, are daunting, Chinese scholars, with access to archival materials, have a comparative advantage in this area, and the Nankai Institute of Economics plans to embark on this massive task.

The predominant attitude remains cautious, however, and leading Academy historian Peng Zeyi argues that one needs a very firm base in hard data before embarking on the task of estimation and that 'reasonable hypotheses' are not enough.[27] In contrast, Wu Chengming calls for the use of statistical tools to develop quantitative measures even where they appear impossible; he also urges Chinese scholars to take up the work of their Western colleagues and estimate growth rates for industry and even agriculture.[28] This attitude has led to criticism that his work is 'not economic history'.

At the same time, many scholars put too much trust in the figures they do find in the sources. For example, a good survey of Republican China's population attempts to develop estimates for benchmark years on the basis of existing data but points out their inconsistency with the 1953 census results, which are clearly more reliable than the Republican figures; having said that, however, the author does not go on to suggest new figures but discusses a series of growth rates calculated from the ones he has just rejected.[29]

In the West, the quantitative revolution has not focused solely, or even mainly, on the compilation of statistical data but rather on the application of statistical and econometric methods to test hypotheses suggested by economic theory. At least in published work, Chinese scholars have moved very little in that direction and none of the articles in this collection apply statistical tests to their data. The increasing amount of work on the economic history of the People's Republic is, however, different in this regard, with much more use of econometric and theoretical models.[30]

KEY ISSUES

The focus of this introduction is narrower than Feuerwerker's survey.
Feuerwerker concentrated heavily on the nature of late traditional Chinese
society and 'the sprouts of capitalism'. While these issues were still of concern in the 1980s,[31] the demands of economic reform and state-sponsored
pluralism have suggested a somewhat different agenda, as reflected in this
collection.

In the 1980s the development of Chinese capitalism and its relationship
to the long process of the country's modernisation has become the central
concern of historians. This is illustrated in a recent controversy in *Studies
in Chinese Economic History* over the central theme of modern Chinese
economic history. In the Maoist period, political orthodoxy held that the
central theme was class struggle, and a recent textbook puts forward the
people's struggle against feudalism and imperialism and to establish a
people's economy as one aspect.[32] An important article in 1984 suggested
a twofold theme: the processes of China moving from independence to
being a semi-colony and from being a feudal society to a semi-feudal one.
In 1989, however, Wang Jingyu, a leading Academy scholar in Beijing,
argued that this latter formulation, while representing a great advance,
set up an unrealistic dichotomy between the two processes; in fact the
impact of foreign capitalism underlay both, and the central theme was
the 'development and non-development of Chinese capitalism'.[33] From
the point of view of the long-term abstract processes analysed by Marx,
development was central but, in terms of the concrete conditions of Chinese
history, non-development bequeathed an even more crucial inheritance to
today's socialist society.

Later that year the same journal published a series of responses by
leading historians,[34] two of which are translated below as Chapter 5. In
those responses a clear dichotomy emerged. Some agreed with Wang that
'non-development', China's failure to develop into a modern industrial
nation, must be given equal or greater prominence. One scholar, for
example, saw the key problem for the Chinese revolution as being the
low level of development of capitalism and the main task of historians
to explain China's economic backwardness (which he strongly differen-
tiated from 'stagnation'). Others have supported the discarding of the
old stagnation paradigm but feel that the pendulum had gone too far
the other way. Why, if China's development was so smooth, have the
problems since 1949 been so great and why is China still such a poor
country?

The opposing view made a clear link between capitalism and early modernisation (*jindaihua*), the forerunner of current socialist modernisation (*xiandaihua*); one author called for the study of the whole course of modernisation from the 1840s to the present as a single process of economic construction. On the basis that the fundamental trend in China over the past century and a half has been towards modernisation, they hold that, for all the difficulties, the central theme was the slow development of capitalism; the idea of 'non-development' is merely a version of the discredited 'stagnation' theory.

This close link between the debate over 'development and non-development' and a general evaluation of the success or failure of China's pre-war socio-economic system was made explicit in Wang Jingyu's response to the debate, where he clearly favours a mainly negative view. The basis of his judgement is political: *economic* development certainly took place but to limit oneself to economics is not enough – one must also take note of the broader political sphere.[35]

More specific demands of the reform programme have prompted re-evaluations on some issues. The increasing use of market or even capitalist methods of economic management has involved a reconsideration of the nature of the pre-liberation capitalist economy. The 'Open Door' policies have also focused attention on the benefits of foreign economic relations and led to a re-evaluation of the foreign role in China's pre-war economy. At the same time, the search for causes of China's immense political and economic problems since 1949 has made it more difficult to attribute all of China's pre-1949 troubles to the foreign impact and has directed attention back to the 'feudal' aspects of Chinese society.

In addition, incipient pluralism has allowed scholars and writers to penetrate 'forbidden zones', such as the Republican, and especially the Nationalist, period. Serious academic attention began to be paid to the Nationalist period only from the mid to late 1980s, at first unofficially among historians, later with official government approval.

Capitalism and China's Modernisation

Reflecting the importance of the Four Modernisations, historians have also focused on modernisation. In the West, of course, modernisation theory, while by no means dead, has been criticised both by radical scholars of the imperialism school and by the new 'China-centred' historians.[36] Although Chinese historians reject some of the theory's questionable assumptions, for instance that of an unchanging traditional society,[37] interest has revived in the key indicators of China's modernisation. Such a focus also directs attention away from the failures which previously dominated discussion:

Wu Chengming explicitly contrasts the 'stagnation theory' with modern-isation theory.[38]

In a debate over the meaning of modernisation,[39] some scholars stressed economic aspects such as industrialisation, the formation of market sys-tems, technical progress, economic growth and urbanisation. Others argued that in addition political democratisation and new value systems form an integral part of the process.[40] Clearly, the latter view had a direct political connotation in the debates over political reform between 1986 and 1989.

Another debate has focused on the relative contributions of internal and external factors to the initial impetus to modernisation and to the process itself. In the early 1980s in particular there was a revival of interest in the 'sprouts of capitalism' in late Imperial China.[41] Some scholars argue that China was beginning to modernise under its own dynamics and would have developed a capitalist society even without the impact of the West. Others more cautiously stress the continuities between the 'sprouts' period and modern industrialisation and the degree to which industrial enterprises were based on pre-modern handicraft workshops.

Many scholars, however, stress the primacy of the Western impact. Ding Richu argues, as does Liu Foding in Chapter 10, that, for all the capitalist sprouts, China was far from any industrial revolution. In the actual process of historical development the West provided the starting point for modernisation and it is merely an 'untestable' hypothesis to say that China could have modernised on its own.[42] Others point out that any continuities between handicraft workshops and modern industry were incidental and that equipment, markets and techniques for the new enterprises were all fundamentally dependent on the West or on the changes induced by the West.[43]

Interest continues, however, in the specifically Chinese features of mod-ernisation. Wu Chengming identifies a 'Chinese road to industrialisation', manifested mainly in the private sector. Capitalists, consciously or unconsciously following the laws of economics, developed economic forms and mixes of techniques that made best use of China's factor endowments, for instance by mixing handicraft and mechanical methods.[44] Shen Zuwei also identifies organisational patterns from traditional China which were relevant not only to China's early twentieth century modernisation but also to the 1990s.[45]

The issue of modernisation is thus closely linked to that of the devel-opment of Chinese capitalism; Wu Chengming has argued that the central facet of China's modernisation was the emergence of a new mode of production (in our period, at least, capitalism). Although Western historians are also interested in the emergence of capitalism and particularly capitalist industry, the centrality of the concept of mode of production for Chinese historians means that they have given it even greater prominence and treat it in a rather different way.

The link with modernisation has focused attention on the success or otherwise of Chinese capitalism before 1937. The previous view was that, after a short spurt of growth in the 1910s, which resulted from the temporary absence of European imperialism, the 1920s and even more the 1930s were characterised by crisis, stagnation and eventually bankruptcy. This was caused both by external factors including Japanese aggression, foreign competition and the impact of the world depression, and by internal factors such as the civil wars, the domination of feudalism in the rural areas and the shortcomings and weakness of capitalism and capitalist management. The bankruptcy of the pre-Communist economy both justified the revolution and put the successes after 1949 in an even more favourable light.

In contrast, many scholars now justifiably point out that, given the long gestation of capitalism in Europe, it is unreasonable to expect Chinese capitalism to emerge fully-fledged in a short period and that in fact the Chinese bourgeoisie had major achievements to its credit. Thus the statistical record of the modern sector up to 1936 shows substantial growth, both of total output and of the Chinese-owned sector. For instance, an important article pointed out that Chinese capital achieved profit levels at least as high as those in the capitalist world and used these as the basis for capital accumulation, even if those profits came from exploitation of the workers and unequal exchange with the rural population.[46]

In this collection, Wu Chengming's authoritative summary written in the early 1980s (Chapter 2) argues that previous views of crisis in the 1920s and 1930s were too pessimistic and that there was merely a market crisis limited to rural areas. In Chapter 3 Zhang Zhongli focuses on the 1920s and also advocates discarding the old orthodoxy of 'crisis', pointing out the many achievements of Chinese capitalism. Finally, a young researcher at the Nankai Institute of Economics, Wang Yuru, puts forward in Chapter 4 a comprehensive series of estimates of economic growth and change between the 1910s and the late 1940s. Although not all Chinese scholars accept the details of Wang's findings, the overall more positive re-evaluation of pre-war economic growth is unlikely to be rejected.

Nevertheless, the record is ambiguous and many studies of individual industries still emphasise the failures even of the modern sector in the 1920s and 1930s. Of course the histories of individual industries differed. Silk was the most obvious case of decline,[47] while 'the period 1922–36 was one when [the flour industry] developed only slowly and fell into difficulties, which became increasingly serious from the early 1930s'.[48] On the other hand, the paper industry succeeded in maintaining its position even in the 1930s.[49]

The previous negative judgement of the fate of Chinese capitalism was partly based on a particular view of the structure of capitalism and the bourgeoisie which excluded any elements linked either to the foreign presence or to the state. China's capitalist sector appears much stronger and larger if one defines it as also encompassing state enterprises and, even more so, foreign enterprises in China. Thus the threefold division of the bourgeoisie into national (private capitalists, the only *real* bourgeoisie), comprador and bureaucratic bourgeoisies has been a troublesome inheritance. At least two major conferences have been held during the 1980s on the bourgeoisie, with the relationship between the national bourgeoisie and the other two groups being the key focus of debate.

The most troublesome concept has been 'bureaucratic capitalism', which received its definitive treatment in Mao's 'The Present Situation and Our Tasks':

> This monopoly capitalism [i.e. that of the Four Great Families], closely tied up with foreign imperialism, the domestic landlord class and the old-type rich peasants, has become comprador, feudal, state-monopoly capitalism. . . . This state-monopoly capitalism oppresses not only the workers and peasants but also the urban petty bourgeoisie, and it injures the middle bourgeoisie. . . . This capital is popularly known in China as bureaucrat-capital. This capitalist class, known as the bureaucrat-capitalist class, is the big bourgeoisie of China.[50]

While Mao's main focus was on the Nationalists in the 1940s, most scholars, even while recognising the problems, extended the use of the concept back to the Self-strengthening Movement of the late nineteenth century and to the warlord period in the early twentieth.

In the 1980s, however, historians have argued that Mao's formulation was merely a political or popular concept, not a rigorous academic or theoretical one, and so does not necessarily have to be adopted in academic writing.[51] Many prefer the term 'state capitalism', used in a more restricted sense of direct state investment, excluding private investment by government officials, which had earlier been an important component of 'bureaucratic capitalism'. State capitalism encompassed the official enterprises of the late Qing and organs such as the National Resources Commission under the Nationalists but not on the whole the intervening warlord period when the state's ability to intervene in the economy was much weaker; within the Nationalist period some also distinguish state investments from the financial empires of the Four Great Families.

This re-interpretation, like others, is far from universally accepted and some scholars still uphold the usefulness of a category of bureaucratic capitalism encompassing investment both by the state and by bureaucrats. An article on the warlords in North-east China denies that there was only a quantitative difference between national capital and the warlords' investments, pointing to the considerable benefits the latter gained in terms of tax rates and transport, which enabled them to take over private enterprises.[52]

As for the comprador bourgeoisie, the issue has been whether their relationship to the national bourgeoisie was an antagonistic or a more organic one. Instead of stressing that compradors served foreign interests in plundering China and oppressing national industry, historians now point out that large portions of comprador profits were invested in modern industry and that the compradors were a, perhaps even the, major component of China's bourgeoisie in the late nineteenth century.[53]

Ma Bohuang's article (Chapter 6) examines the career of one of China's most important comprador capitalists, Liu Hongsheng. It uses archival materials to show how Liu's wealth originated in his role as an agent for a foreign company but how he later reinvested much of his fortune in industrial enterprises.

China's national capitalists, instead of being derided for being backward, are now seen as innovators, for instance in introducing new methods of management and creatively developing the country's own management tradition.[54] Representing this trend, Chapter 7 of this collection, by Xu Dingxin, identifies a number of attributes of pre-war capitalist management (the virtues of competition, the necessity for professional expertise, sales consciousness, careful planning and economising) which the 1980s leadership wished to instill in the current managers of economic enterprises. Chapters 3 and 6 also use Shanghai material to contribute to this debate.

Overall, the pre-war bourgeoisie is now evaluated much more positively, as having bestowed a useful legacy to post-revolutionary China. Such a judgement is of course sensitive politically and, in the context of the 1987 campaign against bourgeois liberalisation, one Shanghai historian wrote an article entitled, 'The way of capitalism is a dead end', arguing that for China independent capitalist development was never a possibility.[55] He concludes, as do most of the articles in this collection, that the socialist revolution was a necessary and inevitable stage in China's modernisation.

The re-evaluation is also important academically and the new interpretation is much closer to current perceptions in the West. Marie-Claire Bergére, for example, has rejected any strict dichotomy between comprador and

national bourgeoisie,[56] and Sherman Cochran among others has shown
the innovativeness and flexibility of Chinese capitalist management.[57]
Particularly in the latter case, however, there must be some question
as to how far Chinese scholarship has developed a balanced picture of
the strengths and weaknesses and the modern and traditional aspects of
pre-war practices.

Agriculture and the Traditional Economy

The state's neglect of agricultural investment since 1949 is paralleled by
the under-representation of agriculture in Chinese scholarship on their
modern economic history. Only 4 per cent of books and 3 per cent of
articles published between 1949 and 1983 dealt with a sector which had
been accounting for substantially more than half of national income.[58]
The reasons for this are various. The immense diversity and complexity
of China's agriculture certainly discourage study, as does the fragmen-
tary nature of the source materials. Other factors are, however, also at
work. One could see this phenomenon, as well as the broader neglect of
agricultural investment, in terms of 'urban bias', with urban intellectuals
having little concern for the fate of the peasants either now or in history.
Beyond this, more immediate political considerations make re-evaluation
of agriculture difficult. The origins and legitimacy of the revolution are
inextricably tied up with the agricultural sector and one survey of the 'land
question' during the 1920s and 1930s was explicitly aimed at showing 'why
only the Communist Party was able to lead the people in solving the land
question'.[59]

Thus the predominant view of the agricultural sector in the early
twentieth century is still one of crisis whereas, as we have seen, that
perception is being discarded for the industry. One article argued that
the century-long chronic crisis was becoming more acute in the 1930s, as
manifested in increasing concentration of land, natural disasters, a decline
in the cultivated area, a fall in agricultural prices, a shortage of rural finance
and a decline in living standards.[60] Many Western scholars would agree
with this picture,[61] but others are challenging it, with Thomas Rawski
providing the most bullish estimates of the success of the agricultural
sector in not only maintaining but actually raising per capita consumption
in the early twentieth century.[62]

Any similar re-evaluation would be very difficult in China; one scholar
attempted to persuade me that Rawski's picture *could not* be correct
because in that case the revolution would not have succeeded. Nevertheless,
Wu Chengming has reviewed the relationship between population, sown

acreage and agricultural production for the whole country, concluding that it is unlikely that per capita output began to decline as early as the mid nineteenth century, though on his figures it did drop steeply in the 1930s.[63] An article on Nationalist policy also produces evidence of growth in the agricultural sector during the Nanjing decade.[64]

Central to agricultural policy and reform since 1978 has been the encouragement of markets and commercialisation in the rural areas. This is reflected in a concentration by historians on twentieth-century trends towards commercialisation and capitalism in agriculture: thus Wu Chengming argued that commercialisation was central to 'modern feudalism'. The degree to which capitalism penetrated agriculture has long been controversial. In the 1930s the Trotskyists argued that Chinese agriculture was basically capitalist and therefore that the tasks of the revolution were fully socialist; the orthodox line held, on the other hand, that China's rural economy was still basically feudal and thus the tasks of the revolution were bourgeois national and anti-feudal.

These key issues on China's rural economy are addressed in Chapters 8 and 9 of this collection. In Chapter 8 Xu Xinwu examines the complex process whereby and the degree to which the old self-sufficient natural economy disintegrated and was replaced by a commodity (commercialised) economy, particularly in terms of a limited increase in the proportion of grain marketed and the gradual replacement of peasant cotton textile production with modern factory production.

The extent of such changes is still controversial. Western scholars such as Rawski and Loren Brandt argue that widespread commercialisation increased the incomes of hundreds of millions of peasants,[65] and among Chinese scholars both Wu Chengming's idea of modern feudalism and the view that commercialisation was a key aspect of the landlord variant of the feudal economy stress the centrality of commerce in China's traditional economy.[66] Other Chinese scholars maintain the link between the feudal economy and the natural economy and stress the degree to which the natural economy survived up to 1949. In their view this phenomenon, not landlord-tenant relations, was the main aspect of feudalism in pre-Liberation China, and the failure to recognise this led to the erroneous agricultural policies of the 1950s.[67]

Chapter 9, by Ding Changqing, examines the degree to which specifically capitalist relations of production emerged. The main capitalist elements were: managerial landlords (who organised the working of their land with hired labour rather than renting it out to tenants); rich peasants, to the extent that they used hired labour; and modern agricultural reclamation companies. Ding concludes that capitalist relations were still very much the

exception in rural China before 1949 but other scholars take an even more
cautious viewpoint. Wang Jingyu argues that none of the three elements
really qualified as capitalist. Reclamation companies still mostly just rented
out land to tenants, while the labour employed by managerial landlords and
rich peasants often lacked the prerequisites of free labour in a capitalist
sense.[68] Similarly an article on hired labour in agriculture defined it as
essentially feudal, involving personal dependence on the employer.[69]

Handicrafts were the other branch of the traditional economy, which was
said to survive on the basis of males practising agriculture and females
spinning. Previous Chinese scholars stressed that foreign trade and later
the rise of modern Chinese industry undermined the traditional handicraft
industries and thus pushed China towards rural crisis. Western scholars,
such as Albert Feuerwerker,[70] have long questioned this picture, which is
now also being rejected in China. Wu Chengming shows that out of thirty
major handicraft industries only eight declined after the opening of the
Treaty ports; twenty-two maintained their level or better, while eighteen
new industries emerged.[71] Although cotton spinning, the largest handicraft
industry, did decline, this is hardly a picture of widespread rural destitution.
Several Shanghai historians have also argued that the self-sufficient natural
economy maintained its strength remarkably well right up to 1949 and even
beyond; those elements of the handicraft industries which were undermined
by foreign trade were those which were already commercialised, while
subsistence production in peasant households maintained its strength.[72]

Foreign Economic Relations

The impact of imperialism has always been seen in China as a two-edged
sword: it put into motion the process of decay of the traditional feudal system but on the other hand (more importantly) it gravely impaired Chinese
sovereignty and prevented a smooth development towards capitalism.[73]
Thus Wang Jingyu argues that 'the existence of foreign capitalist imperialism in China was an important link in the factors hindering the development
of Chinese capitalism'.[74] The whole issue is, of course, very controversial
in both China and the West and is ridden with methodological problems.

Two central issues are addressed by Liu Foding in Chapter 10 of this
book. Liu examines the counterfactual question as to whether China could
have developed industrial capitalism in abstraction from the impact of
the West and the issue of whether, as the dependency theorists in the
West aver, imperialism in underdeveloped countries actually hindered
modernisation through supporting pre-capitalist modes of production. His
negative answers to both these questions challenge Chinese orthodoxy.

Up to the late 1970s studies of imperialism almost always stressed the damage it did to China's economy and society. In the 1980s, however, while imperialism's two-edged nature was still recognised, current policy encouraging opening to the outside world prompted a re-evaluation of China's previous external economic relations.[75] Scholars pointed out, often indirectly, the damage done to China's development throughout the Maoist period by an excessively negative evaluation of foreign economic contacts. The shift in tone is illustrated by a change in the title of the relevant section in the annual bibliography published by *Materials on the Study of Modern Chinese Economic History*, from 'The Imperialist Economic Invasion of China' in 1985 to 'Sino-Foreign Economic Relations' in 1986. Nevertheless a wide divergence remains among Chinese scholars (as among Western) over this issue.

Some scholars argue that it was practically impossible for China to benefit from foreign economic relations when its independence had been compromised. Full independence, sovereignty and equality are necessary preconditions for mutual benefit. A number of examples are given, such as the fact that the Soviet Union was able to benefit from conditions during the world depression while China, which lacked independence, was not, and the notorious case of the Hanyeping Company, which eventually fell under Japanese control. This position seems to me, however, to be illogical and it is never really supported by cogent theoretical arguments. The benefits were no doubt divided unequally and in individual cases (most obviously the opium trade and the indemnities imposed on China in 1895 and 1900) did not exist but there is little reason to suppose that it is necessarily impossible for both sides to benefit. After all the wage contract, while a bargain made on the basis of inequality, can still benefit both sides.

Another group of leading scholars such as Zhang Zhongli and Ding Richu at the Shanghai Academy of Social Sciences argue that, given the unequal treaties, it was still better for China to open to the world than to continue to close its doors.[76] Although to some extent foreign capital in China competed with national capital, it also acted as a stimulus to modernisation, for instance through creating the Chinese working class and through the linkages flowing from modern foreign shipping on the Changjiang (Yangtze). Again the implications for current policy debates need hardly be mentioned.

Chapter 11 of this book, by Ding Richu and Shen Zuwei, gives a positive evaluation of the role of foreign trade in promoting capitalism in China and raising incomes in urban and rural areas. Profits made by Chinese merchants in foreign trade were an important basis for the growth of industry, which developed along the lines of import-substitution. Foreign trade was also the medium for technology transfer and the import of new productive equipment and consumer goods.

Similar points are made about Sino-American trade (which was on a more equal basis than trade with Britain or Japan) by Zhang Zhongli, who in addition identifies a number of benefits which would be familiar to Western students of economics.[77] Thus China gained from the application of comparative advantage, with Sino-American trade following a more-or-less rational pattern of the exchange of semi-processed agricultural products for American machinery and finished products. (Of course the same pattern could also be characterised as a typical example of core-periphery trade in a world systems framework.) China was also able to engage in 'export substitution', that is in building up industries to increase its share of the value of exports – selling reeled silk instead of silk cocoons, vegetable oil instead of seeds.

Foreign investment is also being re-evaluated. While references are still made to 'foreign economic invasion', the positive aspects are also mentioned. An article on Sino-foreign joint enterprises argues 'in the main their role in the modern Chinese economy was of benefit to the investing countries but of no benefit to China'. But they also played some positive role, for instance in expanding capitalist relations, with the compradors becoming an important component of the Chinese bourgeoisie. Moreover foreign investment alleviated to some extent China's shortage of capital and was therefore favoured by many leaders. Joint enterprises also played a part in the modernisation of society, introduced modern technology and trained workers in modern techniques.[78]

Xiong Xingmei, in Chapter 12 of this collection, uses the extensive archives of the Kailuan Mining Administration to provide a more concrete and nuanced picture of one of the most important foreign companies in China than was possible under the Maoist orthodoxy. His central theme is the relationship between the British claims to ownership of the Kailuan mining rights and the management control they enjoyed over the mines.

Foreign trade and investment remains a difficult area to reassess, perhaps because it touches not only on the socialist but also on the nationalist aspect of the Chinese revolution. A leading Shanghai historian, in a memoir of Chinese economic history, suggests that one would be in danger of being denounced as 'too absurd, too bourgeois' if, while admitting that the basic function of the foreign concessions was as a tool of foreign colonisation, one still pointed to their objective role in promoting modernisation. He attributes this to the emotional difficulty of accepting such a position, but concludes that 'in the end emotion cannot replace science': recognition of the positive contribution of the concessions does not obliterate their reactionary and evil aspects, nor should it obscure the distinction between modernisation and independence.[79]

For these reasons, as well as because the issues are difficult and the record can be read either way, many scholars remain unconvinced by the revisionist position. In a study of the silk industry, a Beijing Academy scholar writes of the industry's failures that 'one must stress especially that the control and monopoly exercised by foreign companies over the channels of foreign trade devastated the Chinese silk trade'.[80]

Another recent article criticises the position, put forward in authoritative publications,[81] that foreign capitalism was a component part of Chinese capitalism. In contrast to Liu Foding's article it argues along the lines of dependency theory that foreign capitalism in fact strengthened the feudal aspects of China's economy and society: it forced an increase in the rate of feudal exploitation, for instance by trading in opium and imposing large indemnities; it also helped the feudal authorities through offering government loans. At the same time it destroyed the sprouts of capitalism which might have provided the basis for an independent Chinese road to capitalism. Even productive enterprises were often little more than organs of political invasion; the Japanese-owned South Manchurian Railway Company (this article was written by two scholars from North-east China) was an important example. Thus the overall role of foreign capital was primarily negative and it should not be counted as part of Chinese capitalism.[82]

The Role of the State

The role of the pre-Communist Chinese state has not escaped re-evaluation. Previously the Qing state and to a lesser extent the warlords were seen mainly as feudal and the Nationalist state as bureaucratic capitalist. Now, however, all three are said to have provided essential, though not sufficient, preconditions for China's modernisation.

Ever since 1949 the nineteenth-century Self-strengthening enterprises have been a major focus of discussion and that continues to be the case today, though these enterprises lie outside the period covered by this book. There have been at least five conferences held on the subject since 1980 and the general trend appears to be towards attributing stronger rather than weaker capitalist elements to them.

More important in terms of this book, however, is the new analysis of the economic policies of the Nationalists. One article stresses the extent to which even these direct opponents of the Communists pursued, at least up to 1931, policies which accorded with capitalist interests, for instance in the suppression of the working class, a degree of tax reform and tariff protection, and financial reorganisation; after 1931, however, the economy collapsed and the capitalists became increasingly estranged from the government.[83]

Even post-1931 policy is being re-examined. Scholars have focussed especially on three issues. First, tariff autonomy was previously regarded as an almost complete sham, with foreign control continuing over all major aspects of customs policy and administration. Now such an interpretation is dismissed as not being in accord with historical facts. In the late 1920s and early 1930s China gained real, though limited, autonomy to set levels of tariffs which might protect industry or (more often) maximise revenue, to benefit from the customs revenues, which became the mainstay of Nationalist finances, and also to control the actual operation of the customs service by placing Chinese staff in senior positions.[84]

Second, the currency reform of 1935 has come under the spotlight.[85] Chapter 13, by young Nankai scholar Ci Hongfei, concentrates on this issue. First, Ci argues that China's hyper-inflation was not an inevitable result of the reform, both because inflation had been endemic earlier and because total money supply actually fell following the reform. The later inflation was due to the specific conditions of the war. Second, he rejects the view that the reform created a basis for bureaucratic capitalism, arguing that a state-managed currency and some control over the banking system was a common feature of economic development.

Previously the post-1935 managed currency system had also been denounced as having a completely colonial nature because the currency was tied to the British pound. Now a more balanced view sees it as a sensible response to international conditions prevailing at the time, especially the American silver policy. Finally, the link between the reform and China's ability to prosecute the war with Japan is made: the only way to finance resistance was through inflation, otherwise China's war effort would have collapsed.

Third, the Nationalists' policies of economic construction are being re-examined, with archival research providing new information on, for example, the National Resources Commission.[86] Another article on the quantitative record for the 1930s concludes that, despite the problems of Japanese aggression and the world depression, the Chinese economy did register growth during those years in agriculture, industry and communications.[87]

The debate on the role of the state is yet again a delicate one, for a number of reasons. Of course the failure of the Nationalists is a major plank of the Communist Party's legitimacy; in discussing bureaucratic capital in the 1930s, one article argues, if one makes a positive evaluation of Nationalist policy:

> There would then be no way to explain why the Chinese people demanded the overthrow of and eventually overthrew the reactionary Nationalist rulers or why the confiscation of bureaucratic capital and the protection of national industry and commerce was at the time one of the three main economic programmes of the New Democratic Revolution.[88]

Other articles on the Nationalists also point out, with some justification, that any achievements (including those in the war against Japan) were limited to the 1930s and that by the 1940s they degenerated into a force with no positive role to play.

Beyond that, however, there is a more direct contemporary relevance. In a general way economic development has been mainly state-directed since 1949 and discussions on the costs and benefits of state intervention reflect this. More specifically the tremendous increase in the visibility of corruption in the 1980s and its importance as a political issue, particularly in relation to the activities of the families of senior government officials, make very uncomfortable parallels with the 'bureaucratic capitalism' of the Nationalists. Indeed some people in China believe (with a degree of violence to historical reality) that the situation in the 1980s was worse than that under Jiang Jieshi (Chiang Kai-shek) and the Four Great Families. Because writings on history are so often read as allegories for present politics scholars have to be careful about their choice of research topic in this area.

CONCLUSION

As in the past, the future of Chinese economic history in China will depend on the future of the state and is, therefore, unlikely to be easy. Difficult times lie ahead for all Chinese intellectuals, in terms both of the political climate and of the financial squeeze on universities and research. Nevertheless, there are political and academic reasons for believing that the changes and re-interpretations discussed above will continue and the field will not return to the condition described by Feuerwerker in the 1960s.

Most importantly, on the level of politics, it is likely that the impetus for modernisation, a political programme which can command considerable support and which accords more closely to intellectuals' interests, will reassert itself and provide a basis for at least part of the reform programme, political and economic, to re-emerge. The greater diversity of the Chinese economy which resulted from the reforms can probably not be halted or reversed for more than a short period. This will provide a basis for varying views and also for more open judgements of the contribution of different groups in the past – most particularly of Chinese capitalists but also of foreign enterprise and the pre-Communist state.

On an academic level, increasing diversity will also come from the experimentation with different methodologies particularly by younger scholars, an area in which scholars returning from the West will also have much to offer. The substantial isolation which Feuerwerker argued Chinese scholarship suffered from in relation to the rest of the world is unlikely to return. While nativist sentiments will no doubt remain powerful, no Chinese government will be able to isolate the country, or its academic sector, as completely from foreign contacts as was the case under Mao: despite the events of 1989 and the subsequent political freeze, Chinese scholars remain determined to resist isolation and retain contacts with the outside world.

Diversity and opening to the West will not, however, erase the particularly Chinese aspects of their scholarship. Chinese intellectuals in the future as in the past will not see the function of their work in exactly the same way as do Western scholars, and will continue to want to make a contribution to their country's search for wealth and power through drawing lessons from the recent past.

Notes

1. Albert Feuerwerker, 'China's Modern Economic History in Communist Chinese Historiography', pp. 216–46 in Albert Feuerwerker (ed.), *History in Communist China* (Cambridge, Mass., 1968).
2. There are three major survey articles of the new trends, at least up to the early 1980s. Their influence will be visible throughout this introduction, and I do not in general make specific references to them elsewhere. Mi Rucheng, 'Jianguo yilai Zhongguo jindai jingji shi yanjiu pingshu', *Jindai shi yanjiu*, 1984, no. 5 (September 1984): 82–112; Shi Jijin, 'San zhong quanhui yilai Zhongguo jindai jingji shi yanjiu zai ruogan wenti shang de xin jinzhan', *Zhongguo jindai jingji shi yanjiu ziliao* [hereafter *JJYZ*], 1984, no. 2 (September 1984): 135–58; Okamoto Satoshi, 'Zhongguo zuijin dui Minguo shiqi jingji shi de yanjiu shuping', *JJYZ* 3 (May 1985): 90–115, and 4 (December 1985): 114–32.

3. Feuerwerker, 'China's Modern Economic History', p. 216.
4. Colin Mackerras, 'Conclusion', p. 150 in Michael B. Yahuda (ed.), *New Directions in the Social Sciences and Humanities in China* (New York, 1987).
5. Perry Link, 'The Limits of Cultural Reform in Deng Xiaoping's China', *Modern China* 13.2 (April 1987): 117.
6. Li Baozhu, 'Lun zhangai Zhongguo minzu zibenzhuyi gongye fazhan de yuanyin – Fu Zhufu jiaoshou de tanhua zhuiji', *Nankai jingji yanjiu* 1985.2 (June 1985): 23.
7. Li Shiyue, as quoted in Lin Youneng, 'Zhongguo jindai shehui xingzhi de zai renshi', *Xueshu yanjiu* 1988.6 (December 1988): 51.
8. Andrew Watson, 'Social Science Research and Economic Policy Formulation: The Academic Side of Economic Reform', p. 83 in Yahuda, *New Directions in the Social Sciences.*
9. Yan Zhongping, 'Zai Zhongguo jingji shi xuehui chengli dahui shang de kaimuci', *Zhongguo jingji shi yanjiu*, 1987.1 (February 1987): 155; emphasis mine.
10. John P. Burns, *The Chinese Communist Party's Nomenklatura System* (Armonk, New York, 1989), pp. xx, xxxi–xxxii.
11. See Wang Yuru, 'Nankai jingji yanjiu suo xuezhe jituan dui jiu Zhongguo jingji yanjiu de gongxian', *Nankai jingji yanjiu suo jikan* 1987.1 (March 1987): 1–7.
12. Mi Rucheng, 'Zhongguo jindai jingji shi yanjiu pingshu', p. 88.
13. Huang Yiping, 'Zhongguo jindai jingji shi yanjiu huigu', *Xueshu yuekan* 1989.4 (April 1989): 18.
14. That is, *Fuyin baokan ziliao, F7, jingji shi* [hereafter *FBZ*].
15. Bill Brugger and David Kelly, *Chinese Marxism in the Post-Mao Era* (Stanford, 1990), ch. 4.
16. 'Jianchi he fazhan Makesizhuyi, tuijin jingji shi yanjiu', *Zhongguo jingji shi yanjiu* 1990.1 (March 1990): 1–3.
17. This section relies primarily on Wu Chengming, 'Zhongguo jingji shi yanjiu fangfa zatan', *JJYZ* 6 (April 1987): 1–23.
18. Ling Feng, 'Li Shiyue guanyu jindai Zhongguo shehui xingzhi wenti da jizhe wen', *Xueshu yanjiu* 1988.6 (December 1988): 56–7; see also Ma Hongmo in 'Guanyu Zhongguo jindai jingji shi de zhongxin xiansuo', *Zhongguo jingji shi yanjiu* 1989.3 (September 1989): 77.
19. Liu Feng, '1989 nian Zhongguo jingji shi yanjiu zongshu – jindai jingji shi', *Zhongguo jingji shi yanjiu* 1990.2 (June 1990): 153.
20. Wu Chengming, 'Tan fengjianzhuyi er ti', *Zhongguo jingji shi yanjiu* 1989.4 (November 1989): 5.
21. Ma Ding, 'Ten Major Changes in China's Study of Economics', *Beijing Review* 28.49 (9 December 1985): 18.
22. Wu Chengming, 'Guanyu yanjiu Zhongguo jindai jingji shi de yijian', *Jinyang xuekan* 1982.1 (January 1982): 59.
23. Sun Jian, *Zhongguo jingji shi, jindai bufen (1840–1949 nian)* (Beijing, 1989), p. 3.

24. Wu Chengming, 'Fangfa zatan', pp. 6–12.
25. Notably Peng Zeyi, 'Zhongguo jingji shi yanjiu zhong de jiliang wenti', *Lishi yanjiu* 1985.3 (June 1985): 24–45.
26. Yan Zhongping, *Zhongguo jindai jingji shi tongji ziliao xuanji* (Beijing, 1955).
27. Peng Zeyi, 'Jiliang wenti', pp. 43–4.
28. Wu Chengming, 'Guanyu yanjiu Zhongguo jindai jingji shi de yijian', p. 60.
29. Gu Jirui, *Zhongguo 1911 nian – 1949 nian renkou zhuangkuang* (Nanjing, 1986).
30. Duan Bin, 'Xin Zhongguo jingji shi de hongguan shuliang fenxi', *Zhongguo jingji shi yanjiu* 1989.3 (September 1989): 32–52.
31. For surveys of such work, see William T. Rowe, 'Approaches to Modern Chinese Social History', in Olivier Zunz (ed.), *Reliving the Past: The Worlds of Social History* (Chapel Hill, 1985), pp. 271–83; Timothy Brook (ed)., *The Asiatic Mode of Production in China* (Armonk, New York, 1989).
32. Sun Jian, *Zhongguo jingji shi*, p. 25.
33. Wang Jingyu, 'Lun Zhongguo jindai jingji shi de zhongxin xiansuo', *Zhongguo jingji shi yanjiu* 1989.2 (June 1989): 1–11; for a concrete application of this idea see Zhang Guohui, 'Jiawu zhan hou sishi nian jian Zhongguo xiandai saosi gongye de fazhan he bu fazhan', *Zhongguo jingji shi yanjiu* 1989.1 (March 1989): 91–125.
34. For this and the next paragraph see 'Guanyu Zhongguo jindai jingji shi de zhongxin xiansuo', pp. 62–79.
35. Wang Jingyu, 'Zhongguo jindai jingji shi zhongxin xiansuo wenti de zai sikao', *Zhongguo jingji shi yanjiu* 1990.2 (June 1990): 1–13.
36. Paul A. Cohen, *Discovering History in China: American Historical Writing on the Recent Chinese Past* (New York, 1984), ch. 2.
37. In practice Western modernisation theorists working on China would not accept that assumption either. See Gilbert Rozman (ed.), *The Modernization of China* (New York, 1981).
38. Wu Chengming, 'Zhongguo jindai jingji shi ruogan wenti de sikao', *Zhongguo jingji shi yanjiu* 1988.2 (May 1988): 153–4.
39. See for example Hui Xin, '"Dui-wai jingji guanxi yu Zhongguo jindaihua" guoji xueshu taolunhui xueshu guandian zongshu', *JJYZ* 8 (November 1987): 33–4.
40. Wu Chengming, 'Ruogan wenti de sikao', p. 153.
41. See Xu Dixin and Wu Chengming (eds), *Zhongguo zibenzhuyi fazhan shi*, vol. 1, *Zhongguo zibenzhuyi de mengya* (Beijing, 1985).
42. Ding Richu, 'Guanyu dui-wai jingji guanxi yu Zhongguo jindaihua', *JJYZ* 8 (November 1987): 24.
43. Lu Yan and Yao Xinrong, 'Zhongguo xuezhe lun dui-wai jingji tong Zhongguo jindaihua de guanxi', *JJYZ* 7 (April 1987): 43–5.
44. Wu Chengming, 'Ruogan wenti de sikao', pp. 158–9.
45. See 'Guanyu Zhongguo jindai jingji shi de zhongxin xiansuo', p. 75.

46. Liu Foding, 'Shilun woguo minzu ziben qiye de ziben jilei wenti', *Nankai xuebao* 1982.2 (March 1982): 17.
47. Zhang Guohui, 'Zhongguo xiandai saosi gongye', passim.
48. Xu Xinwu, Yang Gan and Yuan Shushen, 'Zhongguo jindai mianfen gongye lishi gaikuang yu tedian', *Shanghai shehui kexue yuan xueshu jikan* 1987.2 (May 1987): 62.
49. Xu Xinwu, Shen Jianhua and Chen Chengqing, 'Zhongguo jindai zaozhi gongye de lishi gaikuang yu tedian', *JJYZ* 7 (April 1987): 71.
50. Mao Tse-tung (Mao Zedong), *Selected Works of Mao Tse-tung*, vol. 4 (Beijing, 1967), p. 167.
51. Shen Zuwei, 'Jin ji nian guonei jindai Zhongguo zichanjieji yanjiu shuping', *Lishi yanjiu* 1989.4 (December 1989): 88.
52. Fu Xiaofeng, 'Guanyu dongbei guanliao ziben de ruogan wenti', *Jilin daxue shehui kexue xuebao* 1988.5 (September 1988): 17.
53. Ding Richu, 'Guanyu dui-wai jingji guanxi', p. 27.
54. For a fuller treatment of this see Tim Wright, '"The Spiritual Heritage of Chinese Capitalism": Recent Trends in the Historiography of Chinese Enterprise Management', *Australian Journal of Chinese Affairs* 19/20 (1988): 185–214.
55. Jiang Duo, 'Zibenzhuyi ci lu bu tong', *Shanghai jingji yanjiu* 1987.2, pp. 49–55, reprinted in *FBZ* 1987.7 (July 1987): 147–53.
56. In *The Golden Age of the Chinese Bourgeoisie, 1911–1937*, translated by Janet Lloyd (Cambridge, 1989), pp. 243–51.
57. Notably in *Big Business in China: Sino-Foreign Rivalry in the Cigarette Industry, 1890–1930* (Cambridge, Mass., 1980).
58. Mi Rucheng, 'Zhongguo jindai jingji shi yanjiu shuping', pp. 86–7.
59. Lu Zhenxiang, 'Di er ci guonei geming zhanzheng shiqi jizhong tudi zhuzhang pingshu', *Beijing shifan daxue xuebao, she ke ban* 1984.6, pp. 7–16, reprinted in *FBZ* 1985.2 (February 1985): 121.
60. Zheng Qingping, 'Zhongguo jindai de nongye weiji', *Zhongguo nong shi* 1985.4, pp. 54–62, reprinted in *FBZ* 1985.12 (December 1985): 139–47.
61. For some aspects see for example Phillip C. C. Huang, *The Peasant Economy and Social Change in North China* (Stanford, 1985).
62. Thomas G. Rawski, *Economic Growth in Prewar China* (Berkeley, 1989).
63. Wu Chengming, 'Zhongguo jindai nongye shengchan li de kaocha', *Zhongguo jingji shi yanjiu* 1989.2 (May 1989): 63–77.
64. Shi Bolin, 'Guanyu Guomindang zhengfu jianli chuqi jingji zhengce pingjia de jige wenti', *Xiangtan daxue xuebao, she ke ban* 1985.3, pp. 89–94, 29, reprinted in *FBZ* 1985.8 (August 1985): 133.
65. Loren Brandt, *Commercialization and Agricultural Development: Central and Eastern China, 1870–1937* (Cambridge, UK, 1989).
66. Xiao Liang *et al.* (eds), *Zhongguo jingji kexue nianjian (1988)* (Beijing, 1989), pp. 257–8.
67. Liu Foding, 'Zhongguo jindai jingji shi yanjiu de shiwu yu guannian

fangfa de zhuanbian', *Nankai jingji yanjiu suo niankan*, 1987–1988 (Tianjin, 1989), p. 261.
68. Wang Jingyu, 'Zhongxin xiansuo', pp. 6–7.
69. Chen Tingxuan, 'Jindai Zhongguo nongye guyong guanxi de feng-jianxing', *Zhongguo jingji shi yanjiu* 1987.3 (August 1987): 123–7.
70. See Albert Feuerwerker, 'Handicraft and Manufactured Cotton Textiles in China, 1871–1910', *Journal of Economic History* 30.2 (June 1970): 338–78.
71. Wu Chengming, 'Ruogan wenti de sikao', p. 157.
72. Huang Yiping, 'Shijiu shiji mo ershi shiji chu Zhongguo ziran jingji jieti de chengdu', *Xueshu yuekan* 1982.9 (September 1982): 16–22.
73. Feuerwerker, 'China's Modern Economic History', p. 234.
74. Wang Jingyu, 'Zhongxin xiansuo', pp. 1–2.
75. Hui Xin, 'Dui-wai jingji guanxi', passim.
76. Ding Richu, 'Guanyu dui-wai jingji guanxi', passim.
77. Zhang Zhongli and Li Rongchang, 'Zhong-Mei maoyi yu jiu Zhongguo jingji de jindaihua', *JJYZ* 8 (November 1987): 1–23.
78. Cao Junwei, 'Dui jindai Zhong-wai hezi qiye de zai renshi', *Guangdong shehui kexue* 1988.4, pp. 52–6, 62, reprinted in *FBZ* 1989.4 (April 1989): 72–4.
79. Huang Yiping, 'Zhongguo jindai jingji shi yanjiu huigu', p. 22.
80. Zhang Guohui, 'Zhongguo xiandai saosi gongye', p. 121; he does, however, spend considerably more space discussing the failures of the Chinese government.
81. Notably, Xu Dixin and Wu Chengming, *Zhongguo zibenzhuyi fazhan shi*, vol. 1, preface, p. 16; and Wu Chengming, *Zhongguo zibenzhuyi yu guonei shichang* (Beijing, 1985), p. 116.
82. Zhu Xianping and Xu Wenfeng, 'Bu neng ba waiguo ziben zuowei Zhongguo zibenzhuyi de zucheng bufen', *Jilin daxue shehui kexue xuebao* 1989.3 (May 1989): 34–6.
83. Zhang Xiaohui, 'Minzu zichanjieji yu Nanjing guomin zhengfu (1927–1931 nian)', *Shixue jikan* 1987.1 (1987): 29–34.
84. Shi Bolin, 'Guomindang zhengfu', pp. 129–31.
85. Apart from Ci's article, see Chen Kejian, 'Guanyu 1935 nian Guomindang zhengfu fabi zhengce pingjia de jige wenti – yu Huang Rutong deng tongzhi shangque', *Zhongguo jingji wenti* 1987.3, pp. 55–9, reprinted in *FBZ* 1987.7 (July 1987): 60–4.
86. Liu Fangjian, 'Kang-Ri zhanzheng shiqi da houfang jingji xueshu taolunhui zongshu', *JJYZ* 8 (November 1987): 227–30.
87. Shi Bolin, 'Guomindang zhengfu', pp. 132–4.
88. Qing Qingrui, 'Guomindang guanliao ziben de xingcheng dui Zhong-guo jingji fazhan jiujing qi le shenme zuoyong?', *Jiaoxue yu yanjiu* 1986.6 (November 1986): 49.

2 A Brief Account of the Development of Capitalism in China

Wu Chengming

Professor Wu Chengming of the Institute of Economics, Chinese Academy of Social Sciences, is probably the most influential scholar of modern China's economic history.

This translation is from a longer article published in 1981, and republished in 1985 in Wu's book, Chinese Capitalism and the National Market. *The sections not translated here were on 'The Sprouts of Capitalism', 'The Disintegration of the Natural Economy and Changes in the Domestic Market', 'The Establishment of Modern Industry and the Three Forms of Chinese Capitalism', and 'The Period of the Sino-Japanese War and the War of Liberation'. The article is probably the single most important reference point for the new work on early twentieth century Chinese economic history. Key points in the analysis include the quantitative estimates for the speed and nature of the growth of capitalism, the reinterpretation of the 1920s and 1930s, and the inclusion of foreign capital in China as part of Chinese capitalism.*

While the overall interpretation in the article stands, Professor Wu wants to point out that many of the specific estimates have been superseded by those in the latest volume of The History of Chinese Capitalism, *published in early 1991. The new estimates both include additional material and in some cases, for example in that of foreign railway loans, use a different methodology for categorising the different types of capital.*[1]

THE INITIAL AND FURTHER STAGES OF THE DEVELOPMENT OF CAPITALISM IN CHINA

The Initial Stage of the Development of Capitalism

Chinese capitalism first developed in the period from 1895 to 1913. Wang Jingyu's statistics show that during this period 549 newly-built industrial and mining establishments were established by Chinese capital, each with a capital of over Ch$10 000. The total capital amounted to Ch$120 297 000. On the average, 28.9 enterprises were set up each year, with new investment of Ch$6 331 000.[2] The annual growth rate of some leading industries reached 15–20 per cent, which not only was unprecedented but also surpassed the so-called golden age during the First World War. But that was due to the fact that new industries such as tobacco, flour, power, and cement were starting from a very low base. In the cotton textile industry, which had already begun to develop before 1894, the number of spindles increased by 6.3 per cent per year.

During this period, new investment in government-owned enterprises was only Ch$20 132 000, while that in private enterprises amounted to Ch$100 165 000 (calculating investment in joint enterprises as half each). Thus the nature of Chinese industrial capital changed. Before the Sino-Japanese War of 1894–5 most industrial investment had come from the Qing Government. However, from this period on private investment by far surpassed that by the government and gradually became the main component of Chinese industrial capital.

There are a number of important aspects of the development of Chinese capitalism in this period. At the beginning, the stimulus of the Sino-Japanese War of 1894–5 led to an upsurge of investment. The Meiji Restoration in Japan had taken place only thirty years before and now Japan defeated China! The whole country was badly shaken; the demand to save China by establishing factories soon spread all over the country, and consequently the Reform Movement of 1898 was launched. The Chinese bourgeoisie for the first time mounted the political stage. Although the Reform Movement failed, the Qing Government had to slacken its control over the establishment of private enterprises and adopt certain measures to promote industry and commerce. Soon afterwards the democratic revolutionary movement led by Dr Sun Yat-sen emerged. From 1905 another upsurge of investment began, linked with the anti-American boycott. After that there was the campaign to boycott Japanese commodities in 1908, the large-scale movement to recover railway and mining rights, and finally the overthrow of the Qing Dynasty. Therefore, the development of national industry in this period emerged under the stimulus of the bourgeois revolutionary movement and represented the path of laissez-faire capitalist development. However, later history took a different road.

Broader historical conditions must also be examined. In the period of the Sino-Japanese War, both international and domestic conditions suggested that capitalism was the only way to save China, to win independence and to built a stronger nation, and at that time the best way to develop Chinese capitalism was to allow private enterprises to develop without interference and to follow the path of laissez-faire capitalism. This was somewhat different from the situation after the First World War. Consequently, any kind of control or monopoly could only harm economic development. Similarly in Japan, the Meiji government at first devoted major efforts to building up military and some civilian industries. But after 1880 the government sold off all its major enterprises, including some military industries, to private investors at cheap prices. Soon afterwards Japan's industrial revolution began to take place: between 1884 and 1890 the total capital invested in Japanese joint-stock companies increased by thirteen times.

In China also private investment was by no means weak in this period. During the upsurge of factory establishment between 1905 and 1910 new investment amounted to over Ch$15 million annually; in the rights-recovery movement of 1903–10 many privately-owned railway companies emerged and attracted a total investment of Ch$60 million. But because of the impediments put in their way by the Qing Government most of the railways built were taken over by imperialism or by the Government.

Bureaucratic capital had few achievements in this period as far as establishing new industrial and mining enterprises was concerned. However, the partly government-owned Hanyeping Company alone added Ch$48 million to its assets through foreign loans. Up to 1913, if one calculates net assets including new and original investments, industrial and mining investment by bureaucratic capital amounted to about Ch$83 947 000, whereas that of national capital ('National capital' means private capital, excluding government and 'bureaucratic' capital) was Ch$139 609 000. In the area of transport and communications, including railways, shipping and telecommunications, total investment by bureaucratic capital amounted to Ch$69 328 000, that by national capital, including the Chaozhou-Shantou Railway, the Xinning-Xinhui Railway and twelve shipping lines, to Ch$15 378 000. Total Chinese investment in productive enterprises

TABLE 2.1   *Estimate of productive capital in China, 1913 (Ch$ million)*

	Total	Foreign capital	Chinese capital		
			Total	Bureaucratic	National
Manufacturing	267.35*	113.54	153.81	36.32	117.50
Mining	139.70	69.96	69.74	47.63	22.11
Railways	1 008.28	960.00	48.28	37.35	10.93
Shipping	125.62	93.60	33.02	27.58**	4.45
Total	1 540.96	1 237.09	303.86	148.88	154.99

* including public utilities
** including telecommunications

amounted to Ch$303 862 000, eight-and-a-half times as much as that in 1894.

However, if foreign capital in China is taken into account, things are quite different. In this initial stage, foreign capital developed more rapidly than Chinese capital. This was the period when the capitalist great powers entered the stage of imperialism and fought for railway and mining rights in China in order to divide up the country among themselves. Having formally obtained the right to establish factories in China after the Sino-Japanese War of 1894–5, foreign countries rapidly increased their industrial investment in China. Wang Jingyu's statistics show that from 1895 to 1913, 136 mines and factories with a capital of over Ch$100 000 were set up in China by foreign capital, with a total investment of Ch$103 153 000.[3] Together with the original investment in 1894, net assets of foreign capital in industrial and mining enterprises amounted in 1913 to Ch$183 494 000, only a little less those that of Chinese capital.

In transport and communications, however, foreign capital had the absolute predominance. Up to 1911 China built a total of 8900 kilometres of railway lines, 85 per cent of which were run by imperialism or built with loans granted to the Qing Government by imperialist countries. Foreign ships accounted for almost 85 per cent of total tonnage in the Treaty ports, including those along the Yangzi. Foreign investment in Chinese shipping and railways in 1913 has been estimated at a total of Ch$153.6 million.[4] Thus, total foreign productive investment in China amounted to Ch$1237 million, four times as much as that by Chinese capital, whereas in 1894 it had only been 1.5 times as much as Chinese capital. So, as shown in Table 2.1, the relative position of Chinese capital

TABLE 2.2   *Growth rates of major industries run by Chinese capital, 1912–1920*

Industry	Measure	1912	1920	Index, 1912=100	Average annual growth rate (%)
Cotton spinning	index of output of cotton yarn	100.0	422.4	422.4	17.4
Flour	index of output	100.0	516.9	516.9	22.8
Silk reeling	export of reeled silk (piculs)	59 157.0	77 855.0	131.6	3.5
Tobacco	capital (Ch$ million)	0.14	1.68	1 220.0	36.7
Matches	capital (Ch$ million)	2.94	7.46	253.6	12.3
Electric power	output (million KWH)	12.01	29.60	246.4	11.9
Cement	output (Qixin Company) (tons)	59 405	109 741.0	184.7	8.0
Mining	index of output (1913=100)	79.1	158.0	199.7	9.0

was greatly weakened, and it found itself in an even more perilous situation.

The Further Development of Capitalism

In the years between 1914 and 1920, that is during the First World War, capitalism in China developed further. In the six years from 1914 to 1919, the number of new factories or mines established by Chinese capital totalled 379, with a total investment of Ch$85.5 million. On the average, 63 new factories or mines were set up each year, with a new investment of Ch$14.3 million; both figures are more than double those of the previous period. In this period, foreign capital grew only to a limited extent, bureaucratic capital came to a standstill, whereas national capital increased rapidly.

A study of the growth of the major industries run by Chinese capital between 1912 and 1920 has recently been undertaken by Tang Chuansi, and is shown in Table 2.2. Of all these industries, the tobacco industry, with a comparatively low base, had the highest growth rate; growth rates for cotton spinning and flour, which had already reached a certain level in 1911, were 17.4 per cent and 22.8 per cent respectively. The average annual growth rate of the mining industry was 9 per cent, but that for mechanised coal and iron mining reached 13.4 per cent and 25.7 per cent respectively. The average annual growth rate of the eight listed industries, weighted according to investment, was 13.8 per cent, or 15.3 per cent if mining is excluded. Judging from all aspects, this was a period of rapid development of Chinese industry.

However, in this, unlike the previous, period, the rapid development of Chinese industry was due mainly to various contingent factors. The main cause was the war between the imperialist countries, which resulted in reduced imports of foreign commodities, easing of the pressure on Chinese goods. Meanwhile, the price of gold went up while that of silver came down, which in practice meant that China's silver currency was devalued, thus promoting exports. After 1916 the price of silver rose again, but overseas inflation drove China's domestic prices to a higher level, which was still beneficial to industrial production. During this period, the prices of imports rose more quickly than those of exports. In other words, the terms of trade worsened by 55 per cent between 1913 and 1930. This was certainly disadvantageous to the Chinese economy as a whole, and especially to the villages. For China had to export 50 per cent more farm produce to get the same amount of foreign industrial products as it had to before the War. But it was beneficial to the capitalists because, after all, exports did increase, and with them exports of industrial products: the proportion of manufactured products in total exports increased from 19.2 per cent in 1910 to 23.4 per cent in 1920.

Even more importantly, when this price structure was reflected in the domestic market it caused commodity prices to rise faster than wages. For example, between 1915 and 1920 the price of cloth went up by 76 per cent, whereas wages only rose by 35 per cent. This price structure also caused the prices of finished products to rise more quickly than those of raw materials. Therefore, the cotton textile and flour industries made large profits from the relative fall in the prices of agricultural materials. So these two industries experienced the greatest development in this period.

The development of Chinese industry in this period was also stimulated by the people's anti-imperialist patriotic movement, especially by the campaign against the 'Twenty-one Demands' presented by Japan to China in 1915 and by the unprecedented scale of the May Fourth Movement of 1919,

TABLE 2.3   *Estimate of productive capital in China, 1920 (Ch$ million)*

Industry	Total	Foreign capital	Chinese capital		
			Total	Bureaucratic	National
Manufacturing	721.24	306.00	415.24	211.18	204.07
Public utilities	170.34	84.96	85.38		85.38
Mining	213.50	158.50	55.00	11.42	43.58
Railways	1 047.18	968.64	78.54	36.56	41.98
Shipping	215.99	149.36	66.63	11.76	54.87
Total	2 368.25	1 667.46	700.79	270.92	429.87

when merchants went on strike boycotting Japanese goods. However, on the whole, the development of Chinese industry in this period was mainly due to the price factors mentioned above. Once the First World War came to an end, the imperialist forces returned to China and these favourable factors disappeared immediately.

While the Western imperialist countries were fully occupied with the war in these years, Japan greatly expanded its investment in China. In the area of transport and communications, railway building came to a standstill, while the shipping industry underwent considerable development. According to the estimate by Tang Chuansi, by the end of 1920, foreign and Chinese industrial investment in China was as shown in Table 2.3, which uses a different method to estimate Chinese capital from that used in Table 2.1. So some of the items are not directly comparable. But on the whole, it is clear that foreign capital increased by about one third, while Chinese capital more than doubled.

The Level of the Development of Capitalism

After the first two stages of the development of capitalism in China how far had it developed? This question is of vital importance, for it concerns not only the forces and relations of production but also the nature of Chinese society and the direction of the Chinese revolution. Because of the shortage of data and lack of research on this subject, however, we can only make certain preliminary explorations in the hope of arousing the interest of scholars.

Capitalism in China was very weak and never became the major form of social production. To study its backward features, we could use typical enterprises and industries to analyse its productive techniques, organic composition of capital, structure of development, organisation and management. But to determine its level of development, we need comprehensive statistics and macroeconomic comparators. As the concepts of net product and national income have been little studied or used in China, a relatively practical procedure is to assess the proportion of the gross value of industrial and agricultural output accounted for by capitalist enterprises. According to Tang Chuansi's estimate, the gross value of agricultural output around 1920 was about Ch$16 520 million, and the gross value of industrial (including mining) output was about Ch$5383 million; thus total gross value of output was Ch$21 903 million. Using a narrow definition of capitalism, and discounting any capitalist production in agriculture, the gross output value of modern industry reached Ch$1066 million, 4.87 per cent of the total. Thus up to the 1920s capitalism only accounted for around 5 per cent of the Chinese economy.

A second method of calculation might be to say that modern industry accounted for less than 20 per cent of the gross value of industrial (including mining) output in China; more than 80 per cent originated in handicraft industry. Over the years between 1910 and 1920 China also witnessed development in handicraft industries, especially in handicraft workshops. Handicraft workshops were ignored in the estimate of industrial capital above but they cannot be ignored in our estimate of the value of output, as their output was very large, even though their capital was quite small. Around 1920, the gross output value of handicraft industry (including mining) was about Ch$4317 million, of which Ch$1295 million originated in handicraft workshops, if they are considered to account for 30 per cent of the total. If one adds this to the output of modern industry, the total amounts to Ch$2361 million, or 10.8 per cent of the gross value of industrial and agricultural output. Thus by this definition Chinese capitalism accounted for around 10 per cent of the economy in the early 1920s.

In the area of transport and communications, Tang Chuansi estimated that, around 1920, the total income from railways, ships, rickshaws, animal-drawn carts, telecommunications and posts amounted to Ch$747 million, of which the income from modern forms of transport was Ch$341 million, or 45.6 per cent of the total. As this is an estimate of income, it is not directly comparable to the output statistics. But it may be concluded that in transport and communications the level of the development of capitalism was relatively high. However, transport and communications accounted for only a small proportion of China's economy, contributing only some 4.5 per cent of national income.

THE ECONOMIC CRISIS OF THE 1920s AND 1930s

The period between 1921 and 1936, the year before the Sino-Japanese War broke out, witnessed the reactionary coup staged by Jiang Jieshi [Chiang Kai-shek], the Japanese occupation of vast areas of Chinese territory in the North-east, the world economic crisis, and ten years of civil war. China was in great trouble; the people were suffering greatly. But it was also a period of great awakening and great progress for the Chinese nation, a period of great revolution led by the Chinese Communist Party. As has been frequently stated, the Chinese economy faced continual crises and depressions in this period. However, the author is of the opinion that most previous discussions have been too pessimistic.

The Expansion of Capitalist Relations of Production

The path of development of Chinese-owned modern industry was tortuous in this period. In the early 1920s some of the development during the First World War continued. The cotton textile industry in particular continued growing until 1922 because much of the equipment ordered and imported only came into operation after the war. After this a crisis arose and modern industry fell into depression. But from the second half of 1925, stimulated by the revolution and the campaign to boycott foreign goods, the position of modern industry began to improve. Starting from 1926, it began to develop again, though quite slowly. Between 1920 and 1928, over Ch$300 million was newly invested in industry.

The economic crisis in the capitalist world which started in 1929 did not immediately affect China. On the contrary, as the price of silver dropped more rapidly than commodity prices, the Chinese economy was stimulated and industry began to boom, reaching a peak in 1930. As it had already a certain base, capitalist accumulation reached a fairly high level during this period. With the help of bank credit, the tendency towards concentration and centralisation of capital appeared.

Starting from 1931 the capitalist countries successively abandoned the gold standard, thus causing the price of silver to rise again and commodity prices in China to fall. China faced an unprecedentedly serious economic crisis. The Japanese occupation of the vast market and natural resources of North-east China, the dumping of foreign goods at cheap prices and the import of smuggled Japanese goods were the main causes of the crisis. The devaluation of the American dollar and the adoption of the Silver Purchase Act in 1934 deepened the crisis in China; more than 200 million taels of silver flowed out of China. Additional factors were the floods in the Yangzi

River valley and the civil war launched by the Nationalists. Consequently, the peasants were bankrupted and the people reduced to poverty.

The author is of opinion that the economic crisis in the 1920s and 1930s was mainly a market crisis. Its main symptoms were falling prices and stagnating sales, leading to the shut-down of factories and a fall in production. But it was different from the cyclical economic crises in the capitalist countries, for it was a matter of falling purchasing power rather than overproduction; it was also closely bound up with the feudal economy in the vast Chinese countryside. In the stage of rising prices, the rural areas were unable to ship out more products because of the dominance of small-scale peasant farming; when prices dropped, however, rural financial resources became exhausted, and purchasing power in the rural areas declined. The rural economy was much worse hit than the capitalist economy. The exploitation of the peasants actually promoted capitalist accumulation. By the end of 1935, when the Nationalist Government adopted a paper currency, the currency was devalued and prices rose. The capitalist economy revived and in 1936 and the first half of 1937 became prosperous.

Some industries such as silk reeling certainly declined in this period. Some traditional industries came to a standstill. The two major industries, cotton textiles and flour, were the most seriously influenced by the crisis and have attracted attention for this. However, the capital and equipment in the flour industry continued to increase up to 1930; cotton textiles grew even more, continuing to grow to some extent even after 1931. During the two crises the cotton textile industry continued to improve its technology and production management, so that by the end of 1935 its labour productivity had reached the level of the Japanese cotton mills in China.

Meanwhile some new industries emerged, such as the acid and soda ash industries, in which there was considerable investment. The rubber, mechanised silk weaving, knitting, enamelling, daily-use chemicals, and pharmaceutical industries existed in a relatively broad range, though on a small scale. From the 1920s onwards, the popularisation of electric motors and the development of electric power made it easy to set up factories, so that large numbers of small factories sprang up. In addition it induced some handicraft workshops to use electric power, especially in agricultural processing and mining. The machine building industry also began to produce special purpose machines after 1925, which made it easier to set up small factories. Small internal-combustion engines opened up certain markets in the rural areas. These promoted the extension of capitalist production from coastal areas to inland areas and medium-sized and small cities.

TABLE 2.4   *Estimate of productive capital in China, 1936 (Ch$ million)*

	Total	Foreign capital	Chinese capital*		
			Total	Bureaucratic capital	National capital
Manufacturing and mining	4 296	2 920	1 376	206	1 170
Transport and communications	3 914	3 514	400	235	165
Total	8 210	6 434	1 776	441	1 335

* Excluding North-east China

Therefore, the author tends to regard the years from 1921 to 1936 as a period when Chinese capitalism extended its scope, a period when China became increasingly capitalist. Capitalist productive forces were still developed only to a limited extent and the increase in investment was slow, but the relations of capitalist production expanded quite rapidly. That is to say, there emerged both more capitalists and more industrial workers. Capitalism expanded in both sectoral and geographical terms.

The Path of the Development of Capitalism

According to an estimate of industrial capital in China made in 1949 by the author and later revised, by the end of 1936 Chinese industrial capital (including that in mining) amounted to about Ch$1376 million, of which national capital made up Ch$1170 million.[5] Because this estimate excludes North-east China and because the methods of estimation were not entirely the same, the figures are not entirely comparable with those in Table 2.3. But roughly speaking, from 1921 to 1936 Chinese industrial capital more than doubled. The average annual growth rate was only 6 per cent. Most of the increase was accounted for by national capital. So the year of 1936 might be regarded as the peak of the development of national capital.

In transport and communications, there was a rapid increase in investment, owing to the second upsurge in railway building, while shipping also developed to some extent. In addition, a start was made in road and air transportation. But as data in this aspect await checks, we can only make a rough and tentative estimate as shown in Table 2.4.

There was an even greater increase in foreign capital in this period. By 1936 total foreign investment in mining and manufacturing amounted to no

TABLE 2.5   *Chinese and foreign productive capital in China*

Year	Total	Chinese capital		Foreign capital	
	Ch\$ million	Ch\$ million	%	Ch\$ million	%
1894	89.53	35.19	39.3	54.34	60.7
1913	1 540.96	303.86	19.7	1 237.09	80.3
1920	2 368.25	700.79	29.6	1 667.46	70.4
1936	8 210.00	1 776.00*	21.6	6 434.00	78.4

* Excluding the North-east

less than Ch\$2920 million. Including investment in railway and shipping brings the total to about Ch\$6434 million, most of which was Japanese investment in North-east China. If North-east China is excluded, total foreign investment was about Ch\$2843 million.[6]

Table 2.4 presented my estimate of Chinese industrial capital in 1936, which is even rougher and more tentative than the earlier estimates. At the same time, a comparison between Chinese and foreign capital in different years is given in Table 2.5.

Table 2.5 reveals that, over the more than forty years after the Sino-Japanese War of 1894–5, foreign productive capital grew at twice the rate of Chinese capital. Earlier the imperialist countries had focused on controlling Chinese trade and finance, investing little in industry. Starting from the twentieth century, however, they exported to China large amounts of capital to build railways. From the 1930s they began to hold a monopoly position in industry. By 1936, foreign capital controlled roughly 95 per cent of pig iron output in China, 83 per cent of steel output, 66 per cent of the output from mechanised coal mining, and 55 per cent of electric power production. In other words, they controlled the main natural and energy resources. In the textile industry foreign capital accounted for 46 per cent of the spindles and 56 per cent of the looms. The economy of North-east China had become a colonial economy in the full sense; even in China proper the colonial nature of the economy was intensified. Having monopolised the basic industries, the growth of foreign capital was irreversible in the absence of major political changes.

Bureaucratic capital is even more worthy of notice. Before the Anti-Japanese War broke out in 1937, Nationalist bureaucratic capital did not occupy an important position in industry, accounting for less than 15 per cent of total capital. But it had gained a monopoly in the financial sector and, by means of currency, credit and foreign exchange policy, it was able to control the lifelines of national industry and commerce. In short, it had embarked on the road towards state monopoly capitalism. Bureaucratic capital reached this status through a deal with imperialism, which had long looked for a stable dictator to act as their agent and comprador, and found such a person in Jiang Jieshi. So they allowed his government to raise tariffs to some extent, gave up part of their rights over railway administration and helped Jiang to carry out the currency reform so as to tie the Chinese currency to the pound sterling and US dollar. Such measures as the so-called tariff autonomy, the reassertion of control over railway administration, currency reform, and road construction were not without benefits to the development of Chinese capitalism and some of them did promote production and circulation. But they changed the direction of the development of Chinese capitalism. Under the control of state monopoly capitalism the road of laissez-faire capitalism no longer existed.

In addition an entirely new type of national economy had already appeared from 1927 in the revolutionary base areas run by the Chinese Communist Party. This economic formation had not been completely finalised before the War but it already possessed some basic features of the new democratic economy. This economy at that time was still not strong and its national capitalist component was even weaker; nevertheless, it foreshadowed China's future and glimmered with the dawn of the new era. As stated above, at the time of the Sino-Japanese War of 1894–5, the best way to develop capitalism was to take the laissez-faire road. But, in the 1930s, that road was no longer viable either in China or on a global basis. Although in the regions ruled by imperialism and the Nationalists, it was still a task of vital importance to fight against monopoly and for democracy, objectively the development of Chinese capitalism had to change to a new path. If it was not to be not suffocated by comprador-feudal state monopoly capital, it had to enter the new democratic economic system to fulfil its historical mission under the leadership of the socialist economy. Of course, this only became clear in later history and at the time few could foresee this change in direction.

The Level of the Development of Capitalism

The expansion of capitalist relations of production and the great influx of foreign capital led to the rise in the level of the development of capitalism. Ding Shixun estimated that the gross value of industrial and agricultural output in China in 1936 amounted to about Ch\$30 612 million, of which industry (including mining) contributed Ch\$10 689 million; modern industry (including all mining) contributed Ch\$3319 million, or 10.8 per cent

TABLE 2.6   *Level of capitalist development in China*

Year	Share of gross value of industrial and agricultural output accounted for by:		Share of modern transport and communications in gross income of transport and communications
	Modern industry	Modern industry and handicraft workshops	
	%	%	%
1920	4.9	10.8	45.6
1936	10.8	20.5	51.0
1949	17.0	23.1	?

of total industrial and agricultural output. That is to say, the level of the development of capitalism rose from about 5 per cent in 1920 to about 10 per cent in 1936.

The gross value of handicraft output amounted to Ch$7371 million in 1936, of which handicraft workshops, calculated as 40 per cent of handicraft industry, contributed Ch$2948 million. This, together with modern industrial output, amounted to Ch$6267 million, 20.5 per cent of total output. That is to say, by the second definition the level of the development of capitalism rose from about 10 per cent in 1920 to about 20 per cent in 1936. Taking industry alone, modern industry and handicraft workshops accounted for 58.6 per cent of output, which means that more than half was capitalist in character.[7]

In transport and communications, according to the data provided in Wu Baosan's *National Income of China*, the gross income from air transport, water transport, railway transport, car service, rickshaw service, goods transport, telecommunications and posts reached Ch$1350 million, of which 51 per cent was from modern enterprises, 49 per cent from the individual economy. Thus more than half of transport and communications was capitalist in character.

An estimate of the level of the development of capitalism in China in 1920, 1936 and 1949 is given in Table 2.6.

CONCLUDING REMARKS

As mentioned above, by the 1920s, that is after the First World War, the possibilities for the development of capitalism in China had changed objectively. Having no future itself, laissez-faire capitalism had to embark on the transition to socialism through the system of new democratic economy. With the expansion of the Anti-Japanese base areas and liberated areas under the leadership of the Chinese Communist Party, the new democratic economy was expanded day by day. After the liberation of the country in 1949, through the confiscation of bureaucratic capital and the elimination of imperialist economic forces, the new democratic economy was finally established. Under the leadership of the socialist economy, its economic structure was made up of five economic components, as Mao Zedong said:

> The state-owned economy is socialist in character, and the co-operative economy is semi-socialist; these, plus private capitalism, plus individual economy, plus state-capitalist economy in which the state and private capitalists work jointly . . . will constitute the new-democratic economic structure.[8]

In this economic system, private capitalism, guided by the principle adopted by the Chinese Communist Party of 'giving consideration to state and private interests, benefiting both labour and capital', was developed under the leadership of the Party. Over the years from 1949 to 1953, the number of establishments in private capitalist industry increased by 21.4 per cent, the number of staff and workers increased by 25.1 per cent, and the gross value of output increased by 54 per cent.

Notes

1. [Editor's note] This chapter is a translation of sections of Wu Chengming, 'Zhongguo zibenzhuyi fazhan shulue', pp. 100–38 in Wu Chengming, *Zhongguo zibenzhuyi yu guonei shichang* (Beijing, 1985).
2. Wang Jingyu, *Zhongguo jindai gongye shi ziliao, 1895–1914 nian* (Beijing, 1957), vol. 2, p. 657 and passim.
3. Ibid., vol. 1, p. 4 and passim.
4. Estimates adapted from Wu Chengming, *Diguozhuyi zai jiu Zhongguo de touzi* (Beijing, 1955).
5. Wu Chengming, 'Zhongguo gongye ziben de guji he fenxi', *Xinhua yuebao* 1 (November 1949); Wu Chengming, 'Zhongguo minzu ziben de tedian', *Jingji yanjiu* 1956.6 (December 1956): 111–37.
6. Estimates adapted from Wu Chengming, *Diguozhuyi zai jiu Zhongguo de touzi*.
7. Ding Shixun, 'Guanyu Zhongguo zibenzhuyi fazhan shuiping de jige wenti', *Nankai daxue xuebao, zhe she* 1979.4 (October 1979): 20–27.
8. 'Report on the Second Plenary Session of the Seventh Central Committee of the Chinese Communist Party', *Selected Works of Mao Tse-tung*, vol. 4 (Beijing, 1967), p. 369.

3 The Development of Chinese National Capital in the 1920s

Zhang Zhongli

Zhang Zhongli, Research Professor and President of the Shanghai Academy of Social Sciences, is one of the most distinguished Chinese scholars. After working in the United States during the 1950s, when he published two extremely important books in English on the Chinese gentry, he returned to China and joined the Shanghai Academy of Social Sciences. Much of his recent work has been on the business history of Shanghai capitalism, especially the Sassoons; he has also written widely on the implications of history for China's current Open Door policies. Key points in this article, whose central aim is to reinterpret the experience of the 1920s, include the wide use of the abundant company archives held in Shanghai to provide a detailed picture of the growth of the modern sector of China's economy. Whereas Chapters 2 and 4 are concerned primarily with national aggregate statistics, Zhang fills out the picture with specific information for individual enterprises and sectors.[1]

In studies of modern economic history, it was 'generally said that the period of the First World War was the so-called "golden age" of Chinese national industries.'[2] 'After the imperialist countries staged a comeback after the War, however, these industries immediately fell into a state of depression.'[3] This viewpoint seems to be a final conclusion. But, judging from the historical materials I have read, Chinese national capital did achieve some development in the 1920s. Some important industries developed more rapidly than in the past, and it was only in the 1930s that national capital entered its crisis and development stagnated. These phenomena impel us to probe further into the factors promoting development in the 1920s.

SOME HISTORICAL MATERIALS RELATING TO DEVELOPMENT
IN THE 1920s

In the past, there were few historical materials detailing the development
of China's national capital in the 1920s. For instance, *Materials on the
History of the Modern Chinese Industry*[4] gathered materials concerning the
development and depressions of Chinese industries, including development
before the 1920s and a brief account of the depression after 1930, but
it lacked historical materials on the 1920s. Another example is Yan
Zhongping's *History of China's Cotton Textile Industry*[5] which, when
discussing the process of expanded reproduction and accumulation of
national capital, stressed the development of the industry from 1914
to 1922 but the harmful effects of imperialist monopoly capital on the
Chinese-owned textile mills after 1922. In recent years, the publication of
the *Historical Materials on the Rong Family Enterprises*[6] and *Historical
Materials on Liu Hongsheng's Enterprises*[7] has added some historical
data on industrial development in the 1920s. This article introduces some
materials on important industries in this respect.

The Cotton Textile Industry

Chinese national capital invested heavily in this industry. Twenty-one new
cotton mills were set up by national capital (apart from those mills bought
or rented) before 1910, thirteen between 1910 and 1919, and forty-five
between 1920 and 1929.

As the *History of China's Cotton Textile Industry* pointed out, the years
1920–2 saw the high tide of the establishment of cotton mills by national
capital.[8] Among the forty-five newly-established cotton mills in the 1920s,
thirty-two were established in those years. But, judging from the total
number of spindles in Chinese-owned cotton mills throughout the whole
country, there was a notable increase in equipment also after 1922. The
total number of spindles grew by 155 per cent in the 1920s, as against
only 32 per cent in the period 1910–19; between 1914 and 1919 it grew
only 19 per cent, but between 1920 and 1924, 108 per cent; a further 18
per cent increase was registered between 1924 and 1928.

In Shanghai the situation was similar: the total number of spindles grew
by 167 per cent in the 1920s, by only 31 per cent in the 1910s. Between
1914 and 1919 the increase was 34 per cent, between 1920 and 1924, 113
per cent, between 1924 and 1929, 20 per cent.[9]

Among the major enterprises run by national capital, the number of
spindles operated by the Shenxin mills, the mainstay of the Rongs'

enterprises, increased by 278 per cent in the 1920s. Because of the low base in 1916 when the mills had just been established, the growth between 1916 and 1919 was 331 per cent. The Rong group's Shenxin mills expanded more rapidly than the national or the Shanghai average because, aside from establishing new mills, the Rongs also bought or rented a number of old mills. If we exclude spindles which were bought or rented, the number of spindles in mills actually established by Shenxin increased by 82 per cent.[10]

The number of looms owned by national capital also increased more rapidly in the 1920s than in the period 1910–19. In national terms, it increased by 252 per cent in the 1920s, as against only 14 per cent in the 1910s. There was little growth in the weaving industry during the First World War, rather more in 1920–2, but most of all in 1922–9.[11]

As the number of Shanghai's Chinese-owned cotton mills equipped with looms increased substantially in the 1920s, the number of looms increased by 113 per cent between 1920 and 1931, and in fact by 293 per cent between 1919 and 1931.[12] The Shenxin mills began to install looms from 1917, and the number of looms they controlled increased by 100 per cent between 1917 and 1919 and by 144 per cent in the 1920s.[13]

The Silk-Weaving Industry

In 1910 there were forty-six Chinese-owned silk filatures in Shanghai, while this number increased to sixty-five in 1919 and to 104 in 1929. The number of reels grew by about 4000 between 1914 and 1918, and by 6000 between 1920 and 1929. The rates of growth in the two decades were similar, with the number growing by 38 per cent in the 1910s and 35 per cent in the 1920s.[14]

The Tobacco Industry

There was an even more marked development in the Chinese-owned tobacco industry in the 1920s. Up to 1919 Shanghai only had nine tobacco factories under Chinese ownership; at the peak in 1928 there were 101. The number of workers employed increased from 5568 in 1920 to 17 427 in 1928, a 213 per cent increase.[15]

Though the Nanyang Brothers Tobacco Company, the largest Chinese-owned cigarette company, was established in Hong Kong in 1905, it was only in 1916 that they opened a tobacco factory on East Broadway Road in Shanghai. Their Hankou and Pudong branches were opened as their business expanded after the May 30th Movement (1925). The fixed assets controlled by the company increased by 215 per cent between 1920 and 1928, from Ch$4 million to Ch$13 million. This shows that the 1920s were again an important stage of development for Nanyang Brothers.[16]

The Rubber Industry

During the First World War, the Chinese-owned sector of some industries hardly yet existed. The pioneer of Shanghai's Chinese-owned rubber industry, the Da Zhonghua (Great China) Rubber Products Company, only began production in its first factory in Shanghai early in the winter of 1919. Up to 1925, there were only four small Chinese-owned rubber mills in Shanghai, and eight by the end of 1927; but rubber shoes factories sprung up like mushrooms in 1928 and by 1931, excluding those that had been reorganised or closed down, there were forty-eight factories, which accounted for 70 per cent of all the rubber factories in the country. Therefore, the industry saw the late 1920s as a boom period.[17]

The Match Industry

The development of the match industry also came quite late in China. According to a survey conducted in the 1930s, out of fifty-nine match factories currently in operation, only five had been established before 1916; twelve were established between 1917 and 1921.[18] The great majority were set up after 1921. Liu Hongsheng's Hongsheng Match Company, the first of his enterprises, was set up in January 1920.[19]

The Engineering Industry

Parallel with the development of light industry, the Chinese-owned engineering industry also made some progress in the 1920s. Before 1913, there were ninety-one factories producing or repairing machinery for the shipbuilding, cotton-ginning, silk reeling, spinning, weaving and printing industries; by 1919 there were about 200, by 1924, 284. For instance, in 1913 there were only thirteen Chinese-owned factories in Shanghai making or repairing textile and silk reeling machines, but by 1924, excluding those which had closed down, the number reached fifty.[20] Between 1925 and 1931, Chinese-owned machinery factories continued to be established, so that by 1931 their number reached 457. In this period the industry expanded its scope and engaged in copying production machinery in areas such as cigarettes, rubber, electric knitting machines as well as enamelling machines.[21]

The Knitting Industry

Shanghai was also the centre of the Chinese-owned knitting industry; up to 1918, however, there were only eight electric knitting factories in Shanghai, and only ten by 1924. Thereafter, its development accelerated, especially in the form of hosiery factories. By 1928, there were thirty-five electric knitting factories in Shanghai, and from 1920 to 1928 the number of hosiery machines increased by 104 per cent.[22]

The Cement Industry

China began to establish its cement industry at the end of the nineteenth century but, up to the First World War, there were only three Chinese-owned cement factories. During the War the only factory established was the Zhijing Cement Company in Jinan, Shandong, set up in 1917, but it only operated on a small scale. In 1920 Liu Hongsheng established the Shanghai Cement Company with Chinese capital, and the Taihu Cement Company was set up at Wuxi in 1921; the Chinese Cement Company was founded at Longtan in 1922, and after that a small number of small-scale cement factories were also established. On a national basis the production of Chinese-owned cement factories increased by 94 per cent between 1922 and 1929.[23]

The Briquette Industry

The manufacture of machine-made briquettes, blocks of compressed coal dust or charcoal used for domestic fuel, was pioneered by Liu Hongsheng and was another industry developed from the 1920s. Liu established the Zhonghua Briquette Factory in 1926. As a result of a rapid increase in demand, two new briquette factories were opened in 1928, and three in 1929, and other Chinese-owned briquette factories sprang up like mushrooms. The output of Zhonghua increased by twenty-five times between 1926 and 1931.[24]

FACTORS BEHIND DEVELOPMENT IN THE 1920s

First, we must point out that the sharp decline in imports during the First World War did indeed promote the development of the national capital. For instance, total imports of cotton yarn dropped sharply from 2 685 528 piculs in 1915 to 1 131 631 piculs in 1918,[25] thus offering Chinese-owned textile mills good opportunities to sell their products on the market and to make large profits. However, the high tide of establishing textile mills occurred at the beginning of the 1920s, after the end of the war. The *History of China's Cotton Textile Industry* explained this in the following ways: (1) It took quite long time to prepare for the establishment of a large factory; (2) The production of textile machinery in the United Kingdom and USA had been limited during the European War and, moreover, there were difficulties in transportation. Therefore, the high tide of establishing textile mills was in 1921–2.[26] Of course, during the First World War and in the early post-war period the imperialist countries like the United Kingdom had no time to carry out their eastward strategy and slackened their invasion of China, and this was really an important factor in stimulating the development of national capital.

Second, we must point out that, although the influence of the First World War itself was a factor, the Chinese-owned textile industry of course would not have developed so fast if the May 4th Movement anti-Japanese boycott had not limited imports of Japanese goods. At that time, cotton yarn was the main Japanese import into China. The gross value of imports of Japanese yarn decreased sharply from 86 366 000 Japanese yen in 1918 to 47 113 000 in 1921.[27] The quantity of Japanese yarn imports fell from 746 000 piculs in 1918, to 531 000 in 1919. Japanese yarn accounted for 66 per cent of total imports of yarn in 1919, but for only 38 per cent in 1919.[28]

The Shenxin No. 1 Cotton Mill, one of the Rong group, the largest conglomerate of Chinese capital, was established in 1916, with a capital of only Ch$300 000. Net profits were 160 200 taels in 1918, but 754 600 in 1919, 918 630 in 1920, 527 110 in 1921 and 418 770 in 1922. Between 1916 and 1922, the Shenxin No. 1 Cotton Mill earned net profits totalling 2 879 090 taels,[29] and this established the basis of the Shenxin group. Shenxin Nos 2, 3, and 4 Mills were established between 1919 and 1921 when national capital was earning high profits under the influence of the boycott movements. The establishment of industrial enterprises around 1920 by another major Chinese capital group, that of Liu Hongsheng, was also stimulated by the people's patriotic mass movement to boycott Japanese goods, in that they saw profit in the establishment of factories and so began to invest their money in the match industry and cement industries.[30]

The development of national capital was closely linked in the early 1920s to the May 4th Movement, in the mid 1920s to the boycotts surrounding the May 30 Movement, and in the late 1920s to the boycotts provoked by the Jinan Incident in 1928. Over the four industrial sectors of cotton textiles, silk reeling, flour and tobacco there were eighty-two factories in Shanghai in 1915, 109 in 1921; in other words, over seven years, twenty-seven new factories were opened. However, more and more factories were established between 1925 and 1927. By 1927, the total number of the factories had reached 315, an increase of 183 from the 132 factories in 1924.[31]

Taking the cotton textile industry as an example, 'after the May 30th Massacre, the Movement to boycott Japanese and British goods gained momentum, and Chinese yarn sold well on the market',[32] and 'unsold Chinese cloth immediately began to move.'[33] As soon as the movement began, the Rongs issued a manifesto advocating the use of Chinese goods and published advertisements promoting the sale of Chinese cloth.[34] The net profit of Shenxin No. 1 Cotton Mill reversed the decline of 1923–4 and increased from Ch$129 650 in 1924 to Ch$192 470 in 1925.[35] It was also under the impact of the May 30th Movement that in the summer of 1925 the Rongs set up the Shenxin No. 6 Cotton Mill by leasing the Changzhou Cotton Mill.

The May 30th Movement played an even greater role in stimulating the Chinese-owned tobacco industry. Against the background of the monopoly enjoyed by the British-American Tobacco Company in the market, the Chinese-owned tobacco industry developed only slowly before 1925. After British-American Tobacco first set up factories in China in 1902, its production and sales increased year after year and by 1924 the volume of sales reached 634 624 cases each of 50 000 cigarettes. The impact of the boycott movement between 1925 and 1927, however, reversed the trend and sales dropped to 587 950 cases in 1925, and 562 690 cases in 1927.[36]

In 1924 there were only sixteen Chinese-owned tobacco factories but by 1925 their number had increased to fifty-two, by 1926 to sixty-four and by 1927 to sixty-seven. The total value of sales of the Nanyang Brothers Tobacco Company reached a peak in 1925 at more than Ch$20 000 000, an increase of 46 per cent over 1920.[37]

After the Jinan Incident in 1928, the Chinese people launched another movement boycotting Japanese goods, and the cotton textile, flour and rubber industries enjoyed a certain level of development. Because prices rose following the boycott movement and supply was falling short of demand, the Shenxin cotton mills made large profits, and on this basis each mill expanded its productive capacity. The Shenxin No. 7 Cotton Mill was established through the purchase of the British Dongfang Cotton Mill, and the Shenxin No. 8 Cotton Mill soon followed.[38] The number of spindles operated by the Shenxin group increased from 189 804 in 1927 to 197 896 in 1928 and 280 532 in 1929.

The Maoxin and Fuxin Flour Mills run by the Rongs also made full use of the opportunities presented by the boycotts to increase production and thereby profits, and built new warehouses on the basis of those profits.[39] The major enterprises of the rubber industry in Shanghai, such as the Da Zhonghua Rubber Products Factory, also came into being in 1928. At that time the factory's profits were such that it was said that one box of shoes were worth a [shoe-shaped] ingot of silver and profits on the production of a pair of rubber shoes amounted to 25 per cent.[40] Within three years of its establishment the Da Zhonghua Rubber Products Factory had earned profits of more than Ch$1 million and its annual profits were equal to more than 50 per cent of its capital.[41]

The third factor underlying the development of Chinese national capital in the 1920s was the vigorous entrepreneurial spirit shown by some Chinese capitalists. Just as in other capitalist countries, Chinese capitalists were on the look out for opportunities for profit. They were ready to take risks, to reinvest the large profits of their enterprises and to use internal funds to buy more machinery in order to expand production. Thus they hoped to achieve their goals of reducing production costs and maximising profits. They believed that the greater the volume of output, the easier it would be to purchase raw materials and sell their products and the more they could economise on management and business costs.[42] The Shenxin No. 1 Cotton Mill had a total capital of CH$1.5 million in 1920 and in that year profits were Ch$975 000, of which only Ch$75 000 was distributed, Ch$900 000 being used to increase the share capital to Ch$2.4 million. In 1922, the 1921 profit of Ch$0.6 million was added to share capital, raising it to Ch$3 million.[43] This was a difference between the Rongs and some share-holders who had earlier collaborated with them. Earlier, Rong Zongjing and Rong Desheng had established a joint venture, the Zhenxin Cotton Mill, in Wuxi. The Rong brothers advocated continuous expansion of the scale of production but some other shareholders wanted to draw more cash out of the business. At the meeting of the Board of Directors, Rong Desheng pointed out: 'We want to make big money, so we must produce on a big scale; how much would we earn from 30 000 spindles?'[44] In the end the Rongs parted company with these shareholders and founded the Shenxin No. 1 Cotton Mill in Shanghai.

Rong Zongjing and Rong Desheng were not only willing continuously to reinvest their enterprises' profits but they were also good at expanding the scale of their enterprises with the use of the loan capital available in pre-Communist China. Because in the 1920s the Rongs borrowed continuously from the banks and *qianzhuang* (old style Chinese private banks) to buy or rent factories, by 1929 the ratio between loan capital and share capital reached to 4.17:1.[45] Rong Zongjing even said that one should not worry about more debts, just as one should not scratch an itch caused by more lice. This was an effective way of sharing the risks of their enterprises with the banks and *qianzhuang*. Later, when the Rongs faced an impasse because of lack of liquidity, in the end they were able to secure support.

The main purpose of capitalists in buying up factories was to reduce competition and increase their own strength. Therefore Rong Zongjing even said: 'No matter whether a factory is good or bad, I will buy it so long as someone is ready to sell. Buying one more spindle is like getting one more gun.'[46] Between 1922 and 1931, as many as 68.4 per cent of the new spindles in the Shenxin group were purchased.[47] On the basis both of purchase and of new establishment, by 1932 the Shenxin group accounted for 20 per cent of the spindles and 28 per cent of the looms run by Chinese-owned mills outside the North-east. The productive capacity of the twelve flour mills in Shanghai, of which 50 per cent was accounted for by the Fuxin Flour Mills, made up one-third of the total in China proper.[48]

The development of the Liu Hongsheng's enterprises also took place partly through buying up existing factories. For instance, Liu established the Hongsheng Match Factory in 1920 with a total capital of Ch$120 000 but it lost Ch$50 000 between 1920 and 1924, which accounted approximately for half its total capital. In 1924, he bought the Xiechang Match Company, which had a reputation in the industry as a progressive company, in order to eliminate a competitor and to change loss into profit by opening up markets. 'In the first year after the take-over of the Xiechang factory, profits were enough to make up previous deficits and still have a Ch$100 000 surplus on top.'[49]

Liu Hongsheng also made use of sales agreements, a common practice abroad. For instance, when the Shanghai Cement Company, which he set up in 1920, began to produce, it met with competition from Qixin in Northern China. In order to avoid mutual harm and the better to deal with foreign competition, they signed a contract for cooperation in June, 1925. By allowing Qixin the north and central Chinese markets, the Shanghai Cement Company gained predominance in the area covered by the sales agreement (the south China market). Because of this agreement, the Company turned the 1924 loss into a profit of Ch$120 000 in 1926.[50]

A fourth factor was the measures taken by some national capitalists in the 1920s to promote the development of their enterprises through the adoption of advanced management techniques, the establishment of brand names and the opening of institutions to train management and technical personnel. We may take the Rongs' enterprises as an example. From the early 1920s the Rongs set up the head offices of the Maoxin, Fuxin and Shenxin Companies, through which to buy raw materials, market their products and raise funds for the individual mills.[51] The Renzhong brand cotton yarn and Warship brand flour produced by the Rongs' enterprises gradually became famous brand names well known far and near.

The Rongs also founded a public Industrial and Commercial Middle School in 1919. The school was closed down in 1927 with the five cohorts of graduates totalling more than 400, most of whom became technical personnel, such as engineers or even factory managers, in the Rongs' various factories; they came to play an important role in China and were known as 'Industrial and Commercial faction'. From 1928 the Shenxin Staff and Workers Training Centre was established, where twenty students each year were trained in textile technology; it was a half study half work system and, up to 1932, it graduated four classes who became the technical mainstay of the Rongs' enterprises. For the enterprise to do its own training did not require large funds but imparted a practical emphasis to the learning and brought quick results. Therefore, although the Rongs' enterprises also recruited some graduates from colleges and universities as well as qualified personnel returned from abroad, such people were recruited only in small numbers. The Rongs' technical and managerial personnel mainly came from the training institutions set up within the enterprises themselves in the 1920s.[52]

Liu Hongsheng also paid attention to business management. For example, in order to compete with foreign companies, Liu's match factories engaged Lin Tianyi on a high salary as an expert to improve the safety match. Lin's monthly income was about Ch$1000, which was very rare in enterprises at that time.[53] Liu's cement factory also engaged those 'with specialised business knowledge to undertake the operations of retail sales'.[54] From the very start, his Zhanghua Wool Factory sent people abroad to conduct investigations, engage technicians and buy machinery.[55] The Huafeng Enamel Factory enrolled a large number of apprentices to engage in production, something which Liu believed to be beneficial to management and the reduction of labour costs.[56]

Fifth, the emergence of large conglomerates of national capital in the 1920s enabled them to procure cheap raw materials. Owing to the fact that Chinese industrial investment before 1949 was mainly concentrated in light industry, raw materials accounted for a large proportion of total production costs. So the development of national capital depended heavily upon the procurement of cheap raw materials. Again we take the Rongs as an example. They had a head office which was responsible for the coordinated procurement of the large amounts of raw materials which their many mills needed, and set up procurement offices in the main wheat and cotton producing areas. By 1922, Maoxin, Fuxin and Shenxin had established more than ten wheat or cotton purchasing stations in Jiangsu, Anhui and Shandong. During the harvest seasons they purchased cotton and wheat at low prices, or purchased in advance before the harvest season.

The Rongs also saw that setting up exchanges could play a role in controlling the prices of raw materials and products. Therefore, together with other Shanghai industrialists in the same line of business, they organised a flour exchange and a cotton yarn and cloth exchange at the beginning of 1920.[57] Rong Zongjing was an old hand at controlling the market. When wheat and cotton came on to the market, he intentionally sold flour and cotton through his exchanges in Shanghai so as to force prices down and enable him to purchase cheap raw materials soon afterwards. This of course was an example of the Chinese national capitalists exploiting the peasants through the exchange of unequal values. In addition, these larger national capital groups had advantages in procuring foreign wheat and cotton. For instance, there were many mills in the Maoxin and Fuxin groups and they needed a large amount of foreign wheat. If that wheat could be loaded and transported to China in one cargo ship, then transportation costs could be cut by half.[58]

Liu Hongsheng started his career promoting the sale of coal. After the coal had been sold, much coal dust was left. Liu established a cement factory and a briquette factory to solve the problem of disposing of the coal dust. The briquette factory naturally used coal dust as raw material, while the cement factory needed continually to feed coal dust into the kilns in order to intensify the heat and thus turn into cement the stone powder fed in from the other direction. Therefore, the cement factory used a large amount of coal each year.[59] Apart from selling coal from the Kailuan mines, Liu Hongsheng invested in the Liujiang coal mine at the end of the First World War and later took over the Jiawang coal mine and established the East China Coal Mine Company Ltd. These investments certainly also provided cheap raw materials for his cement and briquette factories.

Another example is the way that capitalists of the Nanyang Brothers Tobacco Company in the 1920s colluded with local feudal forces to buy large amounts of land and establish tobacco leaf purchasing stations in tobacco-producing areas such as Xuchang in Henan and Fangzi in Shandong; this allowed them to purchase tobacco directly from the peasants in the manner of the British-American Tobacco Company. They exploited the peasants by means such as advance purchases, usury, reducing the actual weight and reducing the grade of the tobacco. Between 1920 and 1931, at the Xuchang Tobacco-leaf Purchasing station alone, the 'extra poundage' accounted on average for 12 per cent of total purchases, and for a maximum of 16.3 per cent. The total value of this 'extra poundage' reached Ch$400 000.[60]

This chapter has presented some historical materials illustrating the development of Chinese national capital in the 1920s and analysed the internal and external factors promoting that development. Pre-communist China was, however, a semi-colonial and semi-feudal society. Seriously oppressed and controlled by the three big enemies (imperialism, feudalism and bureaucratic-capitalism), the Chinese national capitalist economy could not develop fully and independently. In particular, after the Japanese occupation of Manchuria in 1931 Chinese national capital was also affected by the deterioration of the international and domestic economic situation, and gradually fell into a dilemma of having too many problems to tackle, exposing its own essential weakness. Just as Comrade Mao Zedong rightly pointed out, 'by and large, it was impossible to develop industry unless China was independent, free, democratic and united'.[61]

Notes

1. [Editor's note] This chapter is a translation of Zhang Zhongli, 'Guanyu Zhongguo minzu ziben zai ershi niandai de fazhan wenti', *Shehui kexue* 1983.10 (October 1983): 42–6.
2. Zhongguo renmin daxue, zhengzhi jingjixue xi, *Zhongguo jindai jingji shi* (Beijing, 1979), vol. 1, p. 249.
3. Ibid., p. 262.
4. Chen Zhen *et al.*, comp., *Zhongguo jindai gongye shi ziliao* (Beijing, 1957), vol. 1.
5. Yan Zhongping, *Zhongguo mianfangzhi shi gao* (Beijing, 1963).
6. *Rong jia qiye shiliao*, Shanghai shehui kexue yuan, jingji yanjiu suo, comp, 2 vols (Shanghai, 1980).
7. *Liu Hongsheng qiye shiliao*, Shanghai shehui kexue yuan, jingji yanjiu suo, comp, 3 vols (Shanghai, 1981).
8. Yan Zhongping, *Mianfangzhi shi gao*, p. 172.
9. See Yan Zhongping, *Zhongguo jindai jingji shi tongji ziliao xuanji* (Beijing, 1955), pp. 134–5, 162–3, and Yan, *Mianfangzhi shi gao*, pp. 354–5.
10. *Rong jia qiye shiliao*, vol. 1, pp. 268, 613.
11. The conclusion was drawn from the figures in Yan Zhongping, *Tongji ziliao xuanji*, pp. 134–5.
12. *Shanghai shi mianbu shangye*, Shanghai shi gongshang xingzheng guanli ju, *et al.*, comp. (Beijing, 1979), p. 99.
13. See *Rong jia qiye shiliao*, vol. 1, p. 613.
14. See Yan Zhongping, *Tongji ziliao xuanji*, pp. 162–3.

15. *Nanyang xiongdi yancao gongsi shiliao*, Shanghai shehui kexue yuan, jingji yanjiu suo, comp. (Shanghai, 1960), pp. 254–5.
16. Ibid., p. 145.
17. *Shanghai minzu xiangjiao gongye*, Shanghai shi gongshang xingzheng guanli ju, comp. (Shanghai, 1979), p. 14.
18. Zhao Cong, 'Zuijin Zhongguo zhi huochaiye', *Gongshang banyuekan* 7.3 (1 February 1935).
19. *Liu Hongsheng qiye shiliao*, vol. 1, p. 76.
20. *Shanghai minzu jiqi gongye*, Shanghai shi gongshang ju, comp. (Shanghai, 1979), vol. 1, pp. 199–220, 256, 303 and 455.
21. Ibid., p. 311.
22. See Gong Jun, *Zhongguo xin gongye fazhan shi dagang* (Shanghai, 1933), pp. 178–80.
23. *Liu Hongsheng qiye shiliao*, vol. 1, pp. 155–6, 169, 184.
24. Ibid., p. 245.
25. Yang Duanliu, *Liushiwu nian lai Zhongguo guoji maoyi tongji* (Shanghai, 1931), p. 46.
26. Yan Zhongping, *Mianfangzhi shi gao*, p. 172.
27. Pu Song, *Comparative Study of Boycotts* (1933), p. 6.
28. Charles Remer, *A Study of Chinese Boycotts* (Baltimore, 1933), p. 72.
29. *Rong jia qiye shiliao*, vol. 1, pp. 622–3, table 8.
30. See *Liu Hongsheng qiye shiliao*, vol. 1, p. 76.
31. *Shanghai zibenzhuyi gongshang ye de shehuizhuyi gaizao*, Shanghai shehui kexue yuan, jingji yanjiu suo (Shanghai, 1980), p. 12.
32. Di Xian, 'Minguo shisi nian zhi mianye', *Yinhang zhoubao* 10.7 (2 March 1926).
33. See *Fangzhi shibao*, 2 July 1925.
34. See *Rong jia qiye shiliao*, vol. 1, pp. 185–6.
35. Ibid., table on p. 176.
36. According to the archives of the Yizhong Tobacco Company.
37. *Nanyang xiongdi yancao gongsi*, p. 220.
38. *Rong jia qiye shiliao*, vol. 1, pp. 214–21.
39. Ibid., pp. 223–7.
40. See *Shanghai minzu xiangjiao gongye*, p. 91.
41. Ibid., p. 93.
42. *Rong jia qiye shiliao*, vol. 1, p. 253.
43. Ibid., p. 112.
44. Ibid., p. 52.
45. Ibid., p. 278.
46. Huang Yifeng, 'Jiu Zhongguo Rongjia ziben de fazhan', *Xueshu yuekan* 1964.2 (February 1964).
47. *Rong jia qiye shiliao*, vol. 1, table 1, p. 268.
48. Ibid., pp. 285–6.
49. *Liu Hongsheng qiye shiliao*, vol. 1, p. 84.
50. Ma Bohuang, 'Lun jiu Zhongguo Liu Hongsheng qiye fazhan zhong de jige wenti', *Lishi yanjiu* 1980.3 (June 1980): 53.

51. *Rong jia qiye shiliao*, vol. 1, p. 96.
52. Huang Hanmin, 'Lue lun Rongjia qiye de rencai peiyang wenti', *Jingji xueshu ziliao* 1982.2 (February 1982).
53. *Liu Hongsheng qiye shiliao*, p. 95.
54. Ibid., p. 177.
55. Ibid., p. 249.
56. Ibid., p. 271.
57. *Rong jia qiye shiliao*, vol. 1, p. 69–70.
58. Ibid., p. 82–3.
59. *Liu Hongsheng qiye shiliao*, vol. 1, p. 158.
60. *Nanyang xiongdi yancao gongsi*, p. 203.
61. Mao Tse-tung [Mao Zedong], 'On Coalition Government', *Selected Works of Mao Tse-tung*, vol. 4 (Beijing, 1967), p. 302.

4 Economic Development in China Between the Two World Wars (1920–1936)

Wang Yuru

Wang Yuru is a young scholar from the Institute of Economics, Nankai University; her work reflects the interests of scholars at that Institute. Perhaps the two key points about this chapter are its attempt to develop macro-economic estimates for the whole of the Chinese economy and its complete rejection of the idea of stagnation in the 1920s and 1930s, arguing instead that this was the period of China's most rapid economic development.[1]

What was China's economic situation over the century between the Opium War and liberation in 1949? Was China's economy developing, stagnating or declining? If it was developing, what was its growth rate? Was that rate fast or slow in comparison to other nations at the time? If we divide the period into sub-periods, in which period was growth fastest and development greatest for China? These are questions which concern all researchers on modern Chinese economic history and also all those generally interested in the economic history of China. Unfortunately the textbooks and monographs on modern Chinese economic history published in China do not contain answers to such questions. In this article the author cannot provide a comprehensive analysis of all the above problems but hopes to provide some initial clues through a statistical analysis of the period 1920–36, the most controversial period in modern Chinese economic history and the one where there is the greatest gap between the historical record and the traditional interpretations; we will also compare that period with the preceding (1887–1920) and following (1936–49) periods.

Over the past thirty years, under the influence of political economy, economic historians in China have concentrated on the development and change in the relations of production and neglected, sometimes totally, the growth in the forces of production. Moreover, because of a one-sided comprehension of Marx's ideas about the relations of production, they have also neglected subjects such as circulation, distribution and consumption. Thus the various textbooks on Chinese economic history analyse the Chinese economy according to the type of ownership, such as the foreign capitalist economy, the bureaucratic capitalist economy, the national capitalist economy, the feudal landlord economy. But none offers a comprehensive analysis of the general development of China's economy over that century. This article, therefore, moves from the macro to the micro, from the general to the specific, in using the available data to produce an integrated analysis of the development of the Chinese economy between the two world wars, encompassing both forces and relations of production.

ECONOMIC GROWTH BETWEEN THE TWO WORLD WARS

Although previous works on the economic history of pre-liberation China give no overall analysis of China's economic situation between the two wars, they do express generally similar views on the various sectors of the economy and their interactions. These views are roughly along the following lines: after the First World War the imperialist powers resumed dumping goods and exporting capital to China, thus gaining further control over China's economic lifelines. After the Nationalists came to power, bureaucratic capital rapidly expanded under the control of the Four Great Families: before the outbreak of the Anti-Japanese war, it had gained a monopoly over finance and through the financial sector controlled some branches of industry, mining and transportation. Under oppression by both foreign and bureaucratic capital, Chinese privately-owned industry was declining day by day and sinking into depression, crisis and a state of bankruptcy or semi-bankruptcy. Productive forces in agriculture suffered serious destruction and the rural economy was becoming daily more destitute. In a word, these views impress upon us that China's economy during this period was declining or in a state of stagnation. Such ideas also had considerable currency abroad. Available statistical data, however, suggest that 1936 saw the peak of economic development in pre-Communist China. Moreover many people who lived through those times consider that China's economy in the early 1930s was as healthy as it ever had been up to that time. This must throw some doubt on the conclusions of the works discussed above.

From the late 1960s some overseas scholars began to question this picture. Their studies have concentrated mostly on showing that China's modern industry, mining and transportation expanded quite rapidly

TABLE 4.1   *Gross value of industrial and agricultural output in China, 1887, 1920, 1936 and 1949 (billion 1936 Ch$)*

Sector	1887	1920	1936	1949
Agriculture	11.95	17.35	19.92	13.04
Industry*	2.66	5.65	10.69	5.60
Total	14.61	23.00	30.61	18.64
Implied growth rates (%)		1.38	1.80	–3.74

* including mining

SOURCES: 1887: Chang Chung-li [Zhang Zhongli] in his *The Income of the Chinese Gentry* (Seattle, 1962) was the first to calculate China's gross national product for 1887. Albert Feuerwerker, in his chapter on 'Economic Trends in the Late Ch'ing Empire', in John K. Fairbank (ed.), *The Cambridge History of China*, vol. 11 (Cambridge, 1980), p. 2, relied mainly on Chang's calculations, only adjusting value added in agriculture upwards by 33%. This table is based on Feuerwerker's figures. The figures are converted from net to gross value using the ratios between net and gross value of industrial and agricultural output in Wu Baosan *Zhongguo guomin suode* (Shanghai, 1947), and 'Zhongguo guomin suode, yi jiu san san xiuzheng', *Shehui kexue zazhi* 9.2 (December 1947): 92–153. There is a small error in this procedure because Feuerwerker did not subtract depreciation from the value added of industry and agriculture. We have also converted silver taels into silver dollars at the rate of 1:1.4686 (see Chang, *Income of the Chinese Gentry*, p. 324). We have used the price index for the years 1887–1931 in *Nankai Weekly Statistical Service*, 11 April 1932, and for 1931–36 in Wu Baosan, *Zhongguo guomin suode* to adjust the figures to 1936 prices.
1920: according to Tang Chuansi's figures used Wu Chengming (See Chapter 2), converting 1933 prices into 1936 prices according to the above indices.
1936: See Ding Shixun, 'Guanyu Zhongguo Zibenzhuyi fazhan shuiping de jige wenti', *Nankai daxue xuebao, zhe she* 1979.4 (October 1979): 20–7
1949: *Zhongguo tongji nianjian, 1984*, Guojia tongji ju (Beijing, 1984), p. 20. We have converted the figures to 1936 prices at the ratio of 2.5:1.

between the two world wars. In recent years some articles published in China have also criticised the view that the national economy was bankrupt or semi-bankrupt at that time. Wu Chengming, after describing the tortuous development of China's capitalist economy, came to the belief that the period between 1921 and 1936 was a period of expansion and development of capitalism. He expresses the fear that the views of previous scholars were too pessimistic.[2] Other scholars have also called into question the accepted picture, for instance over the evaluation of the economic policies of the Nanjing government, or over whether or not the bureaucratic capital of the Four Great Families monopolised finance, industry, mining and transportation. But there has still been no overall study and evaluation of the economic development of the inter-war period.

In order to try to make some estimate of the macroeconomic growth rate during this period and then to compare it with those in the preceding and following periods, we have chosen the years 1887, 1920, 1936 and 1949 as benchmarks. We have calculated the gross value of industrial and agricultural output, national income and national income per capita in those years in Tables 4.1, 4.2 and 4.3.

From these tables, we can see that gross value of industrial and agricultural output increased from Ch$23.00 billion (in 1936 prices) in 1920 to Ch$30.61 billion in 1936, an annual growth rate of 1.8 per cent. National income increased from Ch$20.24 to Ch$25.80 billion, a growth rate of 1.53 per cent. Per capita national income increased from Ch$45.99 to Ch$51.60, a growth rate of 0.72 per cent. Each of the three indicators suggest that China's pre-Communist economy peaked in 1936. So it can hardly be that after the First World War China's economy was daily declining into bankruptcy.

During the Anti-Japanese War and the civil war, that is from 1937 to 1949, the Chinese economy declined seriously according to all three indicators. Thus gross value of industrial and agricultural output declined by an average of 3.74 per cent per annum, national income by 2.35 per cent and per capita national income by 2.95 per cent. In the late 1930s both the Japanese and the Chinese devoted themselves to the development of heavy industry in order to strengthen their military forces. So the output of electric power, coal, iron, steel, crude oil, cement, acid, soda and other mineral products peaked in 1942. But in terms of the whole economy, agriculture and light industry, which accounted for a larger proportion of national income than heavy industry, were basically in decline. After the defeat of Japan, there was some improvement in the national economy in 1946 and 1947 but the levels of 1936 were not surpassed. Later the economy declined again under the impact of full-scale civil war so that overall the period 1936–49 was the most difficult one for the pre-Communist Chinese economy.

The first period examined here (1887–1920) was one in which China's modern industry was experiencing its early stages of development. In this period there was a lot of imperialist investment in China. Although none of the past works of economic history has argued on the basis of the development of the whole economy that this was modern China's period of most rapid economic development, the conclusions emerging from studies of individual sectors often give that impression. Such an impression is not

TABLE 4.2   *China's national income, 1887, 1920, 1936 and 1949*
(billion 1936 Ch$)

Sector	1887	1920	1936	1949
Agriculture	9.99	14.49	16.64	9.80
Industry, mining and transportation	1.05	2.04	4.01	2.32
Services	3.87	3.70	5.15	6.83
National Income	14.90	20.24	25.80	18.95
Implied growth rates (% per annum)	0.93	1.53	−2.35	

NOTE: In this and some later tables, the columns appear not to add up because of rounding errors.

SOURCES: 1887: see Table 4.1. Since these figures are for gross value of domestic production, they are not completely comparable statistically with the later figures. As production was almost entirely by traditional methods at the time, depreciation would have been very small. There was some upward bias in Chang's figures on trade and income from gentry services and so the figure for services may be too high.
1920: See Table 4.1 for agriculture, industry, mining and transportation. Net value of output has been calculated using the ratio of gross value of output to net value of output in each sector estimated by Wu Baosan in *Zhongguo guomin suode* and 'Zhongguo guomin suode xiuzheng'. Service income is based on the figures in Dwight H. Perkins, 'Growth and Changing Structure of China's Twentieth Century Economy', in Dwight H. Perkins (ed.), *China's Modern Economy in Historical Perspective* (Stanford, 1975), p. 117, and has been converted to 1936 prices.
1933: Wu Baosan, *Zhongguo guomin suode* and 'Zhongguo guomin suode xiuzheng'.
1949: For agriculture, industry, mining and transportation, see Table 4.1. Service income is based on the 1952 figures in Perkins, 'Growth and Changing Structure', p. 117, and has been converted into 1936 prices.

supported by the figures in Tables 4.1 to 4.3 and the calculations made from them. Thus the rates of growth of all three indicators were clearly lower than those in the later period.

Although Britain and the other Western powers had forced China's door open in the Opium War of the 1840s, their operations still remained in the stage of plunder by force. China's traditional socio-economic structure and mode of production only began to change from the 1870s at the earliest. This was because over the thirty years after 1840 the machine-made products from abroad had not been able really to penetrate Chinese

TABLE 4.3   *Per capita national income, 1887, 1920, 1936 and 1949*
(1936 Ch$)

	1887	*1920*	*1936*	*1949*
National income (Ch$100 million)	148.99	202.37	258.01	189.48
Population (million)	337.50	440.00	500.00	541.67
Per capita national income (Ch$)	39.47	45.99	51.60	34.98
Average annual rate of growth (%)		0.46	0.72	−2.95

SOURCES: for National Income see Table 4.2. For population: 1887: Wang Shida, 'Jindai Zhongguo renkou de guji', *Shehui kexue zazhi* 2.1(March 1931): 51–105; 1920 according to Xu Xinwu, *Zhongguo zibenzhuyi fazhan shi*, vol. 2 (unpublished), ch. 4; 1936: Liu Ta-chung and Yeh Kung-chia, *The Economy of the Chinese Mainland: National Income and Economic Development, 1933–1959* (Princeton, 1965), p. 182, Table 53; 1949, according to *Zhongguo jingji nianjian, 1983*, Zhongguo jingji nianjian bianji weiyuanhui (Beijing, 1983), Section III, p. 5. [Editor's note: after consultation with the author, the population figure for 1936 has been revised from 450 million in the original article to 500 million.]

markets. The opening of the Suez canal, however, greatly shortened the trade route, while the completion of the submarine cable speeded up the transmission of information. Meanwhile the forces of production had obviously been further developed in Britain, and more privileges were gained in China. All these factors greatly increased the competitiveness of British industrial products. Because of these factors, the basis of China's traditional economy – a self-sufficient natural economy combining agriculture with domestic handicraft industries – began to disintegrate and modern Chinese industry, first government-run and later private, began to emerge. So, strictly speaking, the 1870s should be considered the beginning of the development of China's modern economy.

The quantitative analysis in this article takes the mid 1880s as the starting point, both because of availability of data and because of the theoretical issues discussed above. Although the standard view is that China's modern economic history began in 1840, in fact there was little basic change in China's traditional economic structure in the following forty years, and the development of the forces of production in modern Chinese industry was still very limited right up to 1887. Moreover the economy was seriously damaged in the 1850s and 1860s by the Taiping Rebellion and the Qing government's efforts to suppress it. Between ten and thirty million people died during that war.[3] The economy recovered only in the 1880s, when the abandoned land was returned to cultivation. Even with no quantitative data it is not difficult to offer the judgement that the growth rates of our indicators between 1840 and 1887 would have been less than in the later periods between 1887 and 1920 and between 1920 and 1936.

The above analysis shows that, despite the 1931–5 economic depression, on the whole China's economy between 1920 and 1936 experienced considerable development and expanded its economic potential. Indeed the period registered the most rapid growth rate in the history of China's modern economic development and the greatest advance towards industrialisation and the development of capitalism.

THE RAPID DEVELOPMENT OF THE MODERN SECTOR AND THE CHANGES IN THE STRUCTURE OF PRODUCTION

The rapid development of China's economy between the two world wars was mainly due to the rapid growth of industry, mining and transportation, especially the modern sector. The changes in China's traditional mode of production and productive structure which had begun from the end of the nineteenth century underwent a further clear development in this period.

Between 1920 and 1936 the gross value of China's industrial output increased by almost 100 per cent, at an average annual rate of 4.06 per cent (the growth rate of net value of output was 3.98 per cent). Its share in the gross value of industrial and agricultural output rose from 24.58 to 34.92 per cent. At the same time, the gross value of agricultural output increased by less than 15 per cent, at an annual rate of 0.87 per cent. Its share of total gross value of industrial and agricultural output decreased from 75.42 to 65.08 per cent (see Table 4.4).

Although there were examples of the use of mechanised farm equipment such as irrigation or drainage pumps, tractors and threshing machines, and even of chemical fertilisers in Chinese agriculture in this period, such examples were very rare indeed. So production in agriculture can be regarded as using entirely traditional methods and any use of modern methods can be ignored. The same cannot be said of industry, where both modern mechanised and traditional handicraft methods were used. Thus Table 4.4 does not entirely reflect the changing trends in traditional and modern methods in the Chinese economy. Table 4.5 does address this issue.

Between 1920 and 1936 the total value of production by modern methods in China's industry, mining and transportation increased by more than 179 per cent, at an annual growth rate of 6.63 per cent (6.33 per cent

TABLE 4.4   *Growth of agriculture and industry, 1920–1936 (billion 1936 Ch$)*

Sector	1920		1936		Average growth rate, 1920–36 (%)
	gross value of output	% of total	gross value of output	% of total	
Industry	5.65	24.58	10.69	34.92	4.06
Agriculture	17.35	75.42	19.92	65.08	0.87
Total	23.00	100	30.61	100	

SOURCES: see notes to Table 4.1.

TABLE 4.5   *Growth of modern and traditional sectors, 1920–1936 (billion 1936 Ch$)*

Production methods	1920		1936		Average growth rate, 1920–36 (%)
	output value	% of total	output value	% of total	
Modern	1.48	6.21	4.13	12.86	6.63
Traditional	22.31	93.79	27.96	87.14	1.42
Total	23.78	100	32.08	100	

SOURCES: see notes to Tables 4.1 and 4.2.
NOTE: both the modern and the traditional categories include elements of the transportation industry.

TABLE 4.6   *Growth of modern and handicraft industry in China, 1920–1936 (billion 1936 Ch$)*

Type of industry	1920		1936		Average growth rate, 1920–36 (%)
	output value	% of total	output value	% of total	
Modern	1.12	19.80	3.32	31.04	7.03
Handicraft	4.53	80.20	7.37	68.96	3.09
Total	5.65	100	10.69	100	

SOURCES: see notes to Table 4.1.

if calculated in terms of net value). But even at the end of the period its share of national product was still small – only 12.86 per cent. If we disaggregate the figures and consider the proportions of modern and traditional production just within industry, mining and transportation, we get the results shown in Tables 4.6 and 4.7.

Handicraft industries in cities and in the countryside also grew quite rapidly between 1920 and 1936 but their share of total industrial production decreased from 80.20 to 68.96 per cent. Over the period the gross value of the output of modern industry increased by almost 200 per cent, at an annual growth rate of 7.03 per cent (7.11 per cent if using net value),[4] and its share of total industrial output rose from 19.8 to 31.04 per cent. At the same time, the amount of power used by factories in China increased by more than 200 per cent.[5]

Thus there was a clear trend for modern methods to replace traditional methods in some branches of industry. For example, in 1920 coal output by mechanised methods was 14 130 543 tons, a figure which had increased to 33 793 930 tons by 1936 (84.7 per cent of total output), an increase of close to 140 per cent. But at the same time the amount of coal mined by traditional methods decreased by more than one million tons and its share of total output fell to 15.3 per cent. Over the same period there was a 120 per cent growth in the amount of iron ore mined by mechanical methods, which by 1936 accounted for 87 per cent of total production; on the other hand iron ore mined by traditional methods fell both in absolute terms and as a proportion of the total. Similarly pig iron smelted by modern methods rose to 82.7 per cent of the total, that by traditional methods fell by 30 000 tons, to 17.3 per cent of the total.[6] These figures show that, partly through the replacement of traditional methods with power-driven machinery and partly through the establishment of new modern factories and mines, modern production methods were in fact already predominant in most branches of heavy industry by the outbreak of the anti-Japanese war.

Between 1920 and 1936 modern transportation grew more rapidly than did traditional transportation (see Table 4.7). By 1936 it accounted for more than half of total transportation. The tonnage of steamships owned by Chinese businesses increased from 158 150 tons in 1920 to 576 875 tons in 1936,[7] an increase of 260 per cent. Although competition was fierce, they rapidly replaced junk transportation. On the Chuanjiang junks accounted for over half the transport in 1919 but by 1926 they had been completely replaced. Another example is salt transportation on the middle and lower Yangzi where junks had been predominant, but over this period steam shipping was irresistibly driving out traditional transport.

Railway building also reached its height in the period between the two

TABLE 4.7 *Growth of modern and traditional transportation in China, 1920–1936 (million 1936 Ch$)*

Type of transportation	1920		1936		Average growth rate, 1920–36 (%)
	Income	% of total	Income	% of total	
Modern	358	45.66	807	54.94	5.21
Traditional	426	54.34	662	45.06	2.79
Total	784	100	1469	100	4.00

SOURCES: see notes to Table 4.1.

wars. 10 274.56 km of railways were built between 1919 and 1937, an average of 540.77 km per year. This figure was larger than in either the preceding or following periods (see Table 4.8). Moreover the tonnage of goods transported increased from 8.9 billion ton km in 1920 to 17.8 billion ton km in 1936.[8]

A further illustration of the rapid growth of modern transportation is the fact that in this period both highway transport and civil aviation developed from virtually nothing. In 1921 China's highway network was only 736 miles long, but by 1935 it had increased over eighty-one times to 59 900 miles. China's first civil aviation company was established in 1929 but by 1935 three internal air lines operated ten routes with a total length of 1.68 million miles, covering the whole country.[9]

Past studies have largely ignored this record of growth in modern industry, mining and transportation, while at the same time arguing strongly that there occurred undesirable structural change in all sectors. If one only considers the private Chinese-owned sector, such a criticism

TABLE 4.8 *Railway construction in China, 1895–1944*

Period	Railway construction (km)	Average length of railway built per year (km)
1895–1919	10 763.37	430.53
1919–1937	10 274.56	540.77
1937–1944	2 697.47	337.18

SOURCES: Calculations based on Yan Zhongping, *Tongji ziliao*, pp. 172–9. Railways whose date of construction is unknown are not included. There is some overlap in the dates in order to deal conveniently with the construction periods of a few railways.

TABLE 4.9   *Changes in China's industrial structure, 1921–1936*

	Percentage of gross value of industrial output		Index of output, 1921=100	Average annual rate of growth (%)
	1921	*1936*		
Consumer goods	44.1	30.7	222	5.46
Coal	29.8	23.7	253	6.38
Ferrous metals	7.7	8.5	356	8.83
Other mineral products	11.7	8.6	236	5.89
Electric power	5.4	22.1	1301	18.56

SOURCES: Calculations based John Key Chang, *Industrial Development in Pre-Communist China*, pp. 76–9, Tables 20 and 21. Cement and crude oil were of such small importance that they have been omitted; the percentages, therefore, do not add up to 100.

might have some weight. (The development of the production of producer goods was slower than that of consumer goods. Nor did national capital make any great contribution to electric power, transportation, the extraction or processing of raw materials or machine building.) But if one studies Chinese capitalism as a whole, that is including foreign capital, a quite different picture would emerge.

Table 4.9 shows that the growth in the production of producer goods such as coal, ferrous metals, other mineral products and electric power was more rapid than that of consumer goods. Growth was especially rapid in the electric power industry, where output of electricity increased by 18.65 per cent per year, in all increasing thirteen times between 1921 and 1936. Production of ferrous metals also increased at an annual rate of 8.83 per cent, in all more than trebling over the period. But this was from a very small base. Despite the rapid increase (mainly in the Japanese-controlled North-eastern provinces) its contribution to total industrial output was still much lower than in many capitalist countries at the same time. Because of the very low base, cement and crude oil are not included in the table but their output also grew very rapidly. Consumer goods production grew by 2.2 times, but declined as a proportion of total industrial output from 44.1 to 30.7 per cent.[10] Thus China's heavy industry, like that in many other industrialising countries in Europe and America, grew more rapidly than did light industry and therefore the change in China's industrial structure followed the normal pattern. It is, however, necessary to point out that the machine-building industry (which is not included in Table 4.9) made little progress in this period, whether under the aegis of foreign or of Chinese capital. It was the weak link in China's industrialisation.

Between 1920 and 1936 the transportation sector grew about twice as rapidly as did agriculture and industry. Modern transport and communication facilities, such as railways, highways, shipping and aviation, developed even more rapidly. The growth of transportation capacity was coordinated with the development of the material productive sectors and fulfilled a progressive function in relation to domestic commodity exchange as well as import and export trade.

In the period between the two world wars, China's industrial development led to a change in the composition of the country's foreign trade. In 1920 the most important imports were cotton cloth and cotton yarn, amounting to around 247 million Haiguan taels, or about one third of all imports. On the eve of the Anti-Japanese war in 1936, however, the development of China's cotton textile industry had resulted in the reduction of these imports to only 10 million Haiguan taels, only 1.7 per cent of the total, and one twenty-fourth of the level of 1920. On the other hand, imports of raw cotton to supply China's cotton textile mills increased considerably, peaking in 1931 at around 4.7 million piculs. Parallel with this was the rising export of cotton yarn: in 1920 only 70 000 piculs were exported, only one-nineteenth of the amount imported. From 1928, however, exports exceeded imports, peaking in 1931 at 618 000 piculs, or nine times the level of 1920. Cotton cloth exports peaked in 1928 at 16 million Haiguan taels. From the First World War and especially from the 1920s China's cotton yarn entered the markets of south-east Asia and later those of west Asia, Africa and central and south America. Exports of cotton cloth decreased after 1931, however, because of the world economic crisis.[11]

Modern coal mining grew by over 5 per cent per year between the wars, so that, by the outbreak of the Anti-Japanese War, imports of coal were already very limited and their share of the market was only about 2 per cent, whereas exports grew from an average of over 1.6 million tons in 1916–20 to 4.3 million tons in 1936.[12]

With the rapid growth of modern industry and transportation, the importation of producer goods such as machinery, pig iron, steel, other construction materials, chemicals, dyestuffs for industry, transport equipment and liquid fuel naturally increased. The share of the means of production in total imports increased from 28.5 to 44.5 per cent, while that of consumer goods fell from 71.5 to 55.5 per cent.[13] At the same time exports of finished products increased both in absolute terms and as a proportion of total exports and the export of some raw and processed materials

Wang Yuru

Table 4.10 *Changes in the structure of agricultural production
(billion 1933 Ch$)*

	1914–18		1931–37	
	Annual average value of output	%	Annual average value of output	%
Grain crops	10.17	74.59	10.96	70.05
Cash crops	2.32	17.04	3.28	20.97
Livestock	1.14	8.37	1.40	8.98
Total	13.63	100	15.65	100

Sources: adapted from statistics in Dwight H. Perkins, *Agricultural Development in China, 1368–1968* (Edinburgh, 1969), p. 385.

experienced a relative decline since Chinese factories had enlarged their processing capacities.

This rapid growth of modern industry and transportation also resulted in a slight change in the structure of agricultural production. Thus the area sown to cereal crops decreased as a proportion of the total sown area, while that of cash crops such as cotton and oil-bearing crops increased. Value of output also registered corresponding changes. Table 4.10 shows that according to Perkins' statistics the proportion of cereal crops in total agricultural output fell from 75 to 70 per cent, while that of cash crops increased from 17 to 21 per cent.

China's industrial growth rate compared favourably with those of Western countries in their early stages of industrialisation: for instance the United States registered an industrial growth rate of 5.2 per cent (1874–90), Britain 3.3 per cent (1851–73), Germany 4.8 per cent (1891–1900) and France 3.3 per cent (1901–13). Between the wars China's industrial growth rate was 4.06 per cent in terms of gross value of output, 3.98 per cent in terms of net value of output. Japan, on the other hand, was an exception: between 1874 and 1890 its industrial growth rate was 12.1 per cent, between 1891 and 1900, 14.3 per cent,[14] which was much higher than China's growth rate 1920–36.

The situation in agriculture was different. Whereas in China gross value of agricultural output grew by only 0.87 per cent per annum in this period, in other countries the growth rate was much more rapid: 3.01 per cent in the United States (1870–1900), 3.18 per cent in France (1870–90) and 3.29 per cent in Japan (1878–1900).[15]

To sum up, we can conclude that China's modern mining, industrial and transportation sector grew rapidly between 1920 and 1936. As China began the transition towards an industrial society, there were also considerable changes in its economic structure. On the other hand the predominance of traditional production in the rural areas meant that modern production only accounted for 12.86 per cent of national production. Thus there had as yet been no basic change in the traditional mode of production and, on the eve of the Anti-Japanese War, China was still an economically backward agricultural country.

THE GROWTH OF CAPITALIST RELATIONS OF PRODUCTION AND THE RISE AND FALL OF THE VARIOUS ECONOMIC SECTORS

We have studied above the quantity and quality of China's productive forces and the change in its economic structure between the two world wars. We will now go on to analyse the changes in the relations of production.

Marx's theory holds that a major characteristic of the capitalist period is that the products of labor are generalised in the form of commodities. In his study of the development of capitalism in Russia Lenin stressed first of all the extent to which products became integrated into the market economy. Indeed one major standard by which one can judge the level of development of capitalism in rural areas is the degree of commercialisation of agricultural products. The calculations by Wu Chengming and others show that between 1894 and 1919 the value of agricultural commodities traded in China increased by 43.4 per cent in constant prices, with an annual average growth rate of 1.45 per cent.[16] Between 1919 and 1936 commercialisation speeded up, with the value of agricultural products traded rising from Ch$2.17 to 4.5 billion, an increase of 107 per cent and an annual growth rate of nearly 5 per cent; by the end of the period the rate of commercialisation had reached 30 per cent.[17] In 1952 the total value of farm and sideline products traded was Ch$5.63 billion in 1936 prices; thus between 1936 and 1952 there had only been a 1.41 per cent growth rate. Moreover the 1952 figure includes products of forestry, animal husbandry, sideline occupations and fisheries, all of which were relatively commercialised and which had not been included in the 1936 figure. Although the rate of commercialisation was over 30 per cent, the real level of commercialisation had decreased in 1952 as compared with 1936.[18]

Although there was no progress in the modernisation of production techniques in agriculture, from the beginning of the century there was a clear increase in the incidence of the use of hired labor by managerial landlords, rich peasants and agricultural companies. By 1936 the proportion of capitalist management in agriculture reached around 10 per cent but after that it fell back, to about 8.5 per cent in 1949.[19] Thus both the rate of commercialisation and the expansion of capitalist management in agriculture peaked in 1936.

The main increase in capitalist elements in China between the wars was in industry, mining and transportation. In 1920 total output value of capitalist production in industry (including handicraft workshops and small but capitalist coal mines as well as modern industry and mining) was Ch$2.479 billion. By 1936 this figure had increased at an annual average growth rate of 5.97 per cent to Ch$6.227 billion and its proportion of total industrial production rose from 43.9 to 58.6 per cent. Over half of the transportation sector was managed along capitalist lines by 1936.[20] This shows that capitalist production relations expanded rapidly and by the end of the period had gained a dominant position in industry, mining and transportation. The process of the growth of capitalist production relations was even more rapid than the previously discussed modernisation of production methods.

Thus the development of capitalism in China peaked in the mid 1930s. Throughout the Anti-Japanese and Civil Wars, there was little increase in the assets of mining, industrial or transportation enterprises and the total value of capitalist production in 1949 was Ch$4.312 billion (at 1936 prices), a 31 per cent decrease on the 1936 figure. Nevertheless, as non-capitalist production had suffered even more severely, the capitalist proportion of total production still rose from 20.47 to 23.1 per cent,[21] but this does not justify the conclusion that capitalism in China was more developed in 1949 than it had been in 1936.

The structure of capitalist production in industry, mining and transportation encompassed that originating in foreign-owned enterprises, state-owned enterprises and privately owned enterprises. Though total output grew rapidly over the period, each of these groups exhibited somewhat different rates of growth and thus their shares of total output fluctuated over the period. This study, however, comes to the following quite different conclusions over this question from that reached in previous studies.

(a) The production of Chinese-owned enterprises grew more rapidly than that of foreign-owned enterprises
The foreign powers gained the legal right to run factories in China in the Treaty of Shimonoseki of 1895. For the following twenty years there was a surge of imperialist investment in China. Up to 1914 foreign

TABLE 4.11   *Growth of output of Chinese- and foreign-owned enterprises,*
1920–1936 (million 1936 Ch$)

	1920		1936		*Annual average rate of growth (%)*
	value of output	*% of total*	*value of output*	*% of total*	
Chinese enterprises	661	44.8	2 609	63.2	9.0
Foreign enterprises	816	55.2	1 516	36.8	3.9
Total	1 477	100	4 125	100	

NOTE: the statistics include output from Chinese and foreign enterprises engaged in modern industry, mining and transportation.

SOURCES: see notes to Table 4.1, but the statistics do not permit the value of transportation output in 1936 to be divided as between Chinese and foreign enterprises; therefore the ratio holding in 1933 is used, as in Wu Baosan, *Zhongguo guomin suode*.

capital occupied a dominant and monopolistic position in China's modern industry, mining and transportation. But what was the situation after 1913, and particularly after 1920? Table 4.11 shows that the output of foreign enterprises grew by 86 per cent over the period, at an average rate of 3.9 per cent, but their share in total output fell from 55.2 to 36.8 per cent. By contrast, the output of Chinese enterprises grew by 295 per cent at the much higher average rate of 9 per cent and their share in total output grew from 44.8 to 63.2 per cent. If one includes non-modernised Chinese capitalist output (such as handicraft workshops or small coal mines) in the total, then output of Chinese enterprises was some four times that of foreign enterprises. Thus Chinese capital, whether in total or just its modern sector, occupied the dominant position. In many individual industries we also see more rapid growth by Chinese enterprises, which accounted for a rising proportion of total output.

Thus the golden age of foreign direct investment in China was a brief period of ten years or so at the beginning of this century. At that time quite a large proportion of the profits made were reinvested either within the enterprise or in other industries in China. In the subsequent ten years, although some foreign enterprises tended to decline because of political instability in China, most continued to grow, repatriating a large proportion of their profits. Between 1914 and 1930 the annual average foreign investment in China was Ch$73.60 million but the average remittance of profits abroad was Ch$138.80 million.[22] After 1930, Japan rapidly

TABLE 4.12   *Foreign investment in China, 1930–1936 (million Haiguan taels)*

	1930	1931	1932	1933	1934	1935	1936
Profits of foreign enterprises in China	130.2	57.0	35.9	12.8	9.6	6.4	
New foreign investment in China	134.7	28.5	38.5*	19.3*			38.5

SOURCE: Cheng, *Foreign Trade and Industrial Development*, pp. 340–1. The asterisk denotes the total of foreign loans to the Chinese government and foreign investment in new enterprises in China.

increased its investment in the North-east, though for political rather than economic motives. Direct investment in China by other nationalities tended to be on the decline. According to Wu Chengming's calculations, direct foreign investment in China declined by 30 per cent in 1936 as compared with 1930.[23] Zheng Youkui also agrees that both the profits of foreign enterprises and new foreign investment in China tended to decline between 1930 and 1936 (see Table 4.12). The reason for this is complicated, and is related to the changing investment climate in prewar China, which is beyond the scope of this article.

(b) Enterprises run by national capital were the basis of modern industry
Having examined the fluctuations in the relative position of Chinese and foreign enterprises, we need to go on to examine the trend in state-owned and privately owned enterprises.

In 1920, 'state-owned capital' mainly referred to enterprises run by the warlords. Following the political downfall of the people who established and ran these enterprises in the 1920s, most were converted to private companies after 1927. A minority only were taken over and became part of the state enterprises run by the Nationalist government. Thus over this period as far as the total of modern industry, mining and transportation was concerned, the state-owned share of total capital declined from 38.7 to 24.8 per cent, the share of private capital increased from 61.3 to 75.2 per cent. Within industry itself, there was an even sharper decline in the state sector, from 40.1 to 15 per cent, with a decline even in the absolute value of its assets. At the same time private capital expanded rapidly, at an annual rate of 8.17 per cent, so that over sixteen years the net value of its assets increased by 250 per cent and its proportion of Chinese industrial capital rose from 59.9 to 85.0 per cent (see Tables 2.3 and 2.4). This shows that in terms of control over mining, industry and transportation the Nationalist government before 1937 was less prominent than the warlord governments in Beijing and thus there was no base for monopoly. The expansion of state capital in the 1940s was facilitated by the special circumstances of the war and will not be discussed here.

The above analysis shows that private capital showed the most rapid growth of the three components of Chinese capital between 1920 and 1936. By 1936 it had attained the dominant position in modern production in China, with an output value of Ch$1962 million. This was not only much higher than the Ch$647 million output of state enterprises but also higher than the Ch$1516 million output of foreign enterprises.[24] Thus national capital had grown into the main base of China's modern production.

During the early stages of its development (1894–1920), the net value of assets of Chinese private industry grew by Ch$16 255 700 a year on average. But between 1920 and 1936 it grew by Ch$56 570 400 a year, that is 3.48 times the growth in the earlier period. Capital accumulation reached its peak in 1936, and private capital was weakened during the Anti-Japanese and Civil Wars by competition from Japanese and Nationalist monopoly capital. Thus by 1949 its assets totalled only Ch$803 million (at 1936 prices), a 31 per cent decrease on the prewar peak in 1936.[25]

Many scholars have recently discussed the detailed conditions and reasons for the growth of national capitalism in China between the wars.[26] These articles adequately show that the argument that China's national capitalist industry was bankrupt or semi-bankrupt in the years after the First World War is incorrect and there is no need to restate that here.

To sum up, there is no doubt that the period between the two world wars was the period of the most rapid development in China's modern economic history. Obvious progress was made both in industrialisation and in the advance of capitalism. For a full picture we also need to make a cross-sectional analysis, albeit a rough one. In this way, we can draw a comprehensive conclusion.

Between 1920 and 1936 China's national income grew by only 1.53 per cent per annum. In the United States, on the other hand, national income grew at 4.06 per cent between 1920 and 1939, in France 5.74 per cent (1920–39) and in Japan 7.40 per cent (1920–36).[27] Thus their growth rates were higher than China's. In the late 1920s and the early 1930s capitalist countries suffered an unprecedented economic crisis: between 1921 and 1937, the industrial growth rate in the main capitalist countries was as follows: the United States 2.6 per cent, Britain, 2.2 per cent, Germany 3.4 per cent (1921–34), France, 2.9 per cent and Japan 6.2 per cent.[28] China's industrial growth rate between 1920 and 1936 was 4.06 per cent (in terms of net value 3.98 per cent), higher than the United

States, Germany, Britain and France and lower only than Japan. If one only includes modern industry, then China's growth rate was higher even than that of Japan. But the problem was that, despite its very high growth rate, modern industry only accounted for a very small proportion of the national economy. Since agriculture, which made up the bulk of China's economy, made little progress towards using modern production equipment and techniques, the growth of the productive forces could not but be slow. The annual growth rate of agriculture was only 0.87 per cent, slower than those of the United States, France and other Western countries. In addition growth of service income was also slow. These factors meant that China's national income grew more slowly than those of the developed countries in the West. Capitalist production relations by 1936 occupied the predominant position in industry, mining and transportation, but in the countryside feudal relations of exploitation were still dominant. The fetters of the natural economy were much stronger than in the West and went on hampering the modernisation of town and country and the growth of capitalism. Therefore on the whole we can only affirm the achievements in the development of China's economy between the world wars. We should not overstate them.

Notes

* I want to express my appreciation for help given me by my teacher Professor Liu Foding of the Nankai Institute of Economics. I also want to thank Dr Tim Wright for his help with translating the paper and for his suggestions. Needless to say, I alone am responsible for the ideas expressed here. Any errors remain my own.

1. [Editor's note] This chapter is a translation of Wang Yuru, 'Lun liangci shijie dazhan zhi jian Zhongguo jingji de fazhan', *Zhongguo jingji shi yanjiu* 1987.2 (May 1987): 97–110.

2. Wu Chengming, *Zhongguo zibenzhuyi yu guonei shichang* (Beijing, 1985), pp. 129–30; see Chapter 2 above.

3. Jian Youwen, *Taiping jun Guangxi shouyi shi* (Shanghai, 1946), pp. 4–5.

4. The American scholar John Key Chang has calculated gross and net value of output between 1912 and 1949 based on fifteen industries and mining industries in his book *Industrial Development in Pre-Communist China* (Edinburgh, 1969), pp. 60–1. According to his calculations, the average annual rate of growth of gross value of output, 1920–36, was 7.18 per cent, that of net value of output 7.43 per cent. These figures are a little higher than those resulting from our calculations, but they are of the same order of magnitude.

5. Liu Foding, 'Woguo minzu ziben qiye zhaqu shengyu jiazhi de

shouduan he tedian', *Nankai jingji yanjiu suo niankan 1983* (Tianjin, 1984), pp. 202–18.

6. Yan Zhongping, *Zhongguo jindai jingji shi tongji ziliao xuanji* (Beijing, 1955), pp. 102–4.

7. Yan Zhongping, *Tongji ziliao xuanji*, pp. 227, 234.

8. Tim Wright, *Coal Mining in China's Economy and Society, 1895–1937* (Cambridge, 1984), p. 45.

9. Cheng Yu-kwei, *Foreign Trade and Industrial Development in China: An Historical and Integrated Analysis Through 1948* (Washington, 1956), p. 39.

10. Chang's coverage of consumer goods only includes cotton yarn and cotton cloth, so that this discussion of structural change will not be totally accurate.

11. Cheng, *Foreign Trade and Industrial Development*, pp. 41–2.

12. Wright, *Coal Mining*, pp. 49, 71.

13. Yan Zhongping, *Tongji ziliao xuanji*, p. 73.

14. Calculated from Zhongguo kexue yuan jingji yanjiu suo shijie jingji yanjiu shi, *Zhuyao zibenzhuyi guojia jingji tongji ji* (Beijing, 1962), pp. 425–6.

15. Calculated from statistics in ibid.

16. Wu Chengming, *Zhongguo zibenzhuyi yu guonei shichang*, pp. 109–10.

17. Ibid.

18. Ding Changqing, 'Guanyu Zhongguo jindai nongcun shangpin jingji fazhan de jige wenti', *Nankai jingji yanjiu* 1985.3 (June 1985): 42–7.

19. Ding Changqing, 'Shilun Zhongguo jindai nongye zhong zibenzhuyi de fazhan shuiping', *Nankai xuebao* 1984.6 (November 1984): 72–9 (translated as Chapter 10 below).

20. See notes to Table 4.1.

21. Wu Chengming, *Zhongguo zibenzhuyi yu guonei shichang*, pp. 134–5.

22. C. F. Remer, *Foreign Investment in China* (New York, 1933), p. 123.

23. Wu Chengming, *Diguozhuyi zai jiu Zhongguo de touzi* (Beijing, 1955), p. 60. The figure for 1936 excludes the Japanese-occupied north-east.

24. See Table 4.11, using the proportion of state and private capital in Table 2.3 to divide the output of Chinese enterprises into two parts.

25. This calculation is based on Wu Chengming, *Zhongguo zibenzhuyi yu guonei shichang*, pp. 114, 126, 130, 134.

26. In addition to Wu Chengming's book, see Huang Wei, 'Zhongguo minzu zibenzhuyi jingji de fazhan he pochan wenti', *Xueshu yuekan* 1982.2 (February 1982): 21–6, Zhang Zhongli 'Guanyu Zhongguo minzu ziben zai ershi niandai de fazhan wenti', *Shehui kexue* 1983.10 (October 1983): 42–6 (translated as Chapter 3 above) and Liu Foding, 'Shilun woguo minzu ziben qiye de ziben jilei wenti', *Nankai xuebao* 1982.2 (March 1982): 16–26.

27. Calculated from figures in Zhongguo kexue yuan, *Zhuyao zibenzhuyi guojia jingji tongji ji* adjusted to constant prices.

28. Ibid., pp. 425–6.

5   Symposium on the Central Theme of Modern Chinese Economic History

In early 1989, Beijing historian Wang Jingyu from the Institute of Economics in the Chinese Academy of Social Sciences published an article identifying the 'development and non-development of Chinese capitalism' as 'The Central Theme of Modern Chinese Economic History'. *This article sparked off a debate and a symposium was published by* Studies in Chinese Economic History *later that year covering a variety of opinions on the issue. These extracts cover two contributions, both from historians in the Institute of Economics in Shanghai, taking different positions. Du Xuncheng argues that 'non-development', or the failure of the pre-Communist Chinese economy, is the central issue to be addressed. On the other hand Ding Richu, joint author of a chapter translated elsewhere in this collection, argues that the aspects of success, or 'development', were central to the history of China in the early twentieth century. Thankfully, both contributions are free from the invective and absolutism that used to characterise such debates in Chinese public life.*[1]

DU XUNCHENG: STUDYING 'NON-DEVELOPMENT' IS EVEN MORE IMPORTANT THAN STUDYING 'DEVELOPMENT'

I fully concur with the principal theme raised by Wang Jingyu on modern Chinese history – his idea of the 'development and non-development of Chinese capitalism'. Although on the surface this idea is somewhat contradictory, it does grasp the pulse of modern Chinese economic history and so has profound theoretical significance.

Economic history must certainly examine the specific national conditions that limited China's historical development. If the field of vision of our historical research is limited to the 'development of Chinese capitalism', then that would only be a very partial study and one unable to perceive the complete specificity of China's experience. Chinese capitalism was 'transplanted' from the West after the Opium War, and in the one hundred years from that time up to 1949 it is certainly reasonable to say that it reached a place of some strength in the Chinese economic and political worlds, but at the same time it was far from completing its road to prominence. But why was the development of Chinese capitalism so difficult? Why did it go into decline before maturity and die an early death? To try to answer this question means we must also study its 'non-development'. In my opinion the study of its non-development has even more important and profound historical and practical significance than that of its development.

In Wang Jingyu's opinion if one is to study the development and non-development of Chinese capitalism, an important aspect is that one should study the coexistence of development at certain points with non-development overall. In my understanding this means we must study China's dualistic economic structure. In the opinion of the Western economist W. Arthur Lewis, such a dualistic economic structure has general significance for developing countries and centres on the juxtaposition of advanced industry and backward agriculture. In point of fact, the traditional economy is by no means limited to agriculture. The study of the contents and changes of China's dualistic economic structure and of the mutual interactions of the two sectors of the dualistic economy is clearly the basis for studying modern Chinese economic history and indeed modern Chinese history as a whole. This is a formidable research project. In the past, studies of individual cases, industries or areas were relatively numerous, macro or general studies, or those of the interrelations between different economic sectors relatively few. Qualitative studies were more numerous than quantitative ones. Studies of the capitalist economy were more numerous than those of the traditional economy which coexisted with this new economy. Much remains to be done, with everyone working to their strengths, not sticking to one pattern, and everyone enlightening and supplementing each other's work.

The study of the development and non-development of Chinese capitalism cannot be a 'purely economic' study. Particularly in a semi-colonial semi-feudal country like China, politics often had a key influence on economics. So it is very important also to study the relationship between the political situation and government policy on the one hand and the development and non-development of Chinese capitalism on the other. China's dualistic economy created a dualistic set of social interests: the capitalist pole demanded bourgeois political democracy and the 'Westernisation ' of thought and culture, while the traditional pole still demanded centralised government and traditional ethics and morality. These two sets of opposing interests became like two spectres flitting around the process of development of modern Chinese history.

Because the capitalist economy was just a 'transplant' and those responsible for the transplant included the feudal autocratic government and because the development of the new economy was limited, the capitalist economy was unable to create a corresponding independent and strong political force, and it was unable to institute a successful political transition. Apart from being the result of the oppression of Western capitalism, Chinese capitalism failed to develop fully also because of internal conditions including not only the lack of coordination between the corrupt feudal autocracy and the capitalist economy but also the inability of the feudal autocracy to find a way out of the dilemma posed by the 'two spectres'.

The oppression and restriction practised by the corrupt feudal autocracy against capitalism is clear: under all possible circumstances the former tried to make the latter its appendage and to restrict and monopolise capitalist interests. Between 1895 and 1927 the control of the central government was weak and so private capitalism was able to develop to a certain degree but, by the Nationalist period, state monopoly capitalism forcibly broke the regular development of Chinese private capitalism and forced it into a dead end. In the control and monopoly exercised by state monopoly capitalism over private capitalism, it also very much showed its own disease-ridden nature and hastened the process of its own disintegration. On the other hand, in order to survive in a crevice, private capitalism was often forced to compromise itself, such as by seeking special privileges or taking part in speculative management.

Under the difficulties of internal disorder and external disasters, the feudal autocracy had to foster capitalism in order to stop the nation getting ever weaker and its own control ever more precarious. But at a certain stage the fostering of private capitalism became incompatible with the old social formation. That was the dilemma.

The dilemma of the dualistic economic and the old political systems was the chronic disease of modern China. The rulers of pre-Communist China were basically the representatives of imperialism and feudalism and could find no correct path to bring China towards capitalist modernisation.

It was a historical necessity for China to take the socialist road. The social system of China before and after liberation were of course fundamentally different but the rules of historical development have their elements of succession and continuity. The study of the development and non-development of Chinese capitalism and the examination of the reasons why China was unable to realise capitalist modernisation has certainly got many lessons for our current efforts to maintain the socialist road and the implement socialist economic and political reform.

DING RICHU: THE MAINSTREAM WAS THE DEVELOPMENT
OF THE CAPITALIST ECONOMY

In modern China there were both negative and corrupt forces and positive
and progressive ones and these forces both opposed and complemented
each other. Their existence meant that there existed both new and old
forms in China's economic, political and cultural life. But the progressive
forces and the new forms gradually developed, the corrupt forces and old
forms gradually declined. As the central theme of our research, we should
encourage people to study how the progressive forces developed, how
the new and old forms rose and declined. In modern China the capitalist
economy was a new and progressive mode of production, which clearly
developed the forces of production and began to establish the economic
basis for national modernisation and to promote modernisation on the
political and cultural fronts. Therefore I believe that the development of
the capitalist economy is the central thread of modern Chinese economic
history.

Just as Wang Jingyu pointed out, the modern Chinese capitalist economy
both exhibited development and was unable fully to develop, so should we
designate the central thread as the development *and non-development* of
Chinese capitalism? I do not think so. The growth of any new thing is
bound to go through a tortuous process but, however much it is blocked,
however many setbacks or defeats it suffers, it will always struggle through
to overcome difficulties and gradually advance. From the opening of the
port of Shanghai in 1843 to the peak of pre-war national capitalism in
1936, Chinese capitalism, including state and private capitalism, registered
clear growth. My understanding is that, despite the fact that there was
development but not full development, the basic trend was for progress,
and so to take development as the basic thread accords with historical
reality. Of course it hardly needs to be said that this does not mean we
should discard the principle of asking concrete questions and making
concrete analysis, nor that we should fail deeply to study those internal
and external conditions which were unfavourable to Chinese capitalism
or to examine the difficulties and twists and turns of development or the
reasons for its failure to develop fully.

To take the development and non-development of Chinese capitalism as
the central thread is in fact to focus the question on non-development. This
is not totally without reason, because the capitalist economy never occupied
the main position in the national economy. Nevertheless it both influenced
the traditional economy and determined the direction of development of
the Chinese economy, so that the capitalist economy constituted the

leading sector in modern China's national economy; similarly, although the proletariat only constituted a small part of China's population, it was nevertheless the leading force in the new democratic revolution. On this basis, I believe that the development of the capitalist economy was the mainstream of the development process and occupied the leading role. Therefore it is not correct to focus on the question of non-development.

The basis for the argument that the central theme is development and non-development is to counterpose imperialism and the só-called 'bureaucratic capitalism' to private 'national' capitalism, and only to recognise the latter as genuine Chinese capitalism. I will briefly outline my views on this question.

In the situation of China being a semi-colony, foreign capital in China was able to rely on the protection of the military and political power of its metropolis to enjoy various privileges granted by the unequal treaties. It was also able to use its own relatively substantial resources to control or exclude national capitalist enterprises in the same or related lines of business and thus hinder the latter's development. Of course there is a distinction between domestic and foreign and one cannot simply regard foreign capital as national (domestic) capitalism. However, both Chinese and foreign capital took root and grew on Chinese soil and inevitably had to depend on each other; foreign capital of course had considerable influence on China's social and economic life and to some extent promoted and helped the birth and development of national capital. The model provided by foreign enterprises stimulated the creation of Chinese enterprises and also developed the market and commodity economy, creating favourable conditions for national capital to sell its products. In order to make profits, they provided national capitalists with raw materials, machinery, equipment and loans. Foreign enterprises also transferred technology, while their management experience was even more useful to national capitalist enterprises.

So-called 'bureaucratic capitalism' in common usage refers to both enterprises managed by the state authorities and the private investments of high bureaucrats in power. For political reasons in the past these were said to have been 'bureaucratic capitalism' with a strong 'comprador' and 'monopolistic' reactionary nature. But what precisely that 'comprador or 'monopoly' nature entailed was not clearly studied or discussed in detail and for several decades scholars could just define things any way they wanted according to their own understanding. So right up to recent times there have been disagreements on these issues both within China and abroad.[2] I think that we can continue each to hold our own views without forcing any sort of unity but, although there certainly are questions such as those concerning the private investment and state enterprises of the high Nationalist bureaucrats, which had both ties to and contradictions with private capital, nevertheless the only thing we can do is to hold to the principle of 'one China' and accept that they were all component parts of Chinese capitalism.

In the past the majority of works on modern Chinese economic history have excluded three types of Chinese capital from the ranks of national capital: 'comprador' capital, the private investments of high bureaucrats and state capital, all of which had close connections with foreign capital. A few of the most 'radical' works also viewed commercial capital and finance capital as 'comprador' capital because of their substantial 'comprador nature'. Only industry run by private capital was recognised as national capital, and that continually suffered blows and squeeze from foreign capital, 'comprador capital' and 'bureaucratic capital'. Wu Chengming's statement is correct: 'Up to the 1970s some works on modern Chinese economic history mostly gave one a feeling of desolation and decline'; modern Chinese political history and cultural history described the development and victory of the revolutionary movement and the new cultural movement, it was 'only in the area of economic history that people took this view of stagnation, and that is really difficult to explain'. If we admit all varieties of Chinese capital count as national capital, I think that modern Chinese economic history can allow its readers to feel that history consists of uninterrupted advance and so fulfil a function of encouraging people.

When examining the issue of the development of Chinese capitalism, I certainly agree with Wang Jingyu: 'it is not enough to concentrate solely on the actual process of the development and non-development of capitalism, one must take a wider view.' In my opinion we must extent our view into the sphere of politics and intellectual concepts. Here I will just raise an opinion about the sphere of politics. In the hundred or more years of modern Chinese history, although Chinese capitalism had a degree of vigorous growth, there were frequent wars, in approximately one year out of two, while political turmoil was also continuous. This political environment certainly restricted the regular growth of capitalism. If the first or second united fronts had been able to continue over a long period, China would have had the political prerequisites for the smooth development of capitalism. But because of the breakdown of unity, this possibility was lost on both occasions. The fact that capitalism was unable fully to develop was not because it did not have a chance in China, but rather because it did not have favourable political conditions. Again, the breakdown of the second united front, the Nationalist defeat on the mainland and the Communist victory, were made possible because 'the Chinese Communists had been able to mobilize and utilize the potentialities of revolution while the Nationalists had not'.[3] That the Communists rose to power and led the people on the socialist road, while capitalism on the mainland was rapidly reformed out of existence, also happened for political reasons. If economic historians do not study the way politics influenced or even determined the rise and decline of Chinese capitalism but just look to economic factors, this will lead to partial or even downright wrong conclusions.

Notes

1.   [Editor's note] This chapter is a translation of sections of 'Guanyu Zhongguo jindai jingji shi de zhongxin xiansuo', *Zhongguo jingji shi yanjiu* 1989.3 (September 1989): 62–79.
2.   Ding Richu, 'Guanyu "guanliao ziben" yu "guanliao zichanjieji" wenti', pp. 445–50 in *Minguo dang'an yu minguo shi xueshu taolunhui lunwen ji* (Beijing, 1988).
3.   John K. Fairbank, *The United States and China* (Cambridge, Mass., 1971), p. 311.

6 Liu Hongsheng's Enterprise Investment and Management

Ma Bohuang

Professor Ma Bohuang is a senior researcher in the Institute of Economics, Shanghai Academy of Social Sciences. He has published widely on the history of Chinese capitalism. This article examines in detail aspects of the business practices of Liu Hongsheng. Liu was one of the two or three leading capitalists in Shanghai in the 1920s and 1930s, when he became China's 'Match King', and this analysis of his activities represents a major step in the reinterpretation of prewar Chinese capitalism. Liu began as a comprador, selling coal in Shanghai for the Sino-British Kailuan Mining Administration, whose history is examined in Chapter 12. Professor Ma shows how he developed his businesses through vertical and horizontal integration and how he used modern management methods to control those businesses; like Chapter 7, this one has contemporary relevance, holding up Liu's use of cost accounting as an example for managers in the 1980s.[1]

Liu Hongsheng's enterprises developed in pre-Communist China in a situation of imperialist invasion and plunder during the period when China's semi-colonial semi-feudal economy was in decline. However, they still achieved some development in the course of a struggle with foreign monopoly capital and domestic bureaucratic capital. By the 1930s Liu's enterprises had reached a certain scale and continued to struggle through national crisis and economic depression. During the Anti-Japanese War they suffered serious devastation under Japanese occupation and did not recover until China had won the War. In the post-war period, however, the large-scale dumping of foreign goods, runaway inflation and the oppression by the Nationalist authorities meant that the production of his subordinate factories was still bogged down in recession and decline, and Liu's enterprises did not have a real new life until China was liberated.

Liu's enterprises had their own characteristics in terms of primitive capital accumulation, their transformation into national industrial capital and their business management. It could be said that they were typical enterprises in the development of national capitalism in pre-Communist China.

CAPITAL ACCUMULATION BY LIU HONGSHENG AS A COMPRADOR AND IN COMMERCE

Liu Hongsheng's capital in pre-Communist China was neither self-generated in the process of the polarisation of small commodity producers nor gradually formed in 'snail-like' accumulation, as was usually the case in the formative period of capitalist production. It had, however, its 'pioneering period', the process of primitive accumulation.

Liu started out as a comprador working for the British Kailuan Mining Administration. Later on, he took the opportunity to engage, in cooperation with other coal traders, in the sale of Kailuan coal. Thus he became both a comprador and a merchant: one person, two roles. Judging by various available materials, between 1911, when he became a comprador, and the end of the 1920s his total income from the sale of Kailuan coal was around 3 million taels of silver.[2] Of this about 500 000 taels, one sixth of his total accumulation, came from his commission as a comprador. The profits he made through trading in Kailuan coal were about 2.5 million taels.

Towards the end of the First World War there were excess stocks of coal at the Kailuan mines, while it was difficult to ship them out for sale. Liu himself chartered vessels and shipped coal from Qinhuangdao for sale in Shanghai, which was very profitable, and Liu made about 1.95 million taels. Moreover, in the early 1920s he joined with a Chinese coal firm in Shanghai to sell Kailuan coal and in the late 1920s he and the Kailuan Mining Administration jointly organised the Kailuan Sales Office with the exclusive right to sell Kailuan coal. His income from these two sources was no less than 550 000 taels. In a word, dealing in coal was the main source of Liu's family fortune.

Liu's business trading in coal expanded rapidly and its range was quite wide. After he became a comprador, in addition to the commission he received from Kailuan for promoting sales among Chinese customers, he cooperated with Yitaixing, a big coal firm in Shanghai, which signed a coal sale contract with the Kailuan Mining Office in Shanghai; Liu shared 30 per cent of the profits. Soon afterwards, together with other Shanghai coal merchants, Liu set up several other coal firms to sell various kinds of coal, such as Shanxi coal, Japanese Sakifuji coal and Hongay coal from Vietnam. This way he could control the trade and promote his sales. He also cooperated with local merchants in establishing coal firms in Nantong, Jiangyin, Zhenjiang, Nanjing and Wuhu. He joined with local coal firms in Suzhou, Wuxi and Changzhou to establish sales offices for Kailuan coal. Thus with Shanghai as his base, Liu very quickly set up a coal sales network in the main industrial and commercial cities of the Lower Yangzi.

Although the coal-selling establishments which Liu set up in the various Yangzi ports were not highly capitalised, they combined Liu's capital with that of local merchants. Liu used partnerships to penetrate the sphere of influence of local commercial capital. Relying upon his strength and his monopoly of supplies of Kailuan coal, he tried to extend his influence and control to local coal firms; gradually the bosses or managers of those firms became subordinate to him. In order to avoid rivalry among these establishments, he integrated the coal firms in Wuhu, Nanjing and Zhenjiang into one company, and two firms in Nantong were merged into one bureau. Thus, the Kailuan coal sales network was further consolidated and broadened.

At the beginning of this century, Japanese coal dominated the coal market in Shanghai. For example, in 1911 total sales in the Shanghai coal market were 1.1 million tons. Of this, Japanese coal accounted for 74.48 per cent, or 819 000 tons (this excludes the coal sold by various Japanese controlled coal mines in China). Sales of Kailuan coal (including those to foreign businesses) amounted to only 14.08 per cent, or 154 000 tons.[3] At that time, the coal market was not large, since there were few Chinese-owned factories and some urban residents still used firewood for cooking. So Liu tried to open up a new market for coal as a substitute for firewood in the kilns producing bricks, pottery and lime near Shanghai. He not only promoted the advantages of using coal but also changed traditional production methods in the industry by modifying the grates and carrying out burning trials. Within ten years, by 1920, sales of Kailuan coal increased to more than 880 000 tons, 52.19 per cent of total sales in the Shanghai market, an increase paralleled by a steady growth also in the accumulation of Liu's comprador and commercial capital.

There were also other sources for Liu's primitive accumulation of capital. In late 1926, under the name of S. T. Calder, a British staff member of the Kailuan Mining Administration in Shanghai, Liu purchased some land at Rihui Port on the west bank of the Huangpu River (in Shanghai) for use as a dock and warehouse. Soon afterwards it was transferred to Kailuan at a profit of 500 000 taels.[4] The property at Rihui Port was originally public land, belonging to the military. The seller of the property was a bureaucrat,

Fu Xiaoan, who bought it from the warlord Sun Chuanfang and others in
the name of the Japanese firm Mitsui. Later on, again in the name of Mitsui,
he sold it to Liu's agent, S. T. Calder. This shady transaction was enough
to show 'capital comes dripping from head to foot, from every pore, with
blood and dirt'.[5]

THE TRANSFORMATION OF LIU HONGSHENG'S CAPITAL TO NATIONAL INDUSTRIAL CAPITAL

Liu Hongsheng's investment in modern industry began in the early 1920s
after the May 4 Movement. At that time the people of the whole nation
were engaged in widespread patriotic movements resisting imperialism,
promoting national goods and boycotting imported goods. This historical
background no doubt provided an extra objective impetus for the transformation of social capital and the emergence of national enterprises. Liu
himself said that 'during my short life as a comprador, I felt that foreigners
looked down upon Chinese and it was because of their lack of industry and
science that the Chinese people could be bullied. That is why I wanted to
do something with the money in my pocket.'[6] Under such circumstances,
Liu's capital was diverted to the development of national industry.

At the beginning of 1920 Liu started his career in industry by establishing
a match factory in Suzhou, contributing three quarters of the capital of
Ch$120 000. In September of the same year Liu made his largest industrial
investment to date, in the Longhua Cement Factory in Shanghai, supplying
60 per cent of the Ch$1.2 million capital. In addition Liu made large
investments in the Liujiang Coal Mining and Railroad Company in Hebei
Province and the Yusheng Match Factory in Jiujiang. He enjoyed either
complete or majority control over these enterprises. Up to the first half of
1926, Liu's investment in industry, mining, transportation, docks, storage
houses, banking and commercial businesses reached Ch$3.1 million.[7]

At the beginning of 1926, preparations began in Shanghai for the
establishment of the Zhonghua Briquette Factory. The initial capital was
Ch$100 000, of which Liu's share was the largest. In August 1928 Liu
invested Ch$100 000, one-third of the total investment in the new Huafeng
Enamel Factory. In May 1929 Liu organised the Huigong Financial
Syndicate and reorganised the Zhonghua Industrial Company, which had
suffered losses for years and was on the verge of collapse. In October,
he established the Yuhua Woollen Mill (which was later renamed the
Zhanghua Woollen Mill) with a capital of Ch$750 000, on the basis of
the machinery and buildings of the original Rihui Wool Weaving Mill. In

name, this factory was a joint stock company but in reality it was solely owned by Liu. In December of that year Liu organised a new financial syndicate again under the name of the Huigong Financial Syndicate. With Ch\$800 000 that syndicate bought the Jiawang Coal Mine, which had stopped operations because of heavy debts, and reorganised it as the East China Coal Mining Company.

Moreover, in order to control the insurance business of his subordinate enterprises, Liu, together with Chen Guangfu from the Shanghai Bank and others, organised the Dahua Insurance Company in 1927. In addition, in April 1931, in an attempt to allocate capital in a centralised way and absorb unused funds, Liu borrowed Ch\$1 million from the Shanghai Bank on the collateral of his Enterprise Building in order to establish the Enterprise Bank of China. By the end of 1931, Liu's investment in enterprises (including company shares, shares in partnerships and shipping docks) amounted to over Ch\$7.4 million. In the five years from 1927 to 1931 his total investments increased by 136 per cent.[8]

Generally speaking, the scope of Liu's investment in the 1920s was quite wide and his entrepreneurial spirit was quite strong. Liu's factories producing cement, wool, briquettes and matches were pioneers in purchasing machinery and equipment, constructing buildings, introducing science and technology and establishing management systems. This indicates the long-term perspective of Liu's enterprises.

In the process of the transformation of Liu's capital into national industrial capital, he followed the principle of dispersing his investment among medium and small enterprises and did not 'put all his eggs into the one basket'[9]. As a result, each enterprise ran its own business independently and was responsible for its own gains and losses. Overall, however, the gains and losses could balance each other out, maintaining the stability of the whole group. If difficulties appeared, he could use a surplus in one enterprise to balance a deficit in another, thus making it easier for him to avoid risk.

This principle was linked with Liu's basic point of view about pre-Communist China's society and economy. The expansion of foreign monopolistic financial organisations, the running amok of invading forces, superior foreign production technology, fierce market competition and the ruthless exploitation and looting by foreigners greatly spurred on some new and rising capitalists in China. Because of the difficult objective situation and his own weakness, Liu on the one hand admired the capitalist mode of production in foreign countries and on the other felt restricted by domestic social conditions. He thought that the only way for China's society and economy was to maintain a balanced, self-supporting pattern, with agriculture as its base and complemented by medium and small industry.[10] He hoped to be able to survive and develop even in conditions of domination by imperialism and bureaucratic capitalism. Thus it was fully understandable that he should adopt the principle of dispersing his investment, such as was typical among the national bourgeoisie in pre-Communist China.

A favourable condition for Liu's industrial enterprises was that he owned his own docks and warehouses. In 1918 and 1919, in the context of trading in coal, Liu used the name of the Yitaixing Coal Company to entrust the British company, Hopkins, Dunn and Co, with buying real estate along the east bank of Huangpu River in Shanghai, where he set up a series of warehouses. At the same time he established wharves at Jiangyin and Nanjing in the lower Yangzi and rented a dock at Zhenjiang. In 1926, he bought more real estate on the east side of the Huangpu River, in the name of a foreign firm, and built a dock there. Later, he combined his various docks and warehouses together into the Zhonghua Dock Company and became the leading Chinese proprietor of docks and warehouses in pre-Communist Shanghai.

Docks and warehouses played an important role in the accumulation and transformation of Liu's capital. Liu's various subordinate storage yards mainly held coal, which played a pivotal role in his accumulation of comprador and commercial capital and provided his industrial establishments with a source of fuel. Coal piled up in storage yards over a long period became wet with rain and increased in weight. Moreover, a large amount of slack (especially the bituminous slack from Kailuan, which was the basic raw material for cement production) was accumulated at the disposal of Liu himself. His affiliate enterprise, the Shanghai Cement Factory needed more than 2000 tons of slack in its initial stage of producing over 30 000 bags of cement. Thus the establishment of a cement factory created a stable and long-term outlet for the slack accumulated in various storage yards, which in turn provided the cement factory with an endless source of raw materials.

The establishment of the briquette factory was a similar case. The Hongay anthracite in which Liu traded included a lot of dust, the best material for making briquettes. The Nos 1 and 2 Zhonghua Briquette Factories were both located close to Liu's warehouses, so that they could obtain materials on the spot. The various docks on the Huangpu River had warehouses at the back, so that they could provide services such as transportation, loading, unloading and storage of industrial raw material and products. Therefore the Zhanghua Woollen Mill and the Huafeng Enamel Factory were both located close to one of Liu's docks.

However the transformation of Liu's capital into national capital was not completely without problems. This is indicated by Liu's relations with the British-owned Kailuan Mining Administration, which were harmonious on the surface but competitive in reality, and also reflected the contradictions between foreign capital and national capital.

Foreign businessmen did not view with equanimity the way compradors were building up their family fortunes and establishing national industries. At first, when Liu established docks and warehouses, he used the name of the Yitaixing Coal Company instead of his own. This indicates that he attempted to avoid mentioning profits before such profit-hungry people. Later on, together with the Yitaixing Coal Company and the Kailuan Mining Administration, Liu established a joint company, the Kailuan Sales Office. Kailuan then cancelled Liu's salary and post as comprador, so as to reduce his income from coal sales and bring his partnership with Yitaixing into the open. From then on, Liu changed from being a comprador into being a partner in a joint company. His new financial group took over the Jiawang Coal Mine and established East China Coal Mining Company. To avoid arousing suspicion that he would be competing with Kailuan coal, Liu himself did not assume any post in the company but invited somebody else to be the chairman of the board and general manager. In spite of the fact that the details were intricate and the process was delicate, they are sufficient to show how foreign capital restricted and retarded the accumulation and transformation of Liu's capital.

Especially in 1934–5, when Liu's enterprises fell into difficulties, Kailuan employed new Chinese agents and, on the excuse that Liu's position as general manager in the Nationalists' China Merchants Steamship Navigation Company had a negative effect on the business of the Kailuan Sales Office, they demanded the cancellation of the second term of their coal sales contract with the joint company. Liu rejected this and the British in the end did not cancel the contract. They tried to modify it so as to reduce his management rights and earnings but this again was flatly rejected by Liu. The British continued to make all kinds of trouble to force Liu to give up the right to renew the contract but he stuck to his guns and did not give way. As a result, the second term of the contract with the joint company was maintained but the British adopted the method of taking away the firewood from under the cauldron by reducing the sales of Kailuan coal in Shanghai and cutting their personnel in the Sales Office; as a result business declined sharply. The sales of Kailuan coal fell from 1.17 million tons in 1931 to 610 000 in 1935, with profits going down from Ch$1.17 million to Ch$250 000.[11] By 1939, when the contract expired, business had still not improved.

By the 1930s, Liu Hongsheng had become one of China's best-known capitalists. In the eyes of the British-owned Kailuan Mining Administration he had completed his historic task and lost his original value, and so he was not qualified to share their profits any more; thus they tried to replace this old comprador who had changed into a national capitalist with a group of new compradors. The differences and disputes between Liu and Kailuan in the process of his transformation from comprador capitalist to national capitalist in essence reflected the contradiction between foreign capital and national capital.

THE MANAGEMENT OF LIU HONGSHENG'S ENTERPRISES AND THE PLAN FOR CENTRALISATION

In terms of business management, Liu Hongsheng paid great attention to new types of accounting systems, especially cost accounting, and advocated that good industrial management should be based upon cost accounting. He considered that 'in industrial and commercial competition, people should try their best to study how to reduce costs, increase production, reduce prices and use all avenues to sell their commodities. Lack of attention to and study of cost accounting and continuing to follow old patterns will mean certain failure.'[12] Liu employed senior staff with the experience and ability to manage enterprises, giving them excellent pay and conditions. He set up an enterprise management system centring around accounting management and used it to allocate enterprise funds. In order to ensure the independence of accounting, some of the senior accountants were given assurances from the very beginning of their employment that they would not be affected by any internal changes within the enterprise. Every year Liu invited foreign and domestic accountants to audit the accounts of his various affiliated enterprises so as to establish their reputation and prevent malpractice from taking place. In order to implement rigorous cost accounting, forms were drawn up in his affiliate Zhanghua Woollen Mill and sent to the various workshops to be filled in. Details such as volume, unit price, total value of wool for warp and weft were to be entered. When labour and manufacturing costs and returned raw material had been subtracted, the real cost would thus be obtained. An estimate was made by engineers in the first place so as to compare with actual results.[13] This process of cost accounting was considered quite thorough and worth following.

For the purpose of obtaining good results in business management, Liu's group of enterprises often gave accelerated promotion to educated and experienced scientific and technological personnel; they paid attention to the training and cultivation of promising young persons, so as to raise the level of production technology and improve product quality. All his subordinate enterprises like the Hongsheng Match Factory, the China Cement Factory in Shanghai and the Zhanghua Woollen Mill employed foreign technical experts on high salaries and relied on them to direct and improve production. As a result, such personnel had a privileged position in China and this led to some harmful consequences in one or two of Liu's enterprises. Therefore Liu paid attention to the training of personnel within the factories and tried to enlist Chinese experts. He also selected engineers and technicians and sent them abroad for further training, so that he could gradually reduce his reliance on foreign experts.

Especially at critical moments, Liu's group of enterprises gave senior personnel extra payments, expecting them to solve problems and to reverse any decline. Soon after he took it over, the East China Coal Mining Company suffered a series of losses resulting from difficulties in transportation and sales. Liu gave Ch$150 000 of shares each to the new chairman of the board of directors and new general manager, entrusting them with solving the problem of coal transportation on the Tianjin-Pukou and Gansu-Lianyungang railways. There were quite a few cases of such grants of shares and bonuses to important persons in enterprises like the Zhanghua Woollen Mill, the China Cement Factory in Shanghai and the Da Zhonghua Match Company. To use a phrase of Liu's, this was called 'making a lot of money with a little money'.

Liu's management and administration methods had been practised in capitalist countries, some of them reflecting capitalist pragmatism. As described above, he saw accounting as the key link commanding the administration and management of enterprises and used cost accounting to supervise production in enterprises; he paid attention to the use of science and technology to improve production methods; and he trained his own technical personnel. All these played their due role and obtained actual economic results in raising product quality and improving market competitiveness in enterprises producing matches, cement and wool. In their historical development, each of Liu's enterprises had its distinct characteristics in terms of the establishment and implementation of rules and regulations; for example, in the division of rights and duties and their fulfilment among the personnel at all levels; decisions on means of checking up; rewards and punishments and their practice; how to speed up the circulation of capital and products; and the future planning of enterprises and the steps of expansion.

Liu also attempted to imitate the model of foreign monopoly capital in business management, that is to carry out centralised management over dispersed enterprises by means of a holding company but for various reasons he failed to do so.

In 1926, because of the problem of dispersed investment and management, Liu set about preparing for the establishment of a company to exercise centralised management and supervision over his enterprises but it met all kinds of trouble and was put on the shelf because of the lack of necessary conditions.

In 1929, as a result of the development of his business and because of financial problems, the idea of management centralisation was put forward again. Liu planned to invite a senior British staff member from the Kailuan Mining Administration to be general manager of a new holding company. Those in charge of the various enterprises, however, considered that, before the establishment of the planned woollen mill and bank, it was too early to set up such a holding company. The China Enterprise Management Company, which was organised to exercise centralised management and supervision over Liu's enterprises, did not come into being until 1932. Its total capital was set at Ch$200 000, its expected lifespan was 30 years and the board of directors system was adopted inside the company. However even in name it failed after only two or three years.

There were many reasons for Liu's failure to set up a holding company to exercise centralised management over his enterprises. First, such a company is an organisation of monopoly capital. Its purpose is to control other enterprises through a small amount of capital but it must be backed up by strong financial capital. In Chinese industrial circles at the time, such a thing was unprecedented. It was very difficult for people to accept that a company could attempt to control others with only a small amount of capital. Among Liu's enterprises, the Da Zhonghua Match Factory refused to join China Enterprise Management Company because the latter only had a capital of Ch$200 000, while the former had Ch$1 million. That was a very obvious example.[14]

Second, because of Liu's financial weakness, the attempt to impose centralised management over enterprises provided foreign businessmen and bureaucratic capital with an opportunity that they could exploit to their advantage. In November 1933, a British businessman in China came to Liu and told him that he planned to establish a limited-liability company, registered in Britain with the support of British businessmen, as a holding company to direct and keep an eye on all Liu's enterprises. The planned company, called the 'China Industrial Development Trust Company', and its board of directors would consist of four British businessmen and the three Liu brothers. Although this planned holding company never eventuated, the intention of the British was all too clear.

In February 1936, Liu's enterprises had just survived a financial crisis. Song Ziwen [T. V. Soong] sent representatives to discuss with Liu a suggestion to collaborate in setting up a holding company to exercise centralised management over all Liu's enterprises. At that time, Liu already felt that Song intended to seize the opportunity to take over all his businesses. However, because of his difficulties at the time, for a period he dealt with Song courteously but without sincerity. A little later, when his economic situation improved, he stopped doing so.[15]

Although nothing came of these two attempts, they show one thing: national capital in pre-Communist China had insufficient financial strength to carry out centralised management over its enterprises and to expand its business by means of a holding company, nor was it permitted to do so by objective conditions. It was only an illusion without a realistic basis.

Because of the different management conditions in Liu's various enterprises, most of those in charge were suspicious of each other, fearing that they might be involved in trouble and their power might fall into the hands of others. Therefore, they showed different attitudes toward the centralisation of management and it was very difficult to get them to reach a consensus. After the establishment of the China Enterprise Management Company, the system whereby enterprises were supposed invite personnel from that company to act as directors of the board or general managers operated only in name. Usually the original managers were appointed as the 'new' managers sent from the company. In fact, each enterprise was still more or less independent, not controlled by the new company and centralised management was a mere formality. 'Not to put all ones eggs into the one basket' originally was Liu's principle. But with the development of his business, it caused the separation of enterprises and difficulties in their integration.

It can thus be seen that Liu's principle of dispersed investment into medium and small sized enterprises had both positive and negative sides. The positive side meant that, under the changeable economic and political conditions in pre-Communist China, dispersed investment could keep a balance between gains and losses among his enterprises. The negative side was that under the conditions of inadequate accumulation of his own capital and the more general lack of financial resources, dispersed investment inevitably caused enterprises to experience frequent financial shortages and dislocations. Sometimes the enterprises were even in a danger of falling into financial crises. In order to protect themselves, each enterprise sought its own way out and did things independently. In the early 1930s,

Liu's enterprises experienced the problems of leadership being rendered ineffectual by recalcitrant subordinates and a neglect of the interests of the whole. The financial crisis into which he fell in 1935 thoroughly exposed his shortcomings: because of the dispersal in his strength he was unable to cope with the situation. The so-called China Enterprise Management Company was no more than a beautiful blueprint.

Judging from the above problems in the accumulation and transformation of Liu Hongsheng's capital and his business management, Chinese national capitalism was certainly not a favourite child of foreign capitalism and Chinese feudalism. Instead, it came into being as their opposite. In the process of primitive capital accumulation, they were woven together and inextricably linked. From the beginning of the transformation of Liu's comprador capital into national capital, however, their paths diverged, even though they kept a thousand and one economic links with each other. Nevertheless, the central point was the suppression and discrimination which national capitalism suffered and that is why national capitalism could not develop fully in China. Because of the economic and political weakness of the national bourgeoisie, the leadership of the Chinese people's democratic revolution historically fell upon the shoulder of the proletariat and its vanguard, the Chinese Communist Party. Thus the only choice of road for the revolution was socialism.

Notes

1. [Editor's note] This chapter is a translation of Ma Bohuang, 'Liu Hongsheng de qiye touzi yu jingying', *Shehui kexue* 1980.5 (October 1980): 68–72.
2. According to materials from Liu Hongsheng's accounts office, up to the first half of 1926 Liu's total investment in industry, commerce and transportation reached over Ch$3.1 million. This is roughly the same as the estimate made in this article.
3. The statistics for sales of Kailuan coal in Shanghai from 1904 to 1924 compiled by the British Hopkins, Dunn and Co. Ltd; see documents in English from Liu Hongsheng's accounts office.
4. According to survey materials, the price paid by Liu for the Rihui Port was 350 000 taels of silver according to one source, and 450 000 taels of silver according to another. When it was transferred to Kailuan Mining Administration, its price was 900 000 taels of silver. Liu also obtained the rights to sign a contract to sell coal for a second term (1930–9) for Kailuan's Sales Office. The buildings and machinery of the original Rihui Wool Weaving Mill at Rihui Port were dismantled and moved to Zhoujiadu Dock on the east side of the Huangpu river and later became the foundation for Liu's Zhanghua Woollen Mill.

5.   Karl Marx, *Capital*, vol. 1 (Harmondsworth, 1976), p. 926.
6.   Liu Hongsheng, 'Wo wei shenmo yonghu gongchandang?', *Xinwen ribao*, 4 October 1956.
7.   Archives of Liu Hongsheng's accounts office.
8.   Ibid.
9.   A letter from Liu to his fifth son Liu Nianxiao, 11 September 1935, document in English in Liu Hongsheng's archives.
10. A speech given by Wu Qingtai, the manager of the China Cement Factory in Shanghai, on 25 April 1935, in a discussion held to welcome the Delegation of the Foreign Trade and Legislation Committee from the Philippines. See the English language archives of the China Cement Factory in Shanghai.
11. Documents in English in the archives of Liu Hongsheng's accounts office.
12. 'Wo wei shenmo zhuzhong chengben kuaiji', manuscript written by Liu Hongsheng in 1931, in the Liu Hongsheng archives.
13. See the archives of the Joint Survey Department of the Four Banks (the Bank of China, the Central Bank, the Bank of Communications, the Farmers Bank).
14. Liu Hongsheng to P. D. MacFeat, 16 April 1929, letter in English, in the archives of Liu Hongsheng's accounts office.
15. Material provided by Liu Nianzhi in November 1959.

7 The 'Footprints' of Chinese Entrepreneurs in Old Shanghai

Xu Dingxin

Xu Dingxin is a researcher in the Shanghai Academy of Social Sciences. His recent work has focused on the history of Chinese management and this article sums up, better than any other, the recent change in Chinese attitudes towards capitalist management as practised in China before the war.

This article must be read very much in the context of the economic reforms in China in the 1980s, in that its aim is to point the way for contemporary economic managers by distilling the experience of their predecessors. Thus the key issues raised – the virtues of competition, the necessity for professional expertise, sales consciousness, careful planning and economising – are all attributes that the 1980s leadership wished to install in the leaders of economic enterprises in their own period.

A final point to note about this article is that its style, which is retained to some extent in the translation, is more 'literary' than that of the other articles and the author uses many of the colourful phrases which enrich the Chinese language.[1]

Old Shanghai was a metropolis where there were intense rivalries among various powerful capitalists and in the world of capitalism 'competition is emulation with a view to profit'.[2] In order to seek maximum profits, indeed, a number of capitalists, blinded by greed and regardless of their industrial and commercial reputations, tried every means possible to make money by hook or by crook. Especially in the seething waves of speculation, they would rather face the risk of being capsized than give up the opportunity to reap staggering profits.

However, such behaviour was not adopted by those capitalists in China who paid more attention to the management of enterprises and were more experienced in market competition. Although the class nature of capitalists, who are intent on nothing but profit, made it impossible for them completely to abstain from speculative activities, they put most of their effort into trying their best to improve the management of enterprises. They felt the pulse of the rapidly changing international and domestic markets and seized opportunities to learn and master the skills to deal with foreign capitalists and to strengthen the competitiveness of their products. In this way they were able to bear various kinds of foreign and domestic pressure under extremely bad conditions and to make timely reforms and unremitting efforts to improve themselves. Although such efforts were not able to change the fact that imperialism, feudalism and bureaucratic capitalism oppressed and devastated national capitalist enterprises in China, some entrepreneurs managed to develop their enterprises to a certain extent by exploiting the cracks appearing in the internecine rivalry between foreign and domestic reactionary forces. Therefore now, when the thick fog of speculation over the metropolis has cleared, and the sediment accumulated for years washed away, we can still find some experiences in their enterprise management practices which are useful as reference for later generations.

'VICTORY TO THE SUPERIOR, DEFEAT FOR THE INFERIOR' AND 'IT ALL DEPENDS ON HUMAN EFFORTS'

At the end of the nineteenth century the famous bourgeois reformer, Yan Fu, first translated into Chinese a book called *Evolution and Ethics* by Thomas Henry Huxley, a British biologist. The book was entitled *Tian Yan Lun* (On Natural Evolution) in Chinese. Following its publication, the evolutionary point of view, 'in natural selection, survival of the fittest', spread like wildfire all over China. So-called 'natural selection' refers to the fact that in competition for survival the fittest is selected by nature, the unfit eliminated. This idea was very influential among the recently-formed Chinese bourgeoisie. Because of further economic encroachment upon China by the imperialist powers, far-sighted people within and outside the government alike felt the pressure of 'business war' and the serious threat to China's national security, which was as fragile as a pile of eggs.

Many examples proved that victory belonged to the superior and that defeat for the inferior was an irresistible law of nature: the defeat of China in the Sino-Japanese War in 1894–5; the failure of the westernisation movement; and the spate of bankruptcies of national capitalist industrial and commercial enterprises because of poor management. This forced those capitalists who had national pride and dedication and who would not take their defeat lying down to try their best to brace up and fight their way out of adverse conditions. They quickly accepted the idea of evolution and applied it in the management of capitalist enterprises and competition in the market. The idea thus became a driving force promoting enterprise reform and rousing entrepreneurs to vigorous efforts to make their enterprises prosperous.

At the beginning of the Republican period, Mu Ouchu, a capitalist in the cotton textile industry who accepted western capitalist influence quite early, felt deeply that 'there were no advanced countries in the world which did not rouse themselves to vigorous efforts to nurture their spirits and strength, so as to develop their national power'. But when it came to China, not only did everything lag behind but also the people in industrial and commercial circles had neither entrepreneurial spirit nor the means to improve themselves. He argued: 'in this era of economic competition, if one does not try hard to find a proper way to deal with others, if one is not determined to become strong and active in developing ones own resources to make supply meet demand, then others will do it instead.'[3] That meant that if we ourselves did not make a determined effort to make our country strong the imperialist powers would inevitably take over and the vital lifelines of the nation's economy would fall into foreign hands. Such a consequence was unthinkable.

Mu appealed to the public and called on industrial and commercial entrepreneurs over the whole nation to exert their efforts in good time and with one spirit. He himself translated the book *Scientific Management* by Frederick Taylor into Chinese and pioneered its application in his own Deda Cotton Mill. As an innovator in his trade he himself instigated wise policies concerning enterprise management and administration and required the various functional departments to carry out their duties strictly. From the selection of raw materials to the output of finished products, all were subject to strict quality control. After the implementation of 'scientific management' in that factory, results were outstanding. Its products enjoyed great popularity and won first prize in a national competition held in Beijing.[4]

The Guos, a family of overseas Chinese capitalists who ran the Yongan [Wing On] enterprises, understood this point even more clearly. Although they started by selling foreign commodities, they did not wish the domination of the Chinese market by imported goods to last forever. So at the same time as they established the Yongan Department Store they began to raise money to send their children abroad to study in preparation for the establishment of the Yongan Cotton Mill. While selling 'merchandise from around the world, they paid attention to the copying and improvement of such goods so that the development of national industry could be promoted. Their purpose was to enable Chinese peasants and workers to copy, improve and perfect those European and American goods which suited the taste of Chinese people, so as to deny the foreigners the exclusive right to produce such goods.'

Products such as various varieties of 'Three Guns' brand underwear manufactured by the Shanghai Yingyin Weaving Mill were copies and improvements of foreign products, made in accordance with the design, standard and quality specified by the Yongan Company. The perfumed soap produced by the Shanghai Yuhua Chemical Company was also a new product based upon copying Palmolive soap according to Yongan's requirements. In the process of copying, experienced salesmen were sent by the company to help these factories. They compared the merits and demerits of famous brand imported goods and of similar domestic goods and raised suggestions how to improve product quality. Thus a lot of copied products reached the level of similar imported goods and became famous brands.[5]

When the Yongan Textile Company was set up, it had very strict demands in terms of enterprise management and product quality. The Gold City Brand cotton yarn and Roc Brand fine cloth manufactured by its subordinate cotton mill attained the status of famous brands because of their excellent quality and were very competitive in the market.

The Shanghai [Commercial and Savings] Bank developed from a small bank with a capital of only Ch\$100 000 into one with a capital of Ch\$2.5 million, deposits of Ch\$32 million and branches in more than 20 cities over the country; it ranked as the leader of the three southern and four northern banks. This was because Chen Guangfu, who ran the bank, was familiar with the natural law of the survival of the fittest and good at its application. He devoted himself to continually improving the enterprise, preparing for danger in times of peace and constantly striving to become stronger. He considered that 'in the world of today, one can achieve nothing unless one devotes oneself to "business war"'. In an era of natural selection, even if China's business people tried their best to study the ways to achieve victory and to find the means to protect themselves, they might nevertheless fail. How could one give oneself up as hopeless and not rouse oneself to do battle in the field of 'business war'?[6] During all the dozens of years he presided over the bank, he always alerted himself and his colleagues to this matter; he tried to pool wisdom ideas on how to defeat opponents. He required every one, including himself, from managers and directors down to every bank clerk, to pay attention to efficiency, 'to achieve the best result at the minimum cost'.[7] Even after the Shanghai Bank had developed into a large business, Chen Guangfu still closely watched over the international and domestic situation, commercial conditions and monetary changes. He foresaw potential adverse developments and crises and always carefully, cautiously and conscientiously sought a steady development of the enterprise, as if he was treading on thin ice and facing an abyss.

Through painstaking endeavour these entrepreneurs understood the truths, 'victory to the superior, defeat for the inferior' and 'everything depends on human effort'.[8] Of course it must be pointed out that the bourgeoisie mechanically applied the viewpoint of the biologists, 'survival of the fittest' and 'natural selection', into the social field, and explained complicated social phenomena on the same principle as the law of the jungle. Their purpose was simply to write off class contradictions, obscure the class consciousness of the working masses and disguise the criminality of capitalist exploitation. However, with regard to the management of enterprises, 'victory to the superior and defeat for inferior' and 'everything depends on human efforts' are not without value as guides for action.

'EMPTY BAGS CANNOT STAND UP'

The saying 'empty bags cannot stand up' was a vivid metaphor used by some entrepreneurs to ridicule amateurs who were content with ignorance and lacked initiative. Their aim was to arouse and persuade colleagues to study hard and master specialised knowledge. It is impossible to make an empty bag stand up; it cannot stand straight up on the ground until it is full. This simple principle is easy to understand but has often been neglected.

In enterprises controlled by warlords or bureaucrats the people occupying important positions were usually good-for-nothings: they neither had specialised knowledge nor knew anything about management. Relying upon such people no enterprise could succeed. The Hengyuan Textile Company in Tianjin was under the control of the fourth brother of the warlord Cao Kun; he knew nothing about textile technology or industrial administration. What he did do was to lord it over others, to make a modern factory into a disguised form of a government office. The Cao family could squander the enterprise's money at will and the administrative personnel engaged in malpractices, corruption and squeeze. Machines and equipment were not maintained at all, while apparatus and material were thoughtlessly wasted and spoiled. Under the control of such 'empty bags', the factory went bankrupt several times.[9]

The Hengfeng Cotton Mill in Shanghai was established with all its capital coming from the Nie family. Because the factory and family finances were not separated, the system was in chaos. The members of the family could embezzle enterprise funds at will. Their debts to the company were as high as tens or even hundreds of thousands of dollars. Because of the ignorance of the people in charge of the enterprise and the improper appointment of personnel, the development of the enterprise lagged behind others in the same line of business.

Such examples were lessons for those entrepreneurs who showed promise and were exerting themselves. Therefore these entrepreneurs always studied hard and tried to become experts in the specialised knowledge of their trades. They encouraged their subordinates, staff and workers to become familiar with their profession and to enlarge the scope of their knowledge.

In the training of staff and workers carried out in the Shanghai Bank, the slogan 'empty bags cannot stand up' was important. They stressed: 'if one wants to be successful in ones career, one has to prepare oneself fully', and 'if we want to establish a solid position, we must enrich our knowledge and try to put what we learn into practice and add to our experience. Otherwise, there is no hope of success'. Chen Guangfu himself was a very experienced banker but he was not content with what he knew and tried to enlarge the scope of his learning with a thirst for new knowledge.

Because he actively enlisted the services of able people, the Shanghai Bank had a number of technical and administrative personnel with a high level of specialised knowledge. However, Chen keenly felt that a lot of staff, including some senior staff, still remained at the level of the past and were unable to meet the demands of a developing situation. He considered the shortage of able personnel the greatest problem for the Bank. Thus he called on his colleagues to regard ignorance as a disgrace and to acquire knowledge through careful study. A group of senior administrative staff was sent abroad to conduct investigations and pursue study. Training classes were held in a planned way to train talent in reserve. Chen made plans to cultivate able people and gave accelerated promotion and salary increases to those staff who 'studied hard and showed initiative'. He required that, in addition to book knowledge, everyone in the bank should learn on the job. No one should ever feel ashamed to consult their subordinates and, if they learned something, they should keep what they had experienced in mind and make notes about it, no matter how trivial it might seem; 'one should look upon seeking knowledge as an honour for ones whole life'.[10]

As mentioned above, the Guos had rich experience in capitalist commerce, having conducted business abroad for a long time. However they were total amateurs in relation to the textile industry. When they started the preparation for the Yongan Textile Company, they deeply felt their lack of specialised knowledge. They felt that if they were content with an amateur status, did not seek to improve themselves and recklessly established textile enterprises, they would inevitably fail to obtain the results they expected and would be mocked as 'empty bags'. Therefore Guo Le and his colleagues made advance preparations: they sent a number of promising young men in their family to America and Europe to study the engineering aspects of spinning, weaving, printing and dyeing. These young people got to know a lot of classmates during their study abroad. When they finished their studies and returned to China, they became the backbone of the technical and administrative personnel of the Yongan Textile Company and its subordinate factories, and recommended a group of able technical people for employment. In this way, the Yongan Cotton Mill became quite an advanced enterprise in terms of production technology, equipment and management.

The Yongan Company in Shanghai had very strict professional examinations for its staff and workers, stipulating that employees must be familiar with the specialised knowledge necessary in their respective departments, including the names, specifications, varieties, functions and characteristics of various commodities and knowledge of maintenance and repair. They had to master several major foreign languages and local dialects and know the proprieties of receiving customers and understand their psychology. In one word, they 'must win over customers'.

Many capitalists did not become experts in their own trades until they gained professional proficiency through assiduous study. Typical examples were Wu Yunchu from the Tianchu Monosodium Glutamate Factory, Hu Xiyuan from the Chinese Ampere Electrical Equipment Factory, Chen Wanyun and Shen Jiucheng from the Sanyou Industrial Company, Yan Qingxiang from the Dalong Machine Factory, Cai Shangbo from the Meiya Silk Weaving Mill, Xiang Songmou from the Five Continents Soap Factory and others. It was precisely because they were managed by these able and professional specialists that these enterprises were able quickly to change their approach, sail against the current in the stormy sea of 'business war' and win some victories. Whether factories and shops were administrated by experts or were filled with 'empty bags' brought about very clearly different results. This is well worth while pondering over.

'TURNING GOODS OVER LIKE WHEELS'

All industrial and commercial enterprises would like the commodities produced or sold by them to meet market demand, to increase their sales and to accelerate the circulation of capital. Without a market, their goods would be stockpiled, leading to difficulties in the circulation of capital and causing a crisis for the enterprise. This kind of stockpiling of commodities was called 'tied-down capital', a taboo for any industrial or commercial enterprise. Entrepreneurs, therefore, always tried their utmost to make their commodities meet market requirements, thus shortening the time taken for commodities to circulate and increasing the number of times their capital circulated, so as to obtain higher profits. Guo Le, a capitalist in the Yongan group of enterprises, called this process 'turning goods over like wheels'.

In *Capital*, Karl Marx many times expounded the benefits for capitalists of shortening the time of commodity turnover and increasing the number of times capital turned over. He held that, 'a reduction in the turnover time or in one of its two component sections, production time and circulation time, raises the mass of surplus value produced', and would give 'increased effectiveness . . . to the variable portion of capital'. He illustrated it with an example: 'a variable capital of 500 which turns over ten times in the year appropriates just as much surplus value in this period as a variable capital of 5000 with the same rate of surplus value and the same wages, which turns over only once in the year.'[11] Although the Chinese capitalists had not necessarily read *Capital*, it illustrated the law of capitalist production and circulation and summed up the managerial activities of capitalist enterprises.

After setting up the Yongan Company in Shanghai, Guo Le repeatedly admonished the leading managers in every department to take the replenishing of stock as 'the life-line of the company'; he held that the person in charge of the replenishment of goods must know market trends very well and should be far-sighted. One should not over-stock but without stock one can do nothing; therefore the person in charge should ensure that the goods in stock meet market demand, so as to make 'goods turn over like wheels'.[12] In order to avoid overstocking with goods difficult to sell, Guo Le himself paid attention to stocks and appointed several able and experienced assistants capable of reacting quickly to market changes and shouldering the task of replenishment. He was kept well informed on the situation of the sales and stocks of each counter and tried to discover through various channels what consumers were demanding. Using market information as the basis for replenishment, the English word 'return' on Guo's lips was like an invisible whip urging each department to do its best to quicken the turnover of commodities and to reduce stocks. The company had different turnover targets for different commodities. As to those in great demand such as canned food, cloth and articles for daily use, the turnover targets were very high; while some expensive goods not much in demand had a relatively lower target but they still had a target. That was in order to

assess the achievements of each department: for example, it was stipulated
for the ivory department that they should turn over their stock three times
a year, that is, given a capital of Ch\$25 000, the volume of business should
reach more than Ch\$75 000.[13]

The capitalists of Xiedaxiang Silk Cloth Shop also paid great attention
to stocks and looked upon them as the key factor. Their principle was to be
neither out of stock nor overstocked. When they laid down a plan for stocks
and checked its implementation, the general administration department,
those in charge of stock replenishment in various departments and the
managers of the various branch shops took care of it themselves. Besides
the orders they placed for goods at factories, the quota for commodities
in great demand stipulated that this year's stock quota was to be about
70 per cent of the previous year's sales, while 30 per cent was covered
by spot replenishment, which would be carried out flexibly in accordance
with market conditions. They regularly held meetings for stock controllers,
sales assistants and those who looked after stocks in the shop to exchange
information so as to ensure that commodities were neither under-nor
overstocked. Before daily replenishment in various shops and departments
was carried out, persons in charge would go to the warehouse to inquire
about the amount of commodities in stock and the administrators in
the warehouse would regularly inform the departments about changes
in stocks.[14] This kind of effective system guaranteed a high turnover
of merchandise and capital for the enterprise and increased the flow of
profits.

'NOT MINDING TRIFLES AND TRYING TO AIM AT LONG-TERM GAINS'

'Others strive for short-term profits, while I aim at long-term gains; others
disdain trifles, while there is nothing too small to win my attention' was
Chen Guangfu's admonition to the Shanghai Bank. All those entrepreneurs
who were persons of insight, experience and intelligence took that as a
motto. Some businessmen were preoccupied with short-term gains and
losses and paid no attention to setting up their enterprise's long-term
credibility with customers. They tried to reap staggering profits through
various means of cheating. For a short period they might gain profits but in the long run they lost the confidence of customers. Some
industrial and commercial enterprises looked down upon business which
made few or no profits and cold-shouldered customers in word and
deed, driving them away. Therefore wise entrepreneurs were always

far-sighted and started from the small details from which they saw their skill emanating.

To take the management of the Shanghai Bank as an example, they not only paid great attention to industrial loans but also did not neglect small credit loans which other banks disdained to offer. They considered that small factories and shops were not necessarily all unworthy of credit. Because of the shortage of capital, small factories could not improve their products, small shops could not build up stocks, and this directly influenced the survival and development of these enterprises. Therefore the Shanghai Bank made a general investigation of the credit-worthiness of small factories and shops in Shanghai and a partial investigation in some other places. It actively financed any which were promising and credit-worthy. In this way, not only these small industrial and commercial enterprises gained some benefits but also the Shanghai Bank increased its volume of loans and its reputation and prestige in industrial and commercial circles.[15]

The China Travel Service was a tourism service enterprise affiliated to the Shanghai Bank. Its business field was not only large but also on an individually small scale, including booking ship and train tickets on behalf of customers, taking care of luggage, issuing travellers' cheques, organising collective sight-seeing tours to various scenic spots and setting up travel inns, hotels and reception houses for tourists in scenic spots. The bank invested heavily and assigned people to provide very good customer service. After the opening of the China Travel Service, its business developed quickly but it suffered losses for years on end, leading to criticism in some quarters. At a meeting of Shanghai Bank managers, some held that the running of a travel agency was not worth the candle and called for it to be closed down. But Chen Guangfu thought otherwise; he considered that, although short-term profits were small, the travel agency could make 'long-term contributions'. That is, through providing a good service and setting up a wide net of contacts, it made an invaluable good impression; such gains could hardly be evaluated in terms of money. At Chen's insistence, the China Travel Service continued in business and its slogan 'serving society' became famous all over China, thus raising the credibility of the Shanghai Bank as well. Over the years the Shanghai Bank obtained a lot of business such as deposits and loans, storage and entrustment through the reputation and connections of the China Travel Service.[16]

The Yongan Company's home-delivery system aimed to attract foreign and Chinese customers and gained credit through its 'home service'. That company especially established a delivery department with full-time staff and several vehicles. If the customers who purchased commodities in the company's shop wanted their goods delivered to their door-step, large goods would be delivered by trucks, small articles by shop assistants from the various counters. When commodities like electric equipment or radios were delivered to customers' homes, the staff took the trouble to install a switch board, wires and plugs for the customers free of charge.

In one case, a foreign seaman bought a leather case and asked for it to be delivered to his ship moored at Wusong kou, so that he could have a good time out on the town. A shop assistant from the leather goods department was specially sent to deliver it. After changing buses several times and taking a ferry he reached the ship and mounted the gangway with the leather case. Although he was very tired, he still appeared with a friendly and pleasant countenance and was unanimously praised by the foreign seamen. When general manager Guo Linshuang heard about this, he praised the shop assistant as the backbone of the company, giving him both promotion and a wage rise.[17] What Guo Linshuang had seen was not simply one business transaction but rather the increase of the company's reputation and credibility through good service provided in one business transaction; thus more customers would be won over, leading to a situation in which 'people nearby were happy and those far away would come over' and the company would gain lasting 'long-term benefits'.

Of course there was no lack of so-called 'slippery businessmen' in old Shanghai. These merchants completely ignored industrial and commercial credibility, making one speculative deal after another, selling defective goods as good ones like passing off fish eyes as pearls. They did whatever they could, no matter how dirty it might be, so long as they could make money. But reliance upon cheating could not last long. The consumers might be taken in once or twice but after that they would no longer believe them. It was impossible for notorious industrial and commercial enterprises to gain any firm footing in the intense 'business war'. True entrepreneurs always paid attention to the quality of products, the management of enterprises and their industrial and commercial reputation; they laid down a solid base for the survival and development of their enterprises through hard and long-term work. Anyone running an industrial or commercial enterprise was bound to be doomed if, blinded by the lust for profits, they ignored industrial and commercial reputation and plunged headlong into the raging whirlpools of speculation.

'NOT A COIN SHOULD FALL ON BARREN LAND'

'Not a coin should fall on barren land' was a common slogan in industrial and commercial circles. Each year people were judged according to it, and everyone interpreted it in their own way. Actually it did not simply portray the stinginess of capitalists; rather it stressed their shrewdness in running enterprises. 'His function as a capitalist consists in producing surplus value, that is unpaid labour, and in the most economical conditions at that . . . '[18] Because of the restrictions imposed upon them by China's social conditions, the strength of national capitalist industry and commerce was relatively slight in terms of capital and they were in a disadvantageous position. As they were seeking survival and development in adverse circumstances, it was even less possible to allow careless expenditure of hard-earned and limited funds. A shrewd capitalist would always save every coin and try to achieve maximum economic efficiency with minimum investment, to gain maximum profits at minimum cost.

Liu Hongsheng regarded cost accounting as the 'eye' inspecting the good and bad parts of an enterprise's management. He spared no expense in inviting first-rate accounting experts to design accounting systems for the various enterprises that he established. Enterprises under his management such as the Zhanghua Wool Factory, the Shanghai Cement Company and the Da Zhonghua Match Factory were among the first to adopt cost accounting systems. For example, the Da Zhonghua Match Factory spared no effort to reduce non-productive expenditures and costs of production. After adopting a cost accounting system, they compared and analysed the annual production achievements, the consumption of materials, wages, production costs and management fees for all the factories under their control, and the volume of sales, business expenses and profits of each branch office, in order to distinguish the good ones from the poor ones, to enlighten every factory and office and to improve management and raise economic efficiency.[19]

In the period soon after the establishment of the Shanghai Bank, capital was scarce and they had to make economies everywhere. Later on, after it developed and became quite big and well-off, unavoidably some departments became lavish in spending money. For instance, the business of the bank needed a great number of account books, report forms, bills and other kinds of paper and stationery. Such expenditure accounted for quite a large share in the enterprise's costs. Some bank staff considered that, as long as business was developing, there was no harm in increasing the enterprise's expenditures a little. Thus waste of enterprise property happened frequently in various departments. Chen Guangfu, though he was general manager, did not neglect the spread of such malpractice, repeatedly stressing the importance of increasing income and reducing expenditure. He pointed out: 'in order to increase the bank's profits, the only way is to study changes in income so as to broaden its source and to analyse the distribution of expenditure so as to obtain a basis for making economies.'

In order to do this, however, accurate cost accounting was necessary. He believed that the aim of cost accounting in manufacturing industry was to calculate total costs, including materials, labour and other indirect costs, so as to decide the selling price and to determine guidelines for business. In a bank, however, the purpose of cost accounting was to know the true situation of the bank's gains and losses, to measure the efficiency of each department and to check whether there were any extravagant expenditures.

The increase of the Shanghai Bank's expenditure was disclosed very quickly through cost accounting and it was put on the agenda of the general management office. Chen Guangfu repeatedly exhorted members of the bank to practise strict economy and rational expenditure. He stressed that so-called rational expenditure meant that those expenditures linked with the development of the business should not be grudged even though the amount might be quite big. If money was spent inappropriately, however, it was a waste and not even one coin should be spent. Taking aim at waste in the bank, he gave the use of paper as an example, explaining: 'if the expenditure is warranted, hundreds of thousands of sheets of paper are not too much; if it is unnecessary, the use of even one piece of paper is a waste'. He stressed that 'wood can be cut with a string saw, a rock can be worn through by dripping water; economy in trifles ensures abundance; one should pay attention even to the tiniest matters'.[20] The expenditures of the bank decreased rapidly because the leaders attached great importance to it and adopted some quite effective measures. The value of paper, stationery and printing costs saved just between 1931 and early 1933 was more than Ch\$20 000.

Should we simply discard the style of running enterprises with such careful calculation, strict budgeting and not wasting a coin on 'barren land' as 'a worn-out shoe' because the aim of the capitalists was to seek after profits? Should not we take it up as an historic heritage and let it serve today's socialist economic construction after due criticism, discrimination and reform?

Because of the limitations of the sources, what I have said above is only very partial. It is difficult for me to see the whole picture of the history of capitalist enterprise management in pre-Communist China. However, even the odd bits which I have picked up have reflected the value of this historic heritage which is waiting to be further explored and examined. Of course the success or failure of an enterprise did not depend only on the quality of management but also was influenced by other factors. Especially under the historical conditions whereby China was a semi-colonial semi-feudal society, the development of national capitalism could not but be greatly restricted and stifled. Even entrepreneurs of ability, wide knowledge and rich experience in enterprise management could not fully fulfil their aspirations. The enterprises they established were finally driven to the wall by the imperialists and the reactionary Nationalist government and could not escape the fate of decline and bankruptcy.

Notes

1. [Editor's note] This chapter is a translation of Xu Dingxin, 'Zhongguo qiyejia zai jiu Shanghai de huodong zuji', *Shanghai jingji kexue*, 1984.7 (July 1984): 43–8.
2. Karl Marx, *The Poverty of Philosophy* (New York, 1973), p. 146.
3. Mu Ouchu, 'Zhenxing mianye chuyi', in *Ouchu wushi zishu. wenji (Shanghai, 1926)*, p. 25.
4. Ibid., pp. 51–2, and Chen Zhen *et al.*, *Zhongguo jindai gongye shi ziliao*, vol. 1 (Beijing, 1957), p. 453.
5. *Xianggang Yongan youxian gongsi 25 zhounian jinian lu (Xianggang, 1932)*, preface; *Shanghai Yongan gongsi de chansheng, fazhan he gaizao*, Shanghai shehui kexue yuan jingji yanjiu suo (Shanghai, 1981), p. 137, interviews with Liu Jiayan, Liang Caokui and other staff of the Yongan Company.
6. 'Shangren shijie zhi shangren zeren', *Haiguang* 3.3.
7. 'Shiye chengbai zhi genyuan', *Haiguang* 3.5.
8. *Haiguang* 11.8.
9. See Chen Zhen, *Zhongguo jindai gongye shi ziliao*, vol. 1, p. 459–60; *Wenshi ziliao xuanji* 44 (Beijing, 1964), pp. 97–100.
10. A speech given by Chen Guangfu to Shanghai banking colleagues when he returned from a tour of investigation in Europe and USA in June, 1930. Another speech given by Chen Guangfu at the business conference held at the General Headquarters of Shanghai Bank, 15 October 1930. Both speeches are taken from *Chen Guangfu xiansheng yanlun ji* (Shanghai, 1949).
11. Karl Marx, *Capital*, vol. 3 (Harmondsworth, 1981), pp. 163, 165.
12. 'Records of the Preparatory Conference of the Yongan Company, Shanghai, and Records of the Conference of Managerial Personnel'.
13. Interviews with Liu Jiayan, Chen Zhaobao and others, staff of the Yongan Company, Shanghai.

14. Sun Zhaoming, 'Xiedaxiang zhoubu dian shiliao', *Shanghai wenshi ziliao xuanji* 1982.2.
15. *Haiguang* 5.4 and 7.5 contain some records about small loans offered by the Shanghai Bank.
16. Zhu Chengzhang, 'Zhongguo lüxingshe jianshi', *Haiguang* 1.11; speech given by Chen Guangfu at a luncheon attended by the colleagues of Bankers' Association and the China Travel Service on 15 January 1929. See *Chen Guangfu xiansheng yanlun ji*.
17. Interviews with Chen Zhaobao and Xu Menglin, staff of the Yongan Company, Shanghai.
18. Karl Marx, *Capital*, vol. 3, p. 504.
19. Liu Nianzhi, 'Shiyejia Liu Hongsheng zhuanlüe', pp. 65–6; *Zhongguo minzu huochai gongye*, Qingdao shi gongshang guanli ju shiliao zu (Beijing, 1963), pp. 68–70.
20. Talks given by Chen Guangfu at a dinner-party with his colleagues from the Shanghai Bank in November 1930. Also talks by Chen Guangfu with colleagues of the Nanjing Branch of the Shanghai Bank in August 1936. Both from *Chen Guangfu xiansheng yanlun ji*; 'Yinhang chengben zhi jisuan', *Haiguang* 4.2.

8 The Process of the Disintegration of Modern China's Natural Economy

Xu Xinwu

Professor Xu Xinwu is a senior researcher in the Institute of Economics at the Shanghai Academy of Social Sciences. He has published widely on Chinese economic history, including in Western periodicals, and is general editor of the series of industry studies being produced in Shanghai.

This article focuses on one of the most difficult and controversial topics in Chinese history, both in China and in the West: the nature of the prewar Chinese agrarian economy. Its central topic is the complex and incomplete process whereby the 'natural' economy, in which households produced for their own consumption, gave way the 'commodity' economy, in which production was for the market. Professor Xu's macro estimates for the agriculture and handicraft sectors are of major importance and make a great contribution to the debate.[1]

I

A natural economy is the opposite of a commodity economy. Generally speaking, an economy in which the producers produce for their own or their exploiters' direct consumption is a natural economy. Its nature is therefore that it produces only use values.

In China's feudal society, a small-scale agricultural economy which combined farming with weaving was both the basic structure and the basic unit of production; a self-sufficient natural economy was predominant. However, as soon as there was social division of labour, small-scale handicraft production intended for the market developed, as did commercialisation of agricultural products. Moreover, a few of those engaged in the production of handicraft commodities either became independent of agriculture or evolved from government-operated handicraft industries but they were of little importance.

On the eve of the Opium War, the commodity economy was quite prosperous, with quite a large market for some handicraft and agricultural products. At that time the most important commodity traded in terms of value was grain, 10 per cent of which entered the market; second was cotton cloth, of which more than half was marketed;[2] these were the two main commodity flows in the market. The production of other handicraft industries such as silk and silk products, ferrous metallurgy, coal mining, paper-making, ceramic manufacturing and oil pressing was for the market; agricultural sectors such as cane sugar and tea were commercialised, as was cotton production to a certain degree.

The decomposition of the natural economy was, however, very slow and the production of all these commodities accounted for only a small proportion of the total output of industry and agriculture;[3] the proportion of traded handicraft production which came from handicraft workshops was very small; and most trade was in consumer rather than producer goods. This was basically because, in the vast small-scale peasant economy under the feudal ownership of land, small-scale farming and domestic handicrafts were inextricably linked and this formed a strong base for a natural economy.

In the period immediately after the Opium War, the decomposition of China's natural economy still proceeded very slowly and should not be over-estimated. Although some agricultural and handicraft products were traded in considerably greater amounts, these were limited mainly to tea and silk, and secondarily to cotton and soybeans. In all cases the increase in trade resulted from the growth of export demand rather than from domestic industrial development; thus the amount of cotton traded was still very limited, while most silk exports were of hand-made silk. As modern silk filatures had just begun to emerge, the amount of cocoons produced for sale was very small.

Although the volume of imports was increasing steadily, goods such as imported cloth mainly found a market in large and medium cities and did not yet penetrate rural areas. At that time (before 1895) only a few imported goods such as imported cotton yarn in non-cotton producing areas, imported iron (in the form of farm tools made by blacksmiths), kerosene and needles had penetrated the rural areas. The handicraft commodities affected by this were Chinese iron and steel, wax making and oil pressing, and the industries harmed were usually limited to those in cities and towns. Generally speaking, before the Sino-Japanese War of 1894–5, the import of foreign industrial goods only replaced goods produced in already commercialised handicraft sectors and, although the commodity

TABLE 8.1   *The natural and commodity economies in the total value of industrial and agricultural output in 1920 (billion Ch$)*

	Total Industrial and Agricultural Output		Agricultural Output		Individual Handicraft Output		Capitalist Industrial and Mining Output	
	Value	%	Value	%	Value	%	Value	%
Total Value of Output[1]	21.90	100	16.52	100	3.02	100	2.36	100
Commodity Economy	9.77	44.59	6.19[2]	37.55	1.20[3]	40	2.36	10C
Natural Economy	12.13	55.41	10.32	62.45	1.81	60		

SOURCES for Tables 8.1 and 8.2:

[1] For the total value of industrial and agricultural and the value of the output of the various sectors in 1920, see Tang Chuansi, *Zhongguo zibenzhuyi fazhan shi*, vol. 2 (forthcoming), chapter 5 section 1; for those of 1936, see Ding Shixun, 'Guanyu Zhongguo zibenzhuyi fazhan shuiping de jige wenti', *Nankai daxue xuebao, zhe she*, 1979.4 (October 1979): 20–7. The figures quoted exclude transportation. In the value of handicraft output, the output of workshops is estimated as 30 per cent for 1920, 40 per cent in 1936 and is included in the value of capitalist industry and mining output.

[2] For the estimates of the level of commercialisation in agriculture see the various tables in section three of this chapter.

[3] The data of output value of this table was calculated out in accordance with Wu Baosan, *Zhongguo guomin suode, 1933 nian* (Shanghai, 1946). This book's figures for the value of handicraft output obviously included the farmers' household handicrafts in the case of textiles and food products. Therefore, the marketed proportion of individual handicrafts was estimated separately according to the history of the trade concerned.

market was expanding, its effect upon the decomposition of the natural economy was very limited.

After 1895 the decomposition of China's natural economy gathered pace. This was not only because of rapidly growing commodity imports and exports but also increasingly because of the growth of modern industry. Among agricultural products, trade in cotton, tobacco, wheat, oil crops, silk and tea, which were used as inputs by modern industry, continuously developed, while light industrial goods gradually penetrated the rural areas; domestically produced factory yarn in particular became a major force breaking up the integration of spinning and weaving in farm households.

TABLE 8.2   *The natural and commodity economies in the total value of industrial and agricultural output in 1936 (billion Ch$)*

	Total Industrial and Agricultural Output		Agricultural Output		Individual Handicraft Output		Capitalist Industrial and Mining Output	
	Value	%	Value	%	Value	%	Value	%
Total Value of Output[1]	30.61	100	19.92	100	4.42	100	6.27	100
Commodity Economy	17.66	57.68	8.47[2]	43.86	2.65[3]	60	6.27	100
Natural Economy	12.95	42.32	11.19	56.14	1.77	40		

SOURCES see Table 8.1.

It was precisely because more raw materials from rural areas were absorbed by urban industry (or were exported) that some imported and domestically manufactured machine-made industrial goods began to flow in gradually increasing amounts to rural areas. This phenomenon was, however, only on a limited scale.

The degree of decomposition of China's natural economy can be calculated from the ratio between subsistence production (the natural economy) and production for the market (the commodity economy). Any such calculation is, however, a very complicated and difficult process and the author is only able to make a rough and tentative estimate. Up to 1920 the ratio between the natural economy and the commodity economy was roughly 55:45 in terms of the total value of national industrial and agricultural output, so that most goods were still produced for household consumption. By 1936 the ratio between the two was reversed to 42:58 (see Tables 8.1 and 8.2). If the fact that the commodity economy overtook the natural economy showed that the latter was going from decomposition to disintegration, then China's natural economy was already in the process of disintegration. Any such process was, however, very slow. For the period from the outbreak of the Anti-Japanese War in 1937 up to 1949, we lack the materials necessary for such an analysis but there is no doubt that the natural economy still accounted for a large part of the economy for the whole period.

Although the commercialisation of rural handicrafts and agriculture reflected an increase in production, it did not necessarily mean prosperity for China's rural economy or a higher standard of living for the peasants. On the contrary, under the characteristics of China's small-scale peasant economy, to a large extent it represented a kind of 'poor commodity economy'. The clearest case is that of native cloth, which already was quite commercialised but where, in a situation where the broad masses of the peasants were dressed in rags, the increase in commercialisation was achieved at the cost of heavy exploitation of the peasants.

The commercialisation of grain was a similar case. On the one hand there was the problem of grain-producing farmers buying back grain. (Such repurchase was different from the grain sold to rural areas producing cash crops.) Moreover, a rather large percentage of marketed grain came from peasants reducing their consumption, while they lived a life of semi-starvation, eating chaff and wild herbs, or came from peasants economising on the use of higher grade grains and eating coarse grain instead. The fact that wheat was the most highly commercialised grain reflects this phenomenon.

Although peasants sold some agricultural products, they still lacked the purchasing power to buy industrial goods. In the final analysis, under such circumstances, the development of the commodity economy did not greatly hasten the absolute decomposition of the natural economy. Although the amount of grain marketed increased with the growth of production, the rate of commercialisation did not necessarily increase; in a situation where the peasants' standard of living increased somewhat but still remained at a low level, the proportion of grain marketed would not necessarily increase (some grain was used for the development of sideline occupations, but also the peasants increased their consumption of food). This was proved by the experience of the early 1950s.

The decomposition of China's natural economy was reflected most of all in the steady weakening of subsistence production of hand-woven textiles among the broad mass of the peasants and by the increasing commercialisation of agricultural products, especially grain. These will be analysed separately in the following sections.

II

After 1840 a major manifestation of the decomposition of China's natural economy was the devastation of the subsistence cotton spinning and weaving handicraft industries in rural households.

The growing decomposition of the natural economy in China's handicraft cotton textile industry was not manifested in any change in the amount

TABLE 8.3 *The process of replacement of native yarn with machine spun yarn in China's rural cotton textile handicrafts*

	1840	1860	1894	1913	1920	1936
Total output of hand-woven cloth in rural areas (millions of bolts)[1]	597.33	604.71	589.16	497.42	552.32	352.98
Total amount of yarn used in hand-woven cloth in rural areas (million kg)[2]	375.5	380.5	370.5	313.0	347.5	222.0
Machine-spun yarn used in hand-woven cloth[3] (million kg)	1.5	2.0	87.0	226.5	176.5	168.5
As %	0.40	0.56	23.42	72.33	50.76	75.94
Native yarn used in hand-woven cloth (million kg)	374.0	378.0	283.5	65.0	171.5	53.5
As %	99.60	99.44	76.58	27.67	49.24	24.06

SOURCE: Xu Xinwu *et al.*, *Jiangnan tubu shi* (forthcoming), Table B5.
NOTES: [1]The total output of native cotton cloth should be the sum of cloth consumed plus exports, minus imports and minus machine-woven cloth consumed domestically. All amounts are converted into standard bolts of hand-woven cloth, weighing 0.66kg.
[2]Converted from piculs in the original source at the rate of 1 picul = 60.5 kg.
[3]The volume of machine-spun yarn used in hand-woven cloth equals imported yarn plus domestically produced machine-spun yarn minus that proportion used for machine-woven cloth, improved hand-woven cloth and other consuming industries such as knitting.

of hand-woven cloth being marketed. Up to the middle of the nineteenth century, around 45 per cent of China's population spun and wove cloth and they provided the marketed hand-woven cloth needed by the other 55 per cent of the population, including city-dwellers. About 310 of the 600 million bolts of hand-woven cloth produced by peasant households were marketed,[4] with a value of 100 million taels of silver; a roughly similar amount was consumed by the producers. The decomposition of the natural economy should mainly be manifested in a reduction in the subsistence production of cloth by the peasants. Immediately after the Opium War, however, imports of cloth merely replaced hand-woven cloth produced for the market and not yet subsistence production.

The case of cotton yarn was different. At that time Chinese peasant households were more or less self-sufficient in cotton yarn and the market for cotton yarn was very small (in very rare cases in Jiangnan there were a few markets for warp but they were very weak). Therefore imported yarn played a more important role in the decomposition of the natural economy than did imported cloth.

The handicraft spinning and weaving industries in Chinese peasant households were closely linked to small-scale agriculture, and the first step in the decomposition of the natural economy was the emergence of specialised spinning and weaving households who did not themselves produce any cotton at all; this had already developed before the Opium War. These small farmers did not grow their own cotton but instead got it from the market, that is, they moved from a combination of to a separation between cotton cultivation and spinning. After the Opium War, hand-spun yarn was replaced by imported (or factory) yarn, that is, spinning and weaving became separated. Later imported (or machine-woven) cloth replaced native cloth produced for the market and went on to replace subsistence production of hand-woven cloth; in that situation, small farmers could do nothing but give up their shuttles, that is the unity of agriculture and textile production was broken. This process was a trilogy consisting of successive and interlocking stages, but it was never thoroughly completed. The details are discussed below.

The replacement of native yarn with machine-spun yarn (see Table 8.3)
In the early period after 1840 imports of yarn, although increasing steadily, were still limited in volume. Though imports were three times as great in 1883 as in 1870, they were still only 228 000 piculs (1 picul = 133.33 lbs = 60.48 kg.). Imports of coarse Indian yarn, which was more suited to replacing native yarn in Chinese rural areas, far surpassed those of British yarn and became dominant, but most was still sold to spinning and weaving households in areas which did not produce cotton, that is, it first broke into the market in areas where cotton cultivation and spinning had already been separated. In these areas the link between spinning and weaving was weaker and it was easier to break the unity between them. However, such areas were not the centre of China's handicraft cotton textile industry. Moreover what happened was merely the replacement of marketed cotton with imported yarn, so it was not of great significance in the decomposition of China's natural economy.

By 1894 annual imports of yarn reached 701 300 piculs but machine-spun yarn (mostly imported but including a little from Chinese mills) still accounted for only 23.42 per cent of the yarn used in hand-woven cloth. But during the twenty years from 1894 to 1913, imported factory yarn took the offensive. In addition to Indian yarn, imports of coarse yarn

TABLE 8.4   *The process of replacement of hand-woven cloth with machine-woven cloth in rural China (million bolts)*

1840	%	1860	%	1894	%	1913	%	1920	%	1936	%
Total output of cotton cloth in China, plus imports											
600.6	100	624.59	100	685.25	100	778.59	100	842.95	100	910.42	100
Of which: Imports											
2.73	0.46	19.88	3.18	91.70	13.36	253.61	32.57	203.99	24.20	107.77	11.84
Machine-woven cloth											
		5.39	0.79	17.56	2.26	36.64	4.35	409.67	45.00		
Improved hand-woven cloth											
				10.00	1.28	50.00	5.93	40.00	4.39		
Rural hand-woven cloth											
597.33	99.54	604.71	96.82	589.16	85.85	497.42	63.89	552.32	65.52	352.98	38.77

SOURCES: for Tables 8.4 and 8.5: Appendix to *Jiangnan tubi shi*, Tables B4 and B9.

from Japan increased rapidly and became dominant in Central and North China. Moreover, with the emergence of modern cotton mills in China, their products, which amounted to approximately 62.5 per cent as much as yarn imports, gradually came to play a more important role in replacing home-spun yarn in the countryside. In that period the price of imported and factory yarn increased only slowly, while the price of raw cotton went up rapidly owing to greatly increased demand for cotton from domestic cotton mills and to an increase in exports. As a result the price differential between yarn and cotton became smaller and smaller. In particular, the development of modern cotton mills absorbed cotton produced in areas like Jiangnan and thus deprived the spinning and weaving households of their raw material. Meanwhile, because the total output of hand-woven cloth declined sharply, the proportion of imported and factory yarn used in hand-woven cloth in the whole nation quickly increased to 72 per cent.

However, things never develop in a consistent manner and this trend was briefly reversed during and immediately after the First World War. There was a sharp drop in yarn and cloth imports, while Chinese cotton mills had some difficulties in importing new equipment during the war, so that there was little growth in production. Scholars have mostly neglected the fact that the increase in the price differential between yarn and cotton in this period meant that the production of home-spun yarn revived. Hence the proportion of factory yarn used in hand-woven cloth fell to a little over 50 per cent.

By 1920, however, yarn imports declined considerably but the production of Chinese factory yarn increased rapidly, so that it reached 1.3 times the volume of imports. From then on the production of hand-spun yarn went into a continuous decline, so that by 1936, 76 per cent of the yarn used in

TABLE 8.5   *Native cloth in Chinese villages (million bolts)*

1840	%	1860	%	1894	%	1913	%	1920	%	1936	%
Total output of hand-woven cloth in rural areas											
597.33	100	604.71	100	589.16	100	497.42	100	552.32	100	352.98	100
Of which: production for market											
315.18	52.76	316.90	52.41	290.36	49.28	187.51	37.20	221.26	40.66	91.62	25.96
Subsistence production											
282.15	47.24	287.81	47.59	298.80	50.72	309.91	62.30	331.06	59.94	261.36	74.04

SOURCE: see Table 8.4.

hand-woven cloth was machine spun, mostly in mills in China (including those owned by foreigners).

Even then, yarn spun in peasants' homes, at 53.4 million kg, 24 per cent of the total, still accounted for quite a large proportion and was mostly used in the considerable subsistence production of hand-woven cloth. In particular cloth consumed by households who grew cotton, spun yarn and wove cloth was the best and final asylum for hand spun yarn. Although labour productivity in producing factory yarn was several dozen times higher than for homespun yarn, this stubborn stronghold still could not be captured. Up to 1949 and even for some time beyond, there was still a lot of subsistence production of cloth by peasants using homespun yarn. That was a unique phenomenon emerging in and left over from China's semi-feudal semi-colonial society.

The replacement of hand-woven cloth with machine-woven cloth (see Tables 8.4 and 8.5)
The process of the replacement of hand-woven cloth was even slower and more incomplete. On the eve of the Opium War China's output of hand-woven cloth output was about 600 million bolts. In spite of a steady increase in cloth imports, output changed little up to 1894 when the Sino-Japanese War broke out. This was because increased per capita consumption led to an expansion of the market for cotton cloth. This expansion, which took place mainly in large and medium-sized cities, was completely supplied by imported and machine-woven cloth. Therefore there was little replacement of hand-woven cloth.

From 1894 to 1913 a large increase in imports of coarse American and Japanese cloth meant that the volume of hand-woven cloth produced for sale declined sharply. Subsistence production actually increased slightly, however, because such cloth could compete at almost any cost, in contrast to that produced for the market. Meanwhile the warp used in subsistence production of cloth included a lot of factory yarn, which substantially raised weaving efficiency; however hand-spun weft was still used as much as possible by households who both grew cotton and engaged in spinning and weaving.

From the First World War to the beginning of the 1920s both subsistence and market production of hand-woven cloth increased. This was the result of an increase in yarn and cloth prices and the relatively cheap price of cotton. After that there was a continuous decline in the production of hand-woven cloth but still mostly of cloth produced for the market. The production of hand-woven cloth remained as high as 353 million bolts in 1936, 38.77 per cent of estimated total output of cotton cloth. However, three-quarters of that was subsistence production, only one quarter produced for the market.

At first it was only imported cloth which replaced hand-woven cloth. Up to 1894 there was hardly any domestically manufactured machine-woven cloth and even by 1920 production was only 17.96 per cent as much as cloth imports. From then on production increased. Nevertheless, imports of cloth were still quite high at the beginning of 1930s. After 1931, although imports of cloth declined a great deal, China's production of machine-woven cloth continued to increase by leaps and bounds. Following the path laid out by domestic factory yarn, domestic machine-woven cloth became the major factor in replacing hand-woven cloth. Because only 91 million bolts of hand-woven cloth was produced for sale on the market, it still retained its own specific market, but the main bulwark of resistance was formed by subsistence production, which remained as high as 260 million bolts, so that the momentum of machine-woven cloth was blunted. That was one of the important factors accounting for the market crisis which the weaving industry, especially the Chinese-owned sector, experienced when the market was in the doldrums and purchasing power dropped at the beginning of 1930s.

There are a number of points worth stressing in relation to the above discussion.

First, it is easy to misread and misunderstand the process whereby imported yarn and cloth undermined the production of home-spun yarn and hand-woven cloth if one only considers specific examples in time and place. For example, some writers quote sources from as early as in the 1830s before the Opium War, which reflect the damage done by imported yarn to the cotton spinning industry in the rural areas near Guangzhou. In particular in 1831 it was said that serious disturbances broke out in three villages near Guangzhou because of the replacement of home-spun yarn by imported yarn. It seemed that the problem of the replacement of Chinese homespun yarn was already not a minor one.

It is true that yarn imports into Guangzhou sharply increased in 1831 from 380 000 pounds to 955 000 pounds (433 200 kg). But from a national point of view this amount was only a trivial 0.12 per cent of the over 350 million kg of yarn used in rural areas of China. Only because the imports were concentrated in rural areas near Guangzhou was there a certain pressure locally. However, such incidents happened only because people could not adapt themselves rapidly to changing conditions. After all, it was comparatively easy for the peasants to change from buying cotton to spin yarn to buying yarn to weave cloth.

In another example, writings on modern Chinese economic history have often extensively quoted the 1846 work *Qi Min Si Shu* (Four Techniques of the Common People) by Bao Shichen, which said that in the Songjiang and Taicang areas at that time 'foreign cloth is very prevalent and its price is one-third that of hand-woven cloth. Although our rural areas specialise in spinning and weaving, I have recently heard that yarn is no longer spun and that the cloth markets of Songjiang and Taicang are depressed.' That was because after the Opium War the British blindly imported a huge amount of cotton cloth and other articles like pianos and forks. In 1845 imports of cotton cloth from Britain reached a peak of more than 3 million bolts. There was only one solution to liquidating the mountain of cloth that pi ed up: British cloth was dumped on the market. That was a temporary and exceptional phenomenon.

Thus such source material is misleading in that it leads people to think that after the Opium War the Chinese handicraft spinning and weaving industries were immediately devastated. In fact, up to 1860 imports of cloth amounted to only 3.18 per cent of the volume of cotton cloth produced in China.

Second, the general view that imported yarn first intruded in the coastal regions centring on the treaty ports and then gradually spread to the interior is also incorrect. In fact, imported yarn penetrated first into the regions where cotton cultivation had long disappeared (mainly Fujian and Guangdong). Before the Opium War peasants in these areas at first used cotton from Jiangnan and North China for spinning, while later on they used imported Indian cotton; those imports reached 450 000 piculs between 1830 and 1833 and a peak of 570 000 piculs in 1860, second only to the value of opium imports.

Later, imports of yarn developed in the following way: firstly, in Fujian and Guangdong, British and Indian yarn replaced Indian cotton; for example, the yarn imported by the eight ports of south China accounted for 97.9 per cent of the national total between 1867 and 1871 and 63.6 per cent between 1884 and 1888. Even in 1893–4 they still accounted for 44.76 per cent of the total and so the south remained the main yarn-importing area. Central China, with 27.38 per cent of yarn imports through nine ports, ranked second. In fact, yarn imported through ports like Shanghai was mainly resold to places like Sichuan where cotton was in short supply. Very little yarn was sold in the cotton-textile producing area of Jiangnan. Up to 1894 yarn imports into the Songjiang area were estimated to contribute only one per cent of the yarn used in hand-woven cloth. This area was the most developed area in terms of the household cotton textile industry and in terms of producing for the market; it was, therefore, the most stubborn bulwark in resisting imported yarn.

Third, it was commonly considered in the past that on a national basis the use of factory yarn in hand-woven cloth began by a move from homespun warp and weft through a stage of factory warp and homespun weft finally to factory warp and weft. In very general terms one may say this was the case, but it was not necessarily so in all specific instances. In 1894, in non-cotton producing areas such as Fujian and Guangdong, all of the hand-woven cloth used factory warp and weft, while in the cotton growing area of Jiangnan homespun warp and weft still dominated. At that time, when the Songjiang cloth merchants purchased cloth, they would reject cloth woven with factory warp. Only later did the process go first to factory warp and homespun weft and to factory warp and weft, and at first this was limited to cloth destined for the market. Even in such cloth there were some specific varieties, like those specially demanded by fisherfolk, which were still woven with homespun warp and weft.

Subsistence production of cloth gradually came to use factory warp as well, more rapidly from the 1920s. By 1936 an estimated 110 915 000 kg of factory yarn was consumed in subsistence cloth production. In areas where cotton was not cultivated at all, cloth was woven entirely with factory yarn. In addition, in cotton-growing areas, 64 910 000 kg of factory yarn was used in subsistence cloth production. In the latter areas, however, 53 390 000 kg of homespun yarn was still consumed, or 45.13 per cent of the total. This shows that in cotton-growing areas only a small proportion of subsistence cloth production used factory warp and weft, while most still used factory warp and homespun weft and a small proportion homespun warp and weft. Such uneven development needs to be carefully studied.

Fourth, machine-woven cloth replaced hand-woven cloth to a lesser degree than factory yarn replaced homespun yarn. In 1894, labour productivity in the production of factory yarn in China was estimated at forty-three times higher than that of homespun yarn, while the productivity of machine-woven cloth was merely thirteen times of that of hand-woven cloth. Moreover, when factory yarn was used, the efficiency of weaving native cloth was increased so that it was more difficult to replace.

However, technology and equipment in both machine-spinning and machine-weaving were improving and labour productivity was rising as well. In the end, handicraft spinning and weaving had to give way. New changes took place at the beginning of twentieth century. Native cloth woven in the villages, especially that part destined for the market, gradually increased its use of factory yarn. Some weaving areas developed centred around the cotton-growing areas of Jiangnan and North China. There had been some spinning and weaving in these areas in the past but they were not very developed. The peasants bought cotton from merchants and basically spun and wove for their own consumption. But now either the peasants bought factory yarn from the market, or the merchants gave out yarn and got back cloth. Places like Gaoyang and Baodi in the north and Pinghu in Jiangnan developed the production of cloth for the market. Because they did not limit themselves to their own cotton and yarn, the production in such areas was even more thriving than in the conservative cotton-growing regions which had a textile industry. It enabled the hand-weaving industry in rural areas to achieve some development and stop its ongoing decline, though this was a complex process. From the early 1920s, however, these areas also went into decline.

Fifth, after the Opium War, the ratio between yarn and cotton prices was a key factor determining the fate of rural hand-spinning. Given the dearth of systematic price data for yarn and cotton in the domestic market before the twentieth century and because of the small amount of domestic factory yarn at that time we have used the price of imported cotton yarn for the purpose of comparative analysis. Thereafter the data on the ratio between yarn and cotton prices in the domestic market compiled by Nankai University has been used as the basis; in general these figures are sufficient to show the basic trends.

It can be seen from Table 8.6 that from 1867 to 1888, when the price ratio between imported yarn and raw cotton dropped from 3:1 to 2.5:1, the historical tendency of 'expensive cotton and cheap yarn' began and paved the way for the cotton spinning and weaving households in the non-cotton producing areas in Fujian and Guangdong gradually to change from buying cotton for spinning to buying yarn for weaving. Between 1893 and 1902, when the ratio dropped to 1.5:1, not only did all the weaving households who did not grow cotton in Fujian and Guangdong in general give up hand spinning but factory yarn also began to penetrate into spinning and weaving households in cotton-growing areas. Between 1908 and 1913, the

TABLE 8.6   *Ratio between yarn and cotton prices, 1867–1936*

Period	Years	Ratio of Yarn price to price of raw cotton	Notes
1867–1873	6	3.05	In 1869, yarn imports increased sharply, so that the price of yarn slumped. As this was a special case, it is not included here.
1874–1888	15	2.48	
1889–1892	4	1.66	From 1889, the price ratio dropped to less than 2:1.
1893–1902	10	1.49	From 1893, the price ratio dropped to less than 1.5:1 except for some small fluctuations.
1903–1907	5	1.58	
1908–1913	6	1.28	From 1908, the price ratio fell to 1.4:1 bottoming at 1.17:1 in 1911.
1914–1922	9	1.78	From 1914, the price ratio recovered gradually, passing 2:1 in 1916 and 1919.
1923–1927	5	1.24	
1928–1936	9	1.35	

SOURCES: the prices of imported yarn and cotton from 1867 to 1913 have been calculated from figures in Yang Duanliu, *Liushiwu nian lai Zhongguo guoji maoyi tongji* (Nanjing, 1931), pp. 45–6. For the price ratio between raw cotton and yarn in the domestic market between 1914 and 1936, see *Nankai zhishu ziliao huibian* (Beijing, 1958).

NOTE: *Rong jia qiye shiliao*, Shanghai shehui kexue yuan, jingji yanjiu suo, comp, 2 vols (Shanghai, 1980), vol. 1, p. 617 also has figures for the ratio between yarn and cotton prices in the domestic market between 1921 and 1936. These figures show basically the same trend, except that the ratio was a bit higher. For most of the years after 1923, the price ratio was below 1.5:1 and in 1924–7 and in 1934–6 below 1.4:1.

ratio further dropped to the 'trough' of 1.28:1; thus, the decline of hand spinning in that period was understandable. Then from 1916 to 1920, during the period of the First World War, the price ratio rose sharply, reaching a peak of 2:1 on average. This was not only the 'golden age' for the modern machine textile industry, but homespun yarn also reasserted itself. Although the price ratio declined slightly in 1921–2, it still remained between 1.63:1 to 1.55:1. After 1923, it remained at a long term level of below 1.5:1, that is, below the minimum ratio necessary for the survival of homespun yarn, so that hand spinning retreated once more and went into decline. However, although hand-spun yarn was almost completely driven out of commercialised handicraft weaving, some survived in subsistence weaving. Unless the price ratio between yarn and cotton fell close to parity, whenever the small farmers had some cotton on their hands, they would still struggle to do spinning and weaving themselves and try to be self-sufficient.[5]

III

Another important aspect of the increasing decomposition of China's natural economy after the Opium War was the accelerating commercialisation of agricultural products. However, there is no overall estimate of the degree to which that process had gone by the 1920s and 1930s and we are able only to make some rough estimates, as included in Tables 8.7 and 8.8.

This estimate shows that the total value of agricultural output was Ch$16.5 billion in 1920 and Ch$19.9 billion in 1936. These estimates are almost identical with those made by Dwight Perkins in his book *Agricultural Development in China (1368–1968)*. The value of grain output for the two years was Ch$9.6 billion and Ch$11.6 billion respectively, also close to the estimates in that book. The same is true for soybeans. The author of this paper has made an alternative estimate of Ch$11.1 billion of grain output using the output data for 1936 published by National Statistical Bureau, a result which again is similar. Therefore the general estimates are probably reasonable but the estimates of the marketed proportion of some other agricultural products may still be in need of future correction. Nevertheless, generally speaking, it can be seen that the natural economy was still dominant in agricultural production. As shown by Tables 8.7 and 8.8, the ratio between the commodity economy and the natural economy was 38:62 in 1920 and 44:56 in 1936. Thus it seems untenable for some writers to argue that by that period the market economy was dominant in China's rural areas.

First, in the development in China's national economy grain production has been an important issue. China is a large country but its cultivated area is limited. There are some variations in the statistics for cultivated area in modern China but, generally speaking, from the late nineteenth century to the first half of the twentieth century, cultivated area was between 1.2–1.4 billion mu (15 mu = 1 hectare = 2.471 acres) so that cultivated land per capita was about 3 mu.[6] For social as well as natural reasons it was difficult to expand the cultivated area in pre-Communist China. Moreover, because of the high rate of natural disasters, the proportion of abandoned land was quite high.

Grain crops such as rice, wheat and others were sown on more than 80

TABLE 8.7 *Level of commercialisation of Chinese agriculture in 1920 (Ch$ billion)*

	Total value of agricultural output	%	Value of Farming Output				Value of output from Forestry, Animal Husbandry, Fishery, etc
			Total	Grain	Soybeans	Others	
Total Value of Output	16.52[1]	100	13.71[2]	9.60[3]	0.41[4]	3.70	2.81
Production for the market	6.20	37.55	4.23	2.11[5]	0.27[6]	1.85[7]	1.97[8]
Subsistence production	10.32	62.45	9.48	7.49	0.14	1.85	0.84

NOTES:

[1] See Table 8.1 for the source of the total value of agricultural ouput.

[2] According to the State Statistical Bureau, the value of farming output between 1949 and 1952 was about 83 per cent of the total value of agricultural output; the ratio was probably roughly the same before 1949.

[3] According to Wu Baosan, *Zhongguo guomin suode*, in 1933, the value of grain output (including cereals, sweet potatoes and other grains) accounted for 81.04 per cent of the value of output of 28 farming products but this estimate was incomplete as there were other types of farm products. Therefore we have used post-liberation data published by the Planning Bureau of the Ministry of Agriculture and calculated grain output as 70 per cent of total output of farming products.

[4] The statistics differ as to whether soybeans are included under 'grain', and so they have been treated separately here. Soybeans have been estimated as 3 per cent of farm products in 1920 and 4 per cent in 1936.

[5] The proportion of marketed grain was 22 per cent in 1919, 29 per cent in 1936. See Wu Chengming, *Zhongguo zibenzhuyi yu guonei shichang*, p. 110.

[6] The proportion of soybeans marketed in North-east China was higher than that in the rest of the country. J. L. Buck, *The Chinese Farm Economy* (Nanjing, 1930), p. 199, estimates the latter as only 44 per cent between 1921 and 1925, while the proportion in the North-east was as high as 80 per cent. The output of soybeans in China peaked in 1936. Exports from China proper dropped sharply, while domestic sales increased. But exports from North-east China were still thriving. Thus the proportion of soybeans marketed is estimated as roughly 65 per cent both for 1920 and 1936.

[7] According to Buck, *Chinese Farm Economy*, p. 230, the proportion of oil-bearing crops, cotton, hemp etc, marketed between 1921 and 1925 was 55 per cent; we have estimated it at 50 per cent for 1920 and 60 per cent for 1936.

[8] The proportion of forestry, animal husbandry and fishery products marketed is estimated as 70 per cent.

TABLE 8.8   *Level of commercialisation of Chinese agriculture in 1936 (billion Ch$)*

| | Total value of agricultural output | % | Value of Farming Output | | | | Value of output from Forestry, Animal Husbandry, Fishery, etc |
			Total	Grain	Soybeans	Others	
Total Value of Output	19.92[1]	100	16.54[2]	11.58[3]	0.66[4]	4.30	3.39
Production for the market	8.74	43.86	6.37	3.36[5]	0.43[6]	2.58[7]	2.37[8]
Subsistence production	11.19	56.14	10.17	8.22	0.23	1.72	1.02

NOTES: see notes to Table 8.7.

per cent of the limited cultivated area, oil-bearing crops on 10–15 per cent, cotton on about 3 per cent, with the rest put down to tobacco or other crops.[7] Since it was difficult to overcome the problem of inadequate cultivated area per capita, the solution had mainly to be found in increasing the yield per mu, which had to outgrow population. However, under landlord ownership and the structure of small-scale farming in China, it was difficult to increase grain yields per mu beyond a certain level. In the 1930s the average yield of rice per mu was only about 170 kg, of wheat about 72.5 kg or even less.[8] Thus per capita grain production between 1931 and 1937 was between 281.5 kg[9] and 307.5 kg.[10] If we subtract seed grain and the grain consumed by peasants themselves, only a limited amount was left over for sale on the market.

In China grain accounted for about 70 per cent of crop production and 60 per cent of the total value of agricultural output. In such conditions, the key to China's agricultural commercialisation lay in increasing the amount of grain sold on the market. Under the premise of limited cultivated area in China, there are usually two ways to increase the marketing of grain: (a) when the grain yield per mu and total volume of output are fixed, the proportion marketed must be raised; (b) When the proportion marketed is fixed, grain yield per mu and total volume of output must be increased.[11] But both of these two ways were blind alleys in pre-Communist China. The Chinese grain yield per mu and total volume of output had been stagnant for a long time, at least since the beginning of the twentieth century. The average in the 1930s tended to decline relative to that in the 1920s while it declined even further in the 1940s as a result of the war.

Even if the proportion of grain marketed was increased, total sales could only be very limited. The proportion of grain marketed in 1840 was about 10 per cent, in 1894 16 per cent and in 1919 22 per cent. It increased to 29 per cent in 1936, the highest before liberation.[12] That year also witnessed a record level of grain output at 138.7 million tonnes.[13] However, even in such a unique year, only 40.2 million tonnes (excluding 11.3 million tonnes of soybeans) were marketed.[14] In most years in the 1930s less than 40 million tonnes were marketed. China's inability to increase the amount of grain marketed either through increasing its allocation of arable land or through extra supplies of marketed grain restricted the development of cash crops.

Second, the commercialisation of Chinese agricultural products was determined to a large degree by the rise and fall of exports. The traditional Chinese export commodities were tea and silk. The export of tea increased steadily from 1840. But in a competitive world market it went into a clear decline around the Sino-Japanese War of 1894–5. Only an increase in exports to Russia reduced the decline. After 1917 exports to Russia declined sharply as well, so that the tea trade suffered a disastrous set-back. Exports of tea in 1920 were 18.5 million kg, only 13.8 per cent of the 1886 level of 134.1 million kg, and less even than the 27.2 million kg exported on the eve of the Opium War. Tea production went from a reliance mainly on exports to one chiefly on the domestic market.

The case of silk was similar. It experienced a gradual increase at first but its share of the world market began to shrink even before 1895 and continued to decline later on. Only because world consumption expanded dramatically did the export of raw silk still register a certain increase after 1894, thereby promoting the commercialisation of cocoon production by peasants. In 1920 as many cocoons by value were marketed as were reeled by the farmers themselves. Tussah cocoons, the production of which was not so large, were mainly marketed. After 1920 raw silk exports also declined rapidly, to only 3.19 million kg in 1934, less than one third of the 1929 level.

Tea and silk were always the most important export commodities, accounting for more than 50 per cent of China's exports before 1895. But with their decline by 1929–31 they only accounted for 3.6 per cent and 12.1 per cent of exports respectively, which represented a sharp reduction in the commercialisation of agricultural products.

At that time Chinese agricultural commercialisation was characterised by a decline of the old and a development of the new. The prominent new commodities were oil-bearing crops like soybeans, whose production was stimulated by the growth of exports. Soybeans became the largest export commodity – 14.8 per cent of the total, while bean cakes accounted for 5.5 per cent, peanuts 2.2 per cent. By 1936 exports from China proper, excluding the North-east, had declined sharply and tung oil became the major export, at 10.3 per cent of the total, while eggs contributed 5.9 per cent, hog's bristles 3.5 per cent, and tea and silk dropped to only 4.4 per cent and 5.2 per cent respectively.[15] In the meantime the export of agricultural products gradually expanded to include commodities like leather and wool. Although the variety of export commodities became increasingly diversified, each occupied only a very small proportion of the total.

Third, after 1895, the commercialisation of Chinese agricultural products was influenced not only by the rise and fall in exports but also by the emergence of domestic modern industry. The developing commodities were cotton, tobacco and wheat, as well as cane sugar and oil-bearing crops.

A market for cotton developed quite early in China. It was mainly used as wadding cotton and for hand weaving in areas where cotton was not cultivated at all. The volume of cotton marketed did not increase much until the development of the cotton textile industry and the decline of subsistence hand weaving after 1894. But in the late 1920s and early 1930s there was an unfavourable balance in the cotton trade, which hampered the increase in production of domestic cotton and its commercialisation.

Tobacco growing and its commercialisation developed because of the expansion of the domestic tobacco market. Before the 1920s flue-cured tobacco and home-cured tobacco developed together but after the 1920s it was mainly flue-cured tobacco that steadily developed.

Because of the restriction imposed by the self-sufficient natural economy in rural areas, the commercialisation of wheat appears to have been stagnant already in the 1920s and 1930s. Generally speaking, although the commercialisation of agricultural products in China was greatly influenced by exports, the key factor was the domestic market, that is, the solidity of China's natural economy.

Fourth, in the history of agricultural commercialisation in China, there is the problem of opium. This has usually been omitted in past research and not listed in the statistics. Opium was an extremely destructive factor which should not be neglected. The large import of opium from abroad was a very serious disaster for China. From the beginning of the twentieth century, imports declined noticeably; domestically grown opium developed before 1894 but later declined. The opium growing area of the whole nation has been estimated at as much as over 8 million mu, with an output of about 15 million kg valued at Ch$500 million. That was because China was disunited politically at that time and the warlords were fighting each other, so that opium growing became a financial resource for separatist warlord regimes. Opium was grown widely in China up to the 1930s. This was very harmful to the development of the national economy, and it was not completely uprooted until 1949, when China was liberated.

Notes

1. [Editor's note] This chapter is a translation of Xu Xinwu, 'Jindai Zhongguo ziran jingji jiashen fenjie yu jieti de guocheng', *Zhongguo jingji shi yanjiu* 1988.1 (February 1988): 101–10.
2. Wu Chengming, *Zhongguo zibenzhuyi yu guonei shichang* (Beijing, 1985), p. 25; Xu Xinwu *et al.*, *Jiangnan tubu shi* (unpublished manuscript).
3. In Chinese feudal society, the value of agricultural output accounted for a very large proportion of the total value of agricultural and industrial output, while grain output in turn accounted for a very high percentage of agriculture. The fact that the volume of grain traded was only 10 per cent of total grain output determined the absolute dominance of the natural economy. This is explained in detail below.
4. All hand-woven cloth has been converted into a standard bolt weighing 0.66 kg and measuring 3.633 square yards.
5. See *Jiangnan tubu shi*, vol. 1, section 2, and appendices.
6. See the statistics in Yan Zhongping, *Zhongguo jindai jingji shi tongji ziliao xuanji* (Beijing, 1955); Xu Daofu, *Zhongguo jindai nongye shengchan ji maoyi tongji ziliao* (Shanghai, 1983); and Dwight H. Perkins, *Agricultural Development in China, 1368– 1968* (Edinburgh, 1969).
7. J. L. Buck, *Land Utilization in China*, Ch. VII; Ding Changqing, 'Guanyu Zhongguo jindai nongcun shangpin jingji fazhan de jige wenti', *Nankai jingji yanjiu*, 1985.3 (May 1985): 42–7.
8. Yan Zhongping, *Tongji ziliao xuanji*, p. 361; Perkins, *Agricultural Development*, pp. 358–71. According to *Zhongguo tongji nianjian, 1983*, Guojia tongji ju (Beijing, 1983), p. 171, grain yields per mu have developed unevenly since liberation: the average yield of rice per mu was 260 kg in 1978, wheat 123 kg: these yields were 325 kg and 163 kg respectively in 1982.
9. Xu Daofu, *Jindai nongye shengchan*, p. 341.
10. Perkins, *Agricultural Development*, p. 373.
11. After 1949, the proportion of grain marketed tended to decline instead of rising. According to *Zhongguo tongji nianjian, 1983*, p. 393, the volume of grain purchased from peasants was usually about 20–25 per cent, except for a few years when it was over 30 per cent. The improvement of living standards, an increase in the amount of grain

consumed by the peasants and the development of animal husbandry accounted for this. The net volume purchased was about 15–20 per cent. The reasons accounting for the resale of grain to rural areas included the development of rural industry and cash crops. This situation was entirely different from the years before 1949. However, due to a big increase in yield per unit of area, the volume of purchased grain reached 63.55 billion kg in 1975 and 88.05 billion kg in 1982.

12. Wu Chengming, *Zhongguo zibenzhuyi yu guonei shichang,* p. 110.
13. *Zhongguo tongji nianjian, 1983,* p. 185.
14. Yan Zhongping, *Tongji ziliao xuanji,* p. 361; Perkins, *Agricultural development,* pp. 358–71.
15. Yan Zhongping, *Tongji ziliao xuanji,* p. 76.

9 The Development of Capitalism in Modern Chinese Agriculture

Ding Changqing

Ding Changqing works in the Institute of Economics at Nankai University. He has written widely on the salt and coal industries, as well as having been entrusted with much of the work for the sections on agriculture in a forthcoming work on The Development of Chinese Capitalism *to be published by the Chinese Academy of Social Sciences.*

This important article follows on the previous one by Xu Xinwu by producing quantitative estimates for the specifically capitalist elements in Chinese agriculture. It focuses on three phenomena: managerial landlords, that is landlords who cultivated their land with hired labour, rather than renting it out; rich peasants, who themselves worked their land but also hired labour; and agricultural reclamation companies. The first two of these at least have been major themes also in the Western literature.[1]

Except during the debate in the 1930s about the nature of China's rural society, few scholars have examined the question of the level of the development of capitalism in agriculture in modern China. Quantitative research in this area has been even rarer. Therefore, there is a need for such studies. Different approaches to the questions 'Was there capitalism in agriculture in modern China?' and 'To what degree did it develop?' can be roughly summed up as follows: Liquidationists of the Trotskyite-Chen Duxiu school, who exaggerated the level of capitalism and believed that it dominated China's agriculture while feudalism was merely a remnant force.[2] Another point of view held that capitalism had never existed in any form in China's agriculture.[3] But the majority believed that capitalism had developed to a certain degree in modern Chinese agriculture, though this development was very slow and of an insignificant proportion. From preliminary studies of the history and degree of the development of capitalism in agriculture it is my opinion that the last view conforms to the historical facts.

I

An embryonic form of capitalism had appeared in China's agriculture in one or two areas prior to the Opium War. After the Opium War, the invasion of foreign capitalism led to enormous economic changes. At the turn of the century, with the gradual disintegration of the natural economy and the steady growth of the commodity economy, there emerged signs of capitalist production relations. This development went through two different phases: the first phase from the turn of the century to the mid-1930s (the eve of the Anti-Japanese War), the second from the mid-1930s to the late 1940s (the liberation of China).

In China's agriculture, the main manifestations of capitalism were: within the changing landlord economy, so-called managerial landlords; and in terms of the polarisation of the peasant class, the emergence of capitalist rich peasants and the rise of the modern agricultural reclamation companies. The following are specific observations on these agricultural undertakings which were to varying degrees capitalist.

There are at present only a few regional records of managerial landlords in the early twentieth century. For example, in Shandong Province, according to estimates by Jing Su and Luo Lun based on their investigation of 197 villages in forty-two counties, landlords cultivated approximately 8 per cent of their total holdings, while they rented out approximately 92 per cent. In the early twentieth century, there were 58 landlord households in the counties and prefectures of Fengtian in the North-east whose holdings were over 3000 mu, and their total holdings amounted to 378 163 mu. Of this land, 49 578 mu, or 13.1 per cent, was tilled by hired labourers and 328 590 mu, or 86.6 per cent, was rented out.[4]

In the 1920s and 1930s the Nationalist government and several academic organisations carried out large-scale surveys of land distribution and usage in China. Based on these surveys, the area of land cultivated by landlords with hired labour in the years prior to the War was estimated at around 10 per cent of the landlords' holdings and approximately 5 per cent of the nation's total cultivated area. By the mid and late 1940s, the situation of landlords hiring labourers to work the land was as shown in Table 9.1.

Table 9.1 is based on surveys carried out in villages in Shandong, Jiangsu, Anhui and Fujian provinces, covering a cultivated area of 7 684 757 mu, of which 2 354 028 mu was owned by landlords. Of the landlords' holdings,

Ding Changqing

83.54 per cent or 1 966 581 mu was rented out; land farmed by hired labourers accounted for 16.46 per cent or 387 447 mu, occupying 5.04 per cent of the total cultivated area.

An analysis of relevant sources reveals changes in the proportion of land cultivated by landlords employing hired labour in relation both to their total

TABLE 9.1   *Comparison of land farmed by landlords and land rented out in mid and late 1940s*

Region	Area under cultivation (mu)	Area of land owned by landlords (mu)	Land rented		Area managed by landlords		
			Area (mu)	% of total area	Area (mu)	% of total area	as % of total cultivated area
Heilongjiang							
	21 000 000.00	10 500 000.00	6 300 000.00	60.00	4 200 000.00	40.00	20.00
Shandong (1)							
	38 061.38	6 676.94	4 014.95	60.13	2 661.99	39.87	6.99
Shandong (2)							
	29 697.00	3 838.00	1 595.00	41.56	2 243.00	58.44	7.55
Southern Jiangsu							
	7 393 685.00	2 276 621.00	1 904 501.00	83.65	372 120.00	16.35	5.03
Southern Anhui							
	19 740.89	3 751.95	3 236.96	86.27	514.99	13.73	2.61
Northern Anhui							
	117 832.06	28 979.61	26 213.07	90.45	2 766.54	9.55	2.35
Zhejiang							
	79 038.75	33 618.53	26 515.90	78.87	7 102.63	21.13	7.32
Fujian							
	6 702.00	542.04	503.84	92.95	38.20	7.05	0.57
Total	28 684 757.00	12 854 028.00	8 266 581.00	64.31	4 587 447.00	35.69	15.90

NOTES: Shandong (1): 9 representative villages in Shushui and Linshu counties.
Shandong (2): 13 representative villages in Junan and Ganyu counties.
Southern Jiangsu: 964 townships and 16 counties.
Southern Anhui: 1 village in Tongling; 2 villages each in Xuancheng and Wuhu; 1 village in the city of Benxi.
Northern Anhui: a total of 13 villages in 6 prefectures, 1 mining district, 1 city.
Zhejiang: 3 townships, 49 villages, 2 administrative streets.
Fujian: 5 villages.
SOURCES: For Heilongjiang: 'Heilongjiang shengwei guanyu jingying dizhu de yijian', *Qunzhong*, no. 3 (September 1946). For the other provinces: from materials compiled by the Agrarian Reform Committee of the East China Civil and Military Commission on rural investigations carried out in the provinces of East China.

holdings and to the total area of cultivated land. At the turn of the century some landlords in various regions adopted the method of hiring labourers to farm a part or all of their land. This practice expanded during the period up to the 1920s. In the mid 1930s, just prior to the War, land cultivated by landlords accounted for approximately 5 per cent of the total cultivated area. The situation remained basically unchanged up to 1949.

On the economic nature of landlords hiring labourers to work the land, opinions vary. Basically, I think that managerial landlordism was a partially capitalist form of landlord economy. Its capitalist features were mainly manifested in the comparative sufficiency of funds for production, the hiring of a large number of farm labourers, the use of relatively advanced farm implements in the large-scale agricultural management of vast areas of rich arable land and the marketing of most of the production. Nevertheless, this type of landlord economy remained distinctly feudal, as characterised by the following facts: to a considerable extent its production objective was self-sufficiency; the hiring of farm labourers frequently retained features of serfdom; despite farm management on a comparatively large scale, there was no modern organisation of rural labour; the wealth accumulated was not used in the purchase of new farm tools and fertilisers, soil improvement, advancement of farming techniques or in the carrying out of farmland capital construction and expanded reproduction but was more often used in the acquisition of land, which in turn was the means of exploitation through increased renting of land or through practising usury. Furthermore, farm enterprises employing hired labour, with its capitalist characteristics, accounted for only a very small proportion – about 10 per cent – of total landlord holdings.

In brief, the cultivation of land by landlords employing hired labour constituted a capitalist economy with strong feudal characteristics and was but a minor factor in the landlord economy. All in all, a managerial landlord remained a landlord; he was not a rural capitalist. Therefore, he still belonged to the category of feudal economy, but with capitalist elements. He was a landlord with capitalist colouration.[5]

II

The class polarisation of the peasantry was a historical prerequisite for the development of capitalism. In this polarisation, the emergent rich peasant economy was a rural economy that was capitalist in nature. Lenin pointed out that 'in capitalist production the basis for the formation of a home market is the process of the disintegration of the small cultivators into agricultural entrepreneurs and workers'.[6] Mao Zedong also clearly stated that in China 'a sharp process of polarisation was taking place among the peasantry'.[7]

In modern China the rich peasants that emerged in the process of polarisation within the peasantry had the following distinct economic features: (i) they owned extensive areas of fertile land; they had large families and a strong labour force; (ii) they possessed comparatively good production tools and sizeable liquid capital; (iii) the exploitation of farm labourers by rich peasants constituted a part or the majority of their means of livelihood.

These features were the main characteristic of the rich peasant economy. For example, in three villages in Wuxi, Jiangsu Province, the proportion of labour input on rich peasant farms contributed by family members was 77.2 per cent while hired labour contributed 22.8 per cent. On middle peasant farms the proportions were 91.4 and 8.6 per cent, on poor peasant farms 96.8 and 3.2 per cent.[8] Hired labour was an important part of the rich peasant economy.

In nine villages in three districts in the Junan and Ganyu counties of Shandong province, there were altogether 113 rich peasant families that hired labour. In their cultivation of the land, family labour formed about 53.5 per cent of the total labour and hired labour 46.5 per cent. In contrast, in the 909 poor peasant families, hired labour formed only 0.32 per cent of the total labour and family labour 99.68 per cent.[9] It follows that hired labour had become a common phenomenon in rich peasant economy and was an essential condition for its development.

Similar conditions prevailed in North-east China. Among peasant households farming an area of over 50 *shang*, ([translator's note] 1 shang = 1.0005 hectares) hired labour constituted 56 per cent of the labour force, among those farming 30–50 *shang* 32.2 per cent and among those farming land less than 10 *shang* only 10.5 per cent. Thus 'the more extensive the land cultivated by rich peasants. the greater the number of labourers hired. This was essentially different from the hiring of labour by poor peasants. The former was essentially exploitation, while the latter mainly hired labour during the busy seasons.'[10]

We believe that a new social relationship was embodied in the rich peasant economy which developed from the polarisation of the peasantry. First, among the rich peasants, there were capitalist rich peasants who had adopted capitalist means of agricultural management. These rich peasants 'did not rent out their land, some even rented land from others and hired labour to farm it.'[11] Some of the capitalist rich peasants in this category already exhibited certain similarities to the big farmers of western capitalist countries or the agriculturalists who rent land.[12] For example, in Guangdong Province's Pearl River Delta, the majority of 'tenant farmers in Shatian were rural capitalists'.[13] In Guangxi province, there were also a small number of rich tenant-farmers who hired long-term labourers and seasonal labourers to work their farms.[14] In Hunan province, in the region of Hutian in Anxiang county, tenant-farmers cultivating farms of 100–300 mu were quite common. They employed a large number of hired hands and managed their farms as agricultural capitalist enterprises.[15] In Jilin and Heilongjiang there were tenant-farmers who did not own any land but were 'in terms of the number of households, roughly equal in number to or even slightly larger than the middle class landed peasantry. As for actual economic strength, these families had considerable assets and were in fact much better-off than many small landlords.'[16]

In discussing and summing up the characteristics of the development of capitalism in agriculture, Karl Marx pointed out that 'since capitalist production sets in only sporadically at first, it can in no way be held against the assumption made here that it first of all takes hold of those farms which generally can pay a differential rent, as a result of their special fertility or particularly favourable location.'[17] Capitalism in China's agriculture likewise developed along the path pointed out by Marx. Large-scale capitalist production like the above-mentioned tenant enterprises appeared sporadically in only a few areas such as Shatian, Hutian and in newly reclaimed areas in the North-east where the soil was especially fertile. On the one hand, the land in these areas was, as Marx said, particularly fertile or well located and, on the other hand, because of its late development, feudal relations of production were not deeply rooted. These conditions facilitated the growth of capitalist relations of production.

Marx also stated that, 'this entry of capital into agriculture as an independent and leading power does not take place everywhere all at once, but rather gradually and in particular branches of production. At first it does not take hold of agriculture proper, but rather branches of production such as stock-raising and particularly sheep-farming.'[18] This characteristic is also manifested in the development of a capitalist rich peasant economy in China. It was relatively more highly developed in such branches as animal husbandry, forestry, fishery, agricultural side-line production and the cultivation of industrial crops. But this type of capitalist rich peasant was rare in China, whereas the semi-landlord type was much more common. They 'farm their own land and at the same time rent out their surplus land'.[19]

Mao Zedong gave a vivid description of this class of rich peasants in his *Survey of Xunwu* written in May 1930. He wrote that the so-called 'newly emerged rich families' are peasants who had accumulated their wealth through hard work or tradesmen who have prospered through their trade. This stratum moves in an 'atmosphere of frankness and novelty'. Economically, on the one hand they personally engage in farm labour (with little help from long-term hired hands, but mostly helped by seasonal labourers) while, on the other hand, they rent out for grain their land that was distant and barren. Money is all-important to them. These rich peasants are avaricious and preoccupied with making a fortune, toiling in their fields day in and day out. When the end of the year comes around, they have some surplus grain which many of them, instead of selling, dehusk and then take to the county fair, or even go to Bachi and other places in Pingyuan to sell in the hope of getting a few extra coppers. They also ruthlessly practise usury, often 'adding a five' as interest (that is, charge an interest rate of 50 per cent). The so-called 'newly emerged rich families' mentioned above are not petty landlords but rich peasants, which means 'rich peasants of a semi-landlord character'.[20]

The more land this category of rich peasants possessed, the more land they rented out, and so from capitalist rich peasants they became semi-feudal rich peasants, or even landlords. They practised exploitation of a highly feudal or semi-feudal nature and also engaged in renting out land and in usury; even the conditions for hiring labour were semi-feudal. All the same, in spite of its feudal coating, we have no reason to overlook the capitalist nature of the rich peasant economy, because this form of rural enterprise commonly employed hired labour.

Apart from this, during the Anti-Japanese and Civil Wars, in both the anti-Japanese bases and the liberated areas, there appeared a new type of capitalist rich peasant.[21] It was distinct from the old rich peasant economy in many ways. (1) The new rich peasant economy was a kind of capitalist economy; it did not have the semi-feudal quality of the older one. Established on the basis of self-supporting labour and the exploitation of hired labour, it did not practise feudal exploitation in the form of renting out land, neither was the exploitation of hired labour as ruthless. (2) China's old rich peasant economy was integrated with exploitation through usury, whereas the new rich peasant economy did not practise usury but was closely connected with the commercial economy.

In summary, the agricultural enterprises of rich peasants, whether of the new capitalist type or the old semi-feudal type, possessed certain capitalist qualities. On this question, the 'Decision of the Central Committee of the Chinese Communist Party on Land Policies in Anti-Japanese Base Areas' adopted in 1942 by the Political Bureau of the Central Committee of the

Chinese Communist Party clearly stated: 'It must be acknowledged that the capitalist mode of production is the more advanced production mode in China at present. . . . The mode of production of the rich peasant has certain capitalist qualities; rich peasants are the capitalist class in the countryside.'

Prior to the mid-1920s there had been no investigation of the position of the capitalist-style rich peasant economy in the rural economy or of the proportion of rich peasants in the rural population. Later, according to the 1927 estimate of the Nationalist Government's Department in Charge of Peasant Movements, there were altogether 56 million peasant households (including landlords) in the whole country. Taking an average of six persons per household, the total rural population would be 336 million persons. Among them, rich peasants possessing land of more than 30 mu, small and middle landlords and big landlords constituted 14 per cent.[22]

By the late 1920s and early 1930s the rich peasant economy was declining. This could be observed in several areas. First, there was a relative diminution in the population of rich peasants. According to *Statistics on Modern Chinese Economic History*, compiled by Yan Zhongping, investigations carried out in villages in seventeen counties of Shaanxi and five other provinces for the period 1928–33 indicate that the proportion of rich peasants in the rural population declined in thirteen counties and increased in only four counties.[23] Secondly, the area of land cultivated by rich peasants (including landlord entrepreneurs) diminished relatively. According to investigations carried out in 123 villages in eighteen counties of Shaanxi and six other provinces, from 1928 to 1933 eighty-one villages showed a decrease in the percentage of the total cultivated area cultivated by rich peasants (including landlord entrepreneurs), while forty-two villages showed an increase.[24] As for the situation in the whole country, estimates by Tao Zhifu indicate that around 1934 rich peasants accounted for approximately 6 per cent of the total number of peasant households and they farmed about 18 per cent of the nation's cultivable land,[25] or some 255 052 100 mu.[26]

During the Anti-Japanese War, burning, killing and looting by the Japanese fascists, the oppression and exploitation by the four big monopoly capitalist groups of Jiang Jieshi, Song Ziwen, Kong Xiangxi and Chen Lifu, and the burden of all kinds of exorbitant taxes and levies, led to vast areas of land being laid waste in both enemy-occupied and Nationalist-controlled areas. The population diminished sharply and the rural economy as a whole was on the verge of collapse. The rich peasant economy declined in its wake.

In the anti-Japanese bases, the development of the rich peasant economy

TABLE 9.2   *Reclamation and cultivation companies in 1912*

Classification	Number of companies	Paid-up Capital (Ch$)
Agricultural and animal husbandry ·reclamation and conservation	104	5 625 995
Forestry	9	18 145
Mulberry and tea cultivation	44	476 665
Sericulture	8	35 407
Dairy Farming	1	1 000
Others	5	194 470
Total	171	6 351 672

SOURCE: Nongshang bu, *Minguo yuannian di yi ci nongshang tongji biao* (Beijing, 1912), vol. 1, p. 208.

was not consistent. It expanded in the border region of Shaanxi-Gansu-Ningxia. In the Shanxi-Chahar-Hebei region and in the Beiyue mountain region the rich peasant economy suffered a temporary decline in the early stages but later was stabilised and attained some growth. In the anti-Japanese bases in Shandong the rich peasant economy showed some growth in a few places but in the majority of places there was a decline.

Estimates based on investigations carried out during Land Reform in some regions of Liaoning, Sichuan, Gansu, central Hebei and the provinces of east and southern China show that, on the eve of the national liberation, rich peasants accounted for 4.45 per cent of total rural households. They were in possession of 1 761 864 000 mu of cultivable land, or 12 per cent of the total cultivated area.[27]

Between 1937 and 1949, the percentage of rich peasants in the total rural population fell from approximately 6 to 5 per cent and their holdings decreased sharply from 255 052 100 to 176 186 400 mu; or from approximately 18 to 12 per cent of the total cultivated area.

III

As a new way of farming, the agricultural and animal husbandry reclamation and cultivation companies formed in the early twentieth century merit attention in studies on the development of capitalism in agriculture in modern China (see Table 9.2)

Statistics issued by the Ministry of Agriculture and Commerce indicate that up to 1912 there were 171 registered agricultural reclamation companies, with a total capital of 6 351 672 yuan.[28]

From 1912 to 1920 agricultural reclamation companies prospered. Not only did such companies appear in southern China's Guangdong, Guangxi, Jiangsu and Zhejiang provinces and in Heilongjiang, Jilin, Chahar and other provinces in the north but, according to statistics issued by the Ministry of Agriculture and Commerce, there was also a 550 per cent increase in this type of investment, from Ch$6 million to over Ch$40 million.

The period 1920–28 witnessed the beginning of a decline in the agricultural reclamation companies in regions such as Guangxi and northern Jiangsu. In other regions, namely southern Jiangsu province, Chahar and Suiyuan, however, there was some expansion, while the provinces in the North-east saw no noticeable change. By the late 1920s and early 1930s, agricultural reclamation companies throughout the country began to decline. First, large existing companies successively went bankrupt. For example. in the salt reclamation areas of northern Jiangsu. there were initially more than forty companies of various sizes. Their investments totalled more than Ch$20 million and they reclaimed over 4 million mu of land.[29] Of these companies, six of the bigger ones, Dayu, Yuhua, Dafeng, Taihe, Dabeng and Huacheng, had an invested capital of over one million yuan each, totalling approximately Ch$10.10 million.[30] Most of them fell heavily into debt by the late 1920s.

Similarly, in 1925 in the northern province of Suiyuan 'investors in agricultural enterprises mushroomed'. There were ten companies in Linhe alone with an investment of Ch$260 000. But by the 1930s, apart from 'one or two fighting for survival in much worsened conditions, the remaining had lost everything, including their capital'.[31] Reclamation companies were concentrated in Northern Jiangsu, Chahar and Suiyuan and their decline and bankruptcy reflected nation-wide difficulties.

Second, the number of newly registered agricultural reclamation companies and their capital investment decreased, as shown in Table 9.3.

Although the number of agricultural reclamation companies established up to 1937 was small, the capitalist nature of those companies was clear. First, the companies were engaged in agriculture of a commercial nature and were not part of the natural economy. Second, the majority of investors in the companies were industrial and commercial capitalists. They introduced new methods of labour organisation and farm management from industry and commerce to carry out capitalist production in agriculture. Third, hired labour was used extensively in production. The number of hired labourers varied from a few to a few dozen, sometimes

144 — Ding Changqing

TABLE 9.3 *Registered companies in agriculture and forestry and their capital, 1928–1934*

Year	Number of companies	Capital (Ch$1000)
1928	4	130
1929	7	1 629
1930	6	211
1931	4	210
1932	2	130
1933	4	224
1934	3	160

NOTE: the 1934 figures are for the months from January to June.
SOURCE: *Shenbao nianjian 1936*, p. 806.

reaching over a hundred. Besides long-term labourers, seasonal labourers were also engaged. Fourth, even though most companies still employed rather backward farm implements and followed traditional methods of agricultural production, there were individual companies which purchased or tried out modern farm machinery or even introduced electricity into agricultural production.

Between 1937 and 1945 Japanese encroachment upon the agricultural reclamation companies in China led to enormous changes. Some of those in North China and the south-eastern coastal regions were seized by the enemy, some were destroyed, and others laid waste. In the south-west, north-west, and the interior of China, new agricultural reclamation companies, farms, and experimental farms were set up. Table 9.4 presents statistics from 1948, showing the number of farms taken over by the Nationalist government from Japanese imperialists, the number of Nationalist government-owned farms, reclamation organisations and privately-owned farms, and the number of farmhands and area of land reclaimed after the Japanese defeat.

The period from 1937 to the founding of New China in 1949 saw great changes in the number and location of agricultural reclamation companies and farms in China as well as in the nature of the companies and farms. In the Japanese-occupied areas, some of the farms operated by the Japanese under various guises were privately-owned and capitalist in nature, hiring labourers to work the farms. Others were in reality run by slave owners practising a form of plantation economy.

In the Nationalist controlled areas, the agricultural reclamation organisations and farms operated by the Nationalist Ministry of Agriculture and

Forestry and by different levels of local government were of a bureaucratic-capitalist nature. After the victory over Japan, the enterprises originally seized by the Japanese were expropriated by the Nationalists and became a part of their bureaucratic-capitalist enterprises. In addition companies and farms were set up and operated by national capitalists. According to the 1948 statistics of the Reclamation and Cultivation Department of the Nationalist Ministry of Agriculture and Forestry, state-owned reclamation farms accounted for 33 per cent of the total, privately-owned ones 67 per cent. But the number of farmhands on the state-run farms made up close to 80 per cent of the total, those on privately-owned farms only 20 per cent. Land reclaimed by state farms was 95 per cent of the total, that by privately-owned farms only 5 per cent.[32] Obviously, despite the greater number of privately-owned farms, they were all rather small in scale, and were of small significance in the agricultural reclamation of wasteland. But, compared with the feudal economy and bureaucratic-capitalism, the privately-owned reclamation farm was a kind of new and progressive economic component.

To sum up, in the several dozen years from the early twentieth century to the founding of New China in 1949, modern agricultural reclamation endeavours in China stumbled along on a rough and bumpy road, making slow progress. According to the 1948 statistics of the Reclamation and Cultivation Department of the Nationalist Ministry of Agriculture and Forestry, the total area of land owned by the agricultural reclamation companies and farms was slightly over 14 million mu, or a mere 1 per cent of the nation's total cultivated area of 14 682 200 mu.

IV

The above is based on separate investigations of three different types of rural economy of a capitalist nature, namely: managerial landlords, rich peasants and agricultural reclamation enterprises. What follows is a comprehensive view of the proportion these capitalist factors occupied in total agricultural production.

As our preceding calculations show, before the Anti-Japanese War, enterprises run by managerial landlords farmed an area totalling 70 847 800 mu, about 5 per cent of the total cultivated area; for rich peasant enterprises the figures are 255 052 100 mu and approximately 18 per cent and for agricultural reclamation companies, 14 169 600 mu and approximately one per cent.[33] Together they amounted to approximately 340 069 400 mu, or about 24 per cent of the total. On the eve of Liberation, landlord enterprises

TABLE 9.4   *Statistics of government-owned farms, privately owned farms and reclamation farms, 1948*

	Number of farms	Farmhands	Reclaimed area (mu)
Government-owned	63	181 584	13 686 421
Privately owned	130	45 790	775 670
Total	193	227 374	14 442 091

Compiled and arranged according to Guomindang nonglin bu, kenzhi si, *Zhongguo zhi kenzhi* (mimeographed, 1948). Note to the original table: figures were supplied by the various provinces.

farmed an area of 73 411 000 mu, or approximately 5 per cent of the total cultivated area, rich peasant enterprises 176 186 000 mu (approximately 12 per cent) and agricultural reclamation companies 14 442 000 mu (approximately 1 per cent). Together, they added up to 164 280 000 mu, or approximately 18 per cent of the total cultivated area in the whole country. However, none of these types of rural economy was wholly capitalist, each embodying varying degrees of feudalism and semi-feudalism. In estimating the actual level of development of capitalism in agriculture, it is therefore necessary to eliminate all non-capitalist factors.

Based on material gathered from various investigations, it is estimated that in landlord enterprises hired labour generally constituted 80–90 per cent of the labour force. If we base our calculations on 90 per cent, then before the Anti-Japanese War, production by hired labour in landlord enterprises worked approximately 4.5 per cent of the total cultivated area. In rich peasant enterprises, hired labour contributed 25–40 per cent of total labour input; if we accept the figure of 25 per cent, hired labour also worked approximately 4.5 per cent of the total cultivated area. Farming in agricultural reclamation companies was wholly done by hired labour. Hired labour in the above three types of rural enterprises worked 10 per cent of the total cultivated area in 1937, approximately 8.5 per cent in 1949.

The proportion of the total value of agricultural output accounted for by capitalist enterprises is an important point of reference in measuring the degree of the development of capitalism in agriculture. In 1933, prior to the Anti-Japanese War, the total value of agricultural output in China was 35 230 million (1957) *yuan*;[34] of this sum, the value of capitalist output accounted for approximately 10 per cent, or 3523 million *yuan*. On the eve of Liberation, the total value of agricultural output was 32 600 million (1952) *yuan*;[35] of this figure, the value of capitalist output was approximately 8.5 per cent, or about 2771 million *yuan*.

Karl Marx said: 'The production of commodities and their circulation in its developed form, namely trade, form the historic presuppositions under which capital arises.'[36] Lenin also pointed out that one of the fundamental differences between the capitalist and feudal economic systems is that the former is a monetary economy and the latter a natural economy.[37] Therefore, the degree of commercialisation of agricultural products is another point of reference in measuring the degree of the development of capitalism in agriculture. Investigations show that in the 1920s 50–60 per cent of agricultural output was marketed.[38] It should be noted that the above investigations were carried out in the mid-eastern, northern, and north-eastern parts of China where agricultural products were comparatively highly commercialised. According to Wu Chengming's recent estimates, approximately 30 per cent of China's main agricultural product, grain, was marketed in 1936. Furthermore, surveys carried out by the Ministry of Agriculture of the Central People's Government during the early post-liberation years showed that approximately 25 per cent of grain was marketed in North China for the period 1948–9.[39] Considering the above data and other related materials and the fact that agricultural output from landlord and rich peasant enterprises and agricultural reclamation companies was quite highly commercialised, if we reckon, that before the Anti-Japanese War, 60 per cent of the output of the above three types of agricultural capitalist enterprises was marketed, their marketed products accounted for 14.4 per cent of the total value of agricultural output. During the war and for a certain period afterwards the level of commercialisation of agricultural products declined. If we reckon the percentage to be 50 per cent, then the marketed proportion of the agricultural products produced by the above three types of agricultural capitalist enterprises would have approximated 9 per cent of the total value of agricultural output.[40] This is basically consistent with the preceding estimate of the proportion of the total value of agricultural output accounted for by capitalist enterprises, which was 10 per cent on the eve of the Anti-Japanese War and approximately 8.5 per cent on the eve of the founding of New China.

To sum up, capitalism did attain some development in agriculture in modern China but only at a very slow pace. With feudalism still dominating the scene, the percentage of capitalist elements was very small. This was different from the situation in industry where capitalist relations of production had gained dominance. But since agriculture occupied a far more significant proportion of the Chinese national economy, the total value of agricultural output remained greater than the total value of industrial output. Therefore, the weight of capitalist factors in the national economy was still very slight. That is to say, although capitalism had developed to a certain extent, at no time did it become the dominant form in China's socio-economic system. The basic economic characteristic of modern China's semi-colonial semi-feudal society was the co-existence of a weak capitalist economy with a strong semi-feudal economy. It would be wrong to exaggerate the degree of the development of capitalism and, especially, to exaggerate the degree of capitalist development in agriculture. Likewise, to deny the existence of capitalist economic elements would be to contradict historical reality.

Notes

1.   [Editor's note] This chapter is a translation of Ding Changqing, 'Shilun Zhongguo jindai nongye zhong zibenzhuyi de fazhan shuiping', *Nankai xuebao* 1984.6 (November 1984): 72–9, 39.
2.   Chen Duxiu, 'Women de zhengzhi yijian shu', in Zhongguo renmin jiefang jun zhengzhi xueyuan dangshi jiaoyanshi, *Zhonggong dang shi cankao ziliao*, vol. 5.
3.   Wang Xiaoqiang, 'Zhongguo nongmin de jieji shuxing zouyi', *Xuexi yu tansuo* 1980.5 (September 1980): 4–14.
4.   Li Wenzhi, *Zhongguo jindai nongye shi ziliao* (Beijing, 1957), vol. 1, p. 682.
5.   V. I. Lenin, *The Development of Capitalism in Russia* (Moscow, 1956), p. 194, pointed out that 'capitalist economy could not emerge at once, and the corvee economy could not disappear at once. The only possible system of economy was, accordingly, a transitional one, a system combining the features of both the corvee and the capitalist systems.' The semi-colonial semi-feudal landlord system in China likewise possessed some of the traits distinctive of the transitional period mentioned by Lenin in the combination of the corvee and the capitalist systems. The only difference lay in the fact that throughout the whole period feudal exploitation prevailed in the countryside in China.
6.   Lenin, *The Development of Capitalism in Russia*, p. 50.
7.   Mao Tse-tung [Mao Zedong], *Selected Works of Mao Tse-tung*, vol. 2 (Beijing, 1965) p. 323.
8.   Feng Hefa, comp, *Zhongguo nongcun jingji ziliao* (Shanghai, 1933), p. 684.
9.   Huadong jun zheng weiyuanhui tudi gaige weiyuanhui, *Shandong sheng nongcun diaocha*, pp. 21–2.
10. Xu Xuehan, 'Dongbei nongcun jingji de tezhi', *Zhongguo nongcun*, 1.3 (November 1934): 47–60.

11. See *Geming genjudi caizheng jingji shi changpian, tudi gaige shiqi*, vol. 1, p. 304.
12. V. I. Lenin, 'Preliminary Draft Theses on the Agrarian Question', *Collected Works*, vol. 31 (Moscow, 1966), p. 157. Lenin said: 'The big peasants are capitalist entrepreneurs in agriculture, who as a rule employ several hired labourers and are connected with the "peasantry" only in their low cultural level, habits of life, and the manual labour they themselves perform on their farms'.
13. Feng Hefa, *Zhongguo nongcun jingji ziliao*, pp. 297–8.
14. Xue Muqiao, 'Guangxi nongcun jingji', in Feng Hefa, *Zhongguo nongcun jingji ziliao*, p. 457.
15. Wu Zhongdao, 'Hunan Anxiang xian Hutian quyu zhong de nongtian jingying', *Zhongguo nongcun* 1.5 (February 1934): 70–3.
16. Zhong-Dong lu jingji diaocha ju, *Bei Man nongye* (Harbin, 1928), p. 86.
17. Karl Marx, *Capital*, vol. 3 (Harmondsworth, 1981), pp. 937–8.
18. Ibid., p. 937.
19. *Geming genjudi caizheng jingji shi changpian, tudi gaige shiqi*, vol. 1, p. 304.
20. Mao Zedong, *Mao Zedong nongcun diaocha wenji*, pp. 129–30.
21. Yu Suyun *et al.*, *Zhongguo jindai jingji shi* (Shenyang). In this book, the division of rich peasants in the period 1895–1927 into a new type and an old type is not appropriate because at that time the new type had not emerged. The so-called new type rich peasant or new rich peasant refers to the new form of capitalist rich peasant that emerged during the Anti-Japanese and Civil Wars in the anti-Japanese bases and the liberated areas.
22. *Di yi ci guonei geming zhanzheng shiqi de nongmin yundong* (Beijing, 1953).
23. Ibid., p. 265.
24. Yan Zhongping *et al.*, *Zhongguo jindai jingji shi tongji ziliao xuanji* (Beijing, 1955), p. 282.
25. Tao Zhifu, 'Zhongguo xian jieduan de tudi wenti' in *Zhongguo tudi wenti he shangye gaolidai* (Shanghai, 1937), p. 65.
26. According to statistics compiled by Yan Zhongping, *Tongji ziliao xuanji*, the cultivated area in the whole country prior to the Anti-Japanese War was 1 416 056 300 *mu*. Of this area land owned by rich peasants accounted for approximately 18 per cent or 255 052 100 *mu*.
27. According to statistics in Nongye bu, zhengce yanjiu shi, *Zhongguo nongye jingji gaiyao*, in 1949 China's cultivated acreage was 1 468 220 000 *mu*. Of this land owned by rich peasants accounted for approximately 12 per cent, or 176 186 400 *mu*.
28. Nongshang bu, *Minguo yuannian di yi ci nongshang tongji biao* (Beijing, 1912), vol. 1, p. 208.
29. 'Zhongguo de kenzhi wenti' cited in Feng Hefa, *Zhongguo nongcun jingji lun* (Shanghai, 1934), pp. 303–42.

30. Chen Hongjin, 'Jiangsu yan ken qu nongcun jingji suxie', *Zhongguo nongcun* 1.12 (September 1935): 85–91.

31. Feng Hefa, *Zhongguo nongcun jingji ziliao*, pp. 350–1.

32. Based on the above mentioned table, there was one privately-owned reclamation farm in Jiangsu province in 1948. But according to Hua-Dong junzheng weiyuanhui, *Jiangsu sheng nongcun diaocha*, there were 75 privately-owned agricultural farms in south Jiangsu alone prior to the agrarian reform. Note the inaccuracy of the statistics compiled by the Reclamation and Cultivation Department of the Nationalist Ministry of Agriculture and Forestry.

33. No statistics are available for the area of land farmed by the agricultural reclamation companies prior to the Anti-Japanese War. But taking the area occupied by reclamation companies before the liberation to be approximately one per cent of the total area of cultivated land, and with reference to materials compiled before the War, it is estimated that, prior to that period, the agricultural reclamation companies also occupied about one per cent of the total area of cultivated land, that is 14 169 600 mu of the total of 1 416 956 300 mu.

34. Based on Albert Feuerwerker, *Economic Trends in the Republic of China, 1912–1949* (Ann Arbor, 1977), Table 3.

35. *Zhongguo nongye nianjian, 1980* (Beijing, 1981), p. 41.

36. Karl Marx, *Capital*, vol. 1 (Harmondsworth, 1976), p. 247.

37. V. I. Lenin, 'The Agrarian Question in Russia towards the Close of the Nineteenth Century', *Collected Works*, vol. 15 (Moscow, 1963), p. 84.

38. Reference to John L. Buck, *The Chinese Farm Economy* (Nanjing, 1930), pp. 199–202. Research shows that the percentage of agricultural products kept for personal consumption in north China and mid-eastern China for the period 1921–5 was 47.4 per cent, the percentage for sale was 52.6 per cent. Statistics from *Bei-Man nongye* show that farm families with a cultivated area of less than 14 *shang* in the Heilongjiang basin sold 56.9 per cent of their total yield of farm commodities, those with 15–30 *shang*, 55.5 per cent, those with 30–75 *shang*, 58.2 per cent, and those with over 75 *shang*, 61.9 per cent.

39. Zhongyang renmin zhengfu nongye bu, *Huabei dianxing cun diaocha*.

40. The percentage of commodity production under the three forms of agricultural capitalist enterprises before the Anti-Japanese War and before Liberation in the total agricultural output value was calculated as follows: The area cultivated under the three forms of agricultural capitalist enterprise was approximately 24 per cent of the total cultivated area before the War of Resistance, and approximately 18 per cent on the eve of Liberation; therefore, the value of agricultural products produced should also amount to 24 per cent and 18 per cent respectively of the total value of agricultural products, or slightly higher (because the output value of these three forms of agricultural capitalist enterprises was higher than the average). The percentage of commodity

production under the three forms of agricultural capitalist enterprises before the War of Resistance to the total agricultural output was therefore 24% x 60% = 14.4%. Before the Liberation, the percentage of commodity products produced under the three forms of agricultural capitalist enterprises to the total agricultural output value was 18% x 50% = 9%.

10 Foreign Capitalism and China's Traditional Economy

Liu Foding

Professor Liu Foding is head of the economic history group in the Institute of Economics at Nankai University. He has written widely on Chinese and foreign capitalism in China and has led the work of editing and publishing the archives of the Kailuan Mining Administration. This article makes use of that material as well as of the Institute's work on the salt industry.

This article remains firmly within the Marxist tradition and quotes extensively from Marxist classics. At the same time it represents one of the most careful as well as one of the most imaginative overviews of the problem of the influence of imperialism on the Chinese economy, analysing, for example, the counterfactual implications of many positions taken on the issue. Many of the arguments it criticises will be familiar to those who have read the dependency theorists.[1]

This article aims to put forward ideas different from the current views on the relationship between foreign capitalism and the development of China into a capitalist society and on the attitudes of imperialism towards the system of feudal exploitation in China, in an attempt to encourage discussion and further to deepen research.

FOREIGN CAPITALISM AND CHINA'S DEVELOPMENT INTO A CAPITALIST SOCIETY

Researchers on the disintegration of the feudal economy and on the sprouts of capitalism in China generally conclude that, even without the influence of foreign capitalism, China would have slowly developed into a capitalist society. The author holds that neither the hypothetical premise of this view nor the conclusion drawn conforms to the objective laws of historical development and that it is in contradiction with the observations and analysis of Marx, Engels and Lenin on the relevant periods of Chinese history. The view, therefore, is untenable.

The hypothesis and deduction that China would have developed into a capitalist society were evidently based on the belief that, if historical circumstances had been different, the prerequisite conditions [the disintegration of the natural economy and the sprouts of capitalism] could have appeared, and that, according to the laws of causation, the development of capitalism would inevitably have become a fact. Otherwise it would be a pointless exercise in historical research. Now, this counterfactual hypothesis would need to encompass: either (1) in the mid-nineteenth century and for a considerable period afterwards, foreign capitalism did not invade China by military, political, economic or cultural means, and did not exert its influence over China; or (2) the Qing Government could not only succeed in warding off the various forms of invasion by foreign capitalism but also, by completely cutting off the country from the outside world, stop the Western way of life from having any gradual influence among the Chinese. Under either of the above circumstances, the commodity economy within Chinese feudal society would further develop until the natural economy disintegrated and the seeds of capitalism grew up and were strengthened. Over a considerable period of time, modern production would come to predominate in the national economy and, consequently, capitalist production relations would be established all over the country. Beautiful though this hypothesis is, it is merely an unrealistic notion.

With regard to the process of capitalist industrialisation in various countries and regions in the world, Marx and Engels distinctly stated:

> The specific task of bourgeois society is the establishment of a world market . . . and of production based on this world market.[2] National differences and antagonisms between peoples are daily more and more vanishing, owing to the development of the bourgeoisie, to freedom of commerce, to the world market, to uniformity in the mode of production and in the conditions of life corresponding thereto.[3]

> The lower and lower prices of industrial products brought about by mechanisation totally destroyed in all countries of the world the old system of manufacture or industry based on manual labour. In this way, all semi-barbarian countries, which had hitherto been more or less strangers to historical development and whose industry had been based on manufacture, were forcibly dragged out of their isolation.

They bought the cheaper commodities of the English and allowed their own manufacturing workers to be ruined . . . even China is now on the way to a revolution. We have come to the point where a new machine invented in England today deprives millions of Chinese workers of their livelihood within a year's time. In this way large-scale industry has brought all the peoples of the earth into contact with each other, has absorbed all the small local markets into one world market, has everywhere paved the way for civilisation and progress, and thus ensured that whatever happens in the civilised countries will have repercussions in all other countries.[4]

Lenin further discussed this problem:

. . . Thus, the necessity of seeking a foreign market by no means proves that capitalism is unsound, as the Narodnik economists like to picture matters. Quite the contrary. This necessity demonstrates the progressive historical work of capitalism, which destroys the age-old isolation and seclusion of systems of economy (and, consequently, the narrowness of intellectual and political life), and which links all countries of the world into a single economic whole.[5]

What is important is that capitalism cannot exist and develop without constantly expanding the sphere of its domination, without colonizing new countries and drawing old non-capitalist countries into the whirlpool of world economy.[6]

It can be seen from the above quotations that the classic writers of Marxism hold that: Capitalism takes the whole world as its arena and, as it grows, it is bound to pound at and finally break through the barriers of various relatively closed economic regions, whose previous isolation was determined by geographical and natural conditions, to change their historical processes of independent development, to bring them into a unified whole and to establish a new order in which they are closely related to and interdependent on each other. Such is the case with spiritual civilisation as well as material life. Any nation's attempt to keep itself long isolated from the outside world was bound to be without avail, and China was no exception. Raging waves beat the south-east coast wave upon wave; breeches kept appearing along the dykes; however, while retreating in defeat again and again, China consolidated at every step, and waged the most tenacious struggle in the world, thus forming a most complex interlocking pattern. Such was the history of relations between China and foreign countries in the two hundred years from the mid eighteenth century onwards. This is not a beautiful picture, but it is the real portrayal of history. Although contingent factors might lead to changes in detail, the basic outline of this process reflects an inexorable trend independent of subjective human desires.

In the process of the development of its pre-capitalist traditional economy, China exhibited relatively early many signs that appeared when the Western feudal system disintegrated, such as that the commodity economy developed to a certain extent, land could be bought and sold freely, the relationship of personal dependence on landlords was relaxed, and forms of land rent were changed. From the Northern Song Dynasty (960–1127) onwards, these processes expanded considerably. In the middle of the Qing Dynasty (1644–1911), through repeated adjustment and reforms, the feudal landlord economy grew and matured in terms of the systems of land ownership, tenancy, exploitation and taxation. In comparison with the rigid system of feudal lords in the Middle Ages in the West, China's system showed great flexibility and tenacity. Traditional agriculture (that using no modern technology) reached a fairly high level of perfection in its level of production, and formed a uniquely Chinese mode of agriculture.

The unity of agriculture and domestic handicraft industry, however, which was the basis of China's traditional economy, did not waver or break down. So, although certain economic sectors had long exhibited the sprouts of capitalist production relations, these were unable to grow up and become stronger, and therefore for a long time failed to become strong enough to break through the traditional economic structure. The feudal relations of production could still encompass the development of traditional productive forces to a certain degree without the danger of crisis. If one was to make a counterfactual hypothesis or supposition, the conclusion could only be that, without the influence of foreign capitalism, China would have gone along its original economic path and that, over a fairly long period, social revolution would not have been possible, nor would it have been possible for China to develop into a capitalist society.

From the 1840s onwards China encountered not merely the influence of foreign capitalism in a general sense but the armed invasion of the big powers. Even with the powerful military forces and various privileges gained, however, for nearly thirty years after the Opium War of 1840–42 the export of British industrial products to China increased only to a limited extent. This was especially so in the case of cotton textiles and fabrics, one of the major items of national consumption. Cotton textiles in China had long been a product of peasant sideline production, so that there were no expenses in the management of production or the process of circulation, and labour was not counted as a cost. They were therefore extremely cheap and as a result foreign products were not able to compete with them.

It was not until the late 1860s that, because of the economic crisis, the British were compelled to renew their equipment and improve their techniques, thus further reducing their costs of production. In particular the reduction in the length of the sea route (because of the opening of the Suez Canal) and the laying of submarine cables greatly strengthened the competitive capacity of British cotton textiles. From the 1870s on world capitalism developed to a high level, and only then did it gradually open up the Chinese market. The natural economy in rural areas began to disintegrate, thus creating the objective conditions for modern capitalist industry in China to come into being.

Feudal political forces and feudal ideology, however, still held considerable power and had deep-rooted influence. So, based on their own needs, and guided by the principle of 'Chinese learning as the essence, Western learning for practical application', they adopted, in accordance with specific circumstances, an attitude of obstruction, of assimilation or of absorption towards the introduction of the material and spiritual civilisation of the bourgeoisie, thus once again making self-adjustment under new circumstances. The traditional economic structure, which was extremely resilient, put up a desperate fight against both the Chinese and the foreign capitalist economies, thus seriously hampering the rapid development of modern productive forces and the expansion of capitalist relations of production. As a result, in spite of a whole century of efforts by the newly developed capitalism, not only did the feudal system of exploitation still survive but the natural economy in the country was not entirely destroyed.

Right up to 1949, clothing and food, the two basic daily necessities of the peasants, still mainly depended on hand-weaving and hand-milling. Imported goods which managed to find a market in the villages were of limited variety and limited amount, while Chinese goods were even less successful. Modern industrial production accounted for a very small proportion of the gross output of industry and agriculture and capitalist production never played the leading part in the national economy.

These facts show that even under foreign military invasion and heavy blows from foreign commodities and capital, China was unable to develop into a capitalist society. What would have happened in China without these influences can then easily be imagined. Historical experience tells us: (1) in order for China's traditional economic structure thoroughly to disintegrate, there had first to be fairly developed productive forces in modern industry; (2) in order to modernise its economy, China needed go through repeated struggles for a fairly long period of time. Modernisation could not be carried out until the feudal superstructure was thoroughly overthrown and particularly until the influence of feudal ideology in all its manifestations was removed.

Karl Marx compared Chinese society before the Opium War to a mummy carefully kept in a sealed coffin and said that complete isolation had been the primary condition for the preservation of old China. This was as good as saying that, without the influence of foreign capitalism, the socio-economic structure of China would not have changed. He also pointed out that the innumerable political upheavals in Chinese history resulted only in changes of dynasty, just like figures on a merry-go-round. It was not until after the mid nineteenth century that the original economic structure in China gradually disintegrated, that the traditional economic balance was broken, and that real social changes began to take place. In this sense, the Western bourgeoisie provided a revolutionary impetus, because it was only by breaking the combination of small-scale agriculture and household handicraft industry that the social division of labour could come to replace the household division of labour, that labour could be developed as social labour, and that social labour productivity could be rapidly raised. Marx went even further and held that from one point of view the import of opium into China also played a role in aggravating the crisis of feudal rule in China. He said, 'It would seem as though history had first to make this whole people drunk before it could rouse them out of their hereditary stupidity.'[7] For all its shamelessness and criminality, the opium trade was never mesmeric. On the contrary, it caused the Chinese nation to wake up. Therefore it was also one channel of the influence of foreign capitalism.

The imbalance between the relations of production and productive forces within Chinese feudal society did not directly cause the changes in the nature of Chinese society from the 1870s onwards. Instead, the invasion of foreign capitalism played the decisive role in bringing about those changes. This view may be regarded as the 'Traditional Economic Equilibrium Theory', or 'External Transplant Theory', but it remains historical fact, as was already clear the writings of classical Marxism. Furthermore, the author is of the opinion that it would be extremely harmful to allow the above-mentioned wrong judgement concerning the course of historical development to continue to be held over a long period of time in the future and thus to become the theoretical foundation of a certain propaganda or policy at an opportune moment.

Both the industrial revolution in Britain and the industrialisation of Western Europe, both the rapid development of capitalism in the metropolis and the development of dependent countries sooner or later into capitalism, resulted from the ever strengthening interaction and interdependence between countries and nations. In the history of the development of the world economy no country ever developed into capitalist society while isolated from the world.

ATTITUDES OF IMPERIALISM TOWARD THE SYSTEM OF FEUDAL EXPLOITATION

Those who dissent from the view expressed in the first part of this article may hold that the author sets up a dichotomy between the foreign capitalist economy and the Chinese feudal economy and describes the relationship between the two in an incorrect way. For the current view is that 'Everywhere imperialism attempts to preserve and to perpetuate all those pre-capitalist forms of exploitation (especially in the villages).'[8] In fact, the relationship between imperialism and feudal forces in China was one characterised both by contradictions and by compromise and collusion, as was reflected in the military, political, economic and cultural fields. This is a very complicated issue and needs to be examined and tested with a great amount of material. However, being two entirely different economic systems in nature, the two are opposed to each other in terms of their long-term interest, the former being bound to develop until it gradually replaces the latter. This is an objective law independent of human will. It is true both in the mother countries of capitalism and in their dependencies.

Marx and Engels argued:

> The bourgeoisie, by the rapid improvement of all instruments of production, by the immensely facilitated means of communication, draws all, even the most barbarian, nations into civilisation. The cheap prices of its commodities are the heavy artillery with which at batters down all Chinese walls, with which it forces the barbarian's intensely obstinate hatred of foreigners to capitulate. It compels all nations, on pain of extinction, to adopt the bourgeois mode of production; it compels them to introduce what it calls civilisation into their midst, i.e., to become bourgeoisie themselves. In one word, it creates a world after its own image.[9]

Lenin also pointed out:

> The export of capital influences and greatly accelerates the development of capitalism in those countries to which it is exported.[10]

On a global basis, various kinds of pre-capitalist relations of exploitation in a number of colonial and semi-colonial countries were all smashed by the import of commodities and capital from the metropolis, and capitalism then gradually developed. China was no exception. Foreign capitalism made every effort to reform China's socio-economic structure after its own image and to accelerate the development of capitalism in China. It is a one-sided view simply to sum up the modern history of China as the history of imperialism opposing the development of Chinese capitalism. The main reason why China failed fully to establish the capitalist mode of production over nearly a century before 1949 was that the feudal forces were particularly powerful and obstinate. Many of the agents of imperialism in China felt deeply that those feudal forces were beyond the reach of their power. It was not that they did not want to replace them but that their ability was not equal to their ambition. Imperialism did on the one hand oppress and prevent the Chinese national capitalist economy from developing but, on the other hand, it also promoted its growth and expansion. The import of foreign capital, on the whole, not only caused the modern mode of production in China to grow quite rapidly but also caused the capitalist economy in China to make progress, albeit slowly.

The import of foreign commodities and capital resulted in the gradual disintegration of the natural economy in China's rural areas and in the expansion of commodity and labour markets, thus taking an active part in breaking up the feudal economic base. So much is beyond controversy. The problem lies in estimating the degree of the disintegration of the natural economy.[11] This part of the article will discuss the attitude of imperialism towards the system of feudal exploitation. The author holds that imperialism did not attempt everywhere to preserve the original modes of feudal exploitation in China, still less to perpetuate them. On the contrary, imperialism wished to abolish them immediately if possible; if that was not possible for the time being, it wished to abolish them once the necessary conditions existed. The author illustrates this view below with examples from his own research.

Many of the foreign coal-mining enterprises in old China adopted the contract system. Unskilled workers like those who cut coal underground were recruited, managed and paid by contractors. This system had a strong extra-economic coercive character. Not only were workers exploited by foreign capitalists, they also suffered feudal exploitation by the various levels of contractors. In the early twentieth century this exploitation was very serious. Later things gradually changed. For example in the British-controlled Kailuan Coal Mines, the wages of contract labourers were decided by contractors up to the 1930s. Wages varied not only between mines but also between contract companies in the same mine. After 1931 the mine authorities intensified their control over the contractors and the workers under them. Contract labourers were recruited by mine authorities instead and were handed over to the contractors after they were registered in mines. Minimum wages were fixed through agreements between labour and capital. The supervisors of mines had the right to check, at any time, the payment of contract labourers. After the Anti-Japanese War broke out in 1937, wages in kind (cheap coal and cheap flour, which came to be the main content of workers' wages), part of the supplementary wages and part of the newly-increased currency wages, were given to the workers directly by the mine authorities. The middleman's exploitation was strictly limited.

The contractors' right to contract certain portions of the coal-mining project or other work was passed on from generation to generation. It could also be sold or transferred. This was indeed a kind of feudal privilege with a monopoly character. Foreign capitalists made use of contractors and their subordinates of various ranks to supervise the workers because they were closely connected with the local traditional underworld and many of them were leaders of varying ranks or backbones in the feudal secret societies themselves and were in close collusion with local governments. Relying on their power, they could force workers under harsh discipline to work hard for capitalists under very bad or even dangerous working conditions. But as their middleman's exploitation absorbed a fairly large portion of the surplus value created by workers, this system of management hindered the renewal of production equipment and the improvement of technology and labour productivity, while limiting the growth of output and profits. Consequently, considering their own economic interests, foreign capitalists repeatedly tried to abolish the contract system. Because they failed to recruit enough qualified low- and middle-ranking labour management personnel, however, their attempts to institute group contract and piece rate wages were fiercely opposed both overtly and covertly by the contractors and by the workers under their influence and results were far from ideal. The workers' productivity under the direct management of mine authorities dropped to some extent when compared with that under the coercive management of the contractors so that the contract system was never abolished right up to 1949. However, the powers of the contractors were much more limited than in the early twentieth century and the other profits gained by contractors were also strictly confined within certain limits.

It can therefore be seen clearly that this system of feudal exploitation surviving in foreign enterprises in China was on its way to gradual extinction, as it conflicted with the basic and long-term interests of the capitalists.

Up to the end of the Qing Dynasty the transport and sale of salt for human consumption in China was monopolised by the government and special merchants. Salt produced in various regions had fixed districts for transport and sale, called *xiao an* (districts). Apart from a few places where the transportation and sale of salt was handled by the government, it was generally undertaken by wealthy merchants who registered themselves with the government. These merchants were granted varying numbers of special permits, called *yin piao* (salt licences). With these licences they had the exclusive right to transport a certain amount of salt to assigned districts for sale. The licences they owned could be inherited and so the transport and sale of salt became the privilege of their families. In fact they often leased out the right to others, while they themselves sat idle and enjoyed large profits. In this way, they led a parasitic life.

As salt had to be sold in assigned districts and transported with licences, outsiders' encroachment on the transport and sale of salt was regarded by the government and special merchants as smuggling. Therefore a feudal system was established to allow the special merchants alone to transport and sell salt in assigned districts on the basis of their licences. Relying on this privilege, the merchants used scales which understated the weight, forcing down the prices at will when they bought salt from the salt-making households; when salt was transported to the districts, they mixed sand and earth into the salt and sold it at a high price using scales that overstated the weight. A few salt merchants made fortunes and became rich quickly, while officials of various ranks made money in the form of bribes. Feudal exploitation was indeed very serious.

In order to obtain the £25 million Reorganisation Loan from the Five Nation Consortium after the fall of the Qing Empire, Yuan Shikai did not hesitate to sell out China's sovereignty in salt administration by using the total amount of the salt taxes as guarantee for the loan. He formed the Head Office of the Salt Gabelle as the supreme institution for salt affairs in China, which made it possible for the major powers to control China's salt administration through the foreign personnel who held real power in the bureau.

Sir Richard Dane, an Englishman, was appointed as the first director of the Head Office of the Salt Gabelle. Starting with an increase in salt taxes to ensure that the loan would be paid back on schedule, he vigorously advocated abolishing the system of salt being sold exclusively by the government and special merchants. He advocated levying taxing salt at its source, permitting free transport and sale of salt, free trade and competition. Starting from 1914, the institutions for managing governmental transport and sale were abolished in some areas. In some regions north of Huai River and in the provinces of Sichuan, Guangdong, Hubei, Fujian and Zhejiang, the system of transport and sale of salt with licences was abolished and free sale of salt was allowed.

However, progress in the reforms was slow because of obstruction both from the special merchants, who had had the exclusive rights to transport and sell salt in assigned districts on the basis of licences, and from the officials in the Warlord Government who were in charge of salt affairs. According to an investigation by the Head Office of the Salt Gabelle, up to 1931 the transport and sale of salt in nearly half the regions in China, especially in some important provinces, like the four districts of the Huainan region, were still controlled by the hereditary salt merchants and by the special and contract merchants who were their successors and quite similar in character; in the remaining half of the regions, especially in some remote provinces, the system of free trade had been adopted instead.[12] This shows that, under foreign pressure, the replacement of the traditional feudal system of salt sales by the mode of capitalist management was an irresistible historical trend.

The Jiuda Refinery, the first modern salt making enterprise in China, was established in 1914. In order to open up markets, national capitalists launched into fierce competition with the feudal salt merchants. In response to a company application, the Office of Salt Affairs only permitted allowed it to sell salt in the residential quarters for foreigners in the Treaty ports. Dane, the director of the Head Office of the Salt Gabelle, and his successor Gamble held that sale of the refined salt, which was of excellent quality, should not be restricted. Instead it should be allowed to compete freely with crude salt. With the expansion of refined salt production, the producers ignored the prohibition in the old regulations and began to sell salt beyond the Treaty ports in the inland regions. Although the Head Office of the Salt Gabelle considered as inevitable the end of limitations on the sale of refined salt, it realised that once the old regulation was abolished, it would certainly lead to the abolition of the regional sales system of the districts and licences. To start with, in inland regions of the four districts of the Huainan region and the five regions attached to Jiangsu Province, the sale of refined salt up to a stipulated limit was allowed. This was approved by the Ministry of Finance and was put into effect at the beginning of 1935.

After the outbreak of the Anti-Japanese War in 1937, the transport and sale of salt was monopolised by the Japanese military and the Nationalist Government respectively. It became exclusively official, although its character was slightly different from feudal monopoly. The original division of sale districts broke down and could not be maintained any longer; the system of salt sales monopolised by special merchants was also abolished by formal decree. After the victory in the war, the Nationalist Government restated: 'All the special benefits, rights and interests of salt sales by special merchants and of other salt enterprises monopolised by individuals, whether they are in regions in the rear areas or in the recaptured areas, are to be abolished once and for all.'[13] But in fact, the approved carriers were mostly salt organisations manipulated by the private capital of the Four Big Families. The official monopoly of the Nationalist Government in the rear areas during the war was replaced by the commercial monopoly of the Four Great Families, while the feudal monopoly profits of the special merchants in the earlier licence and district system became the monopoly profits of the private capital of the Four Great Families.

The above mentioned facts show that, in the case of the transport and sale of salt, which was of vital importance to the Chinese economy, international financial capital and its agents in China advocated the replacement of the traditional mode of feudal monopoly exploitation with laissez-faire capitalist operation. When the Nationalist Government decided to adopt the system of salt sold exclusively by the government during the Anti-Japanese War, Walker, the American director in the General Bureau of Salt Affairs, strongly opposed it, for he held that this measure was bound to encroach on the interests of private merchants. He advocated that the government should continue to allow free sale by private capital but his suggestion was rejected.

The view that imperialism attempted everywhere in the villages of China to preserve and perpetuate all forms of feudal exploitation has been cited in all textbooks on modern Chinese economic history but has not been convincingly demonstrated in any one of them. While compiling a textbook, the author tried hard but unsuccessfully over several years to find examples in an attempt to prove this view. But none of the literature or the archives that the author consulted could offer direct support to the idea that imperialism attempted to preserve and to perpetuate the system of feudal exploitation in the villages.

Imperialism bought and seized only a limited amount of land in China's countryside for farming. Only from the early twentieth century onwards did Japan and some other countries encourage their people to migrate to North-east China and Shandong province to run a few farms. These farms generally adopted the mode of capitalist management, employing farm labourers on wages and using some new types of farm machinery to varying degrees. Only on the land occupied by a few foreign churches was the old mode of exploitation which was popular in old China still generally used: the churches rented the land separately to local poor peasants for farming and collected land rent.

Fundamentally, in order to expand its exports of commodities and capital to China in order to make more profit, imperialism found it necessary further to open up the widest market, the villages in China. In doing so, the peasants were expected to change from self-sufficient small producers into wage labourers rather than remain tied for a long period to the relations of feudal exploitation.

Notes

1.	[Editor's note] This chapter is a translation of Liu Foding, 'Lun waiguo zibenzhuyi yingxiang yu Zhongguo chuantong jingji de guanxi', *Nankai jingji yanjiu suo jikan* 1986.2 (June 1986): 64–9.
2.	Marx to Engels, 8 October 1858, in *Karl Marx and Frederick Engels: Selected Correspondence* (Moscow, 1956), p. 134.
3.	'Manifesto of the Communist Party', in Karl Marx, *The Revolutions of 1848* (Harmondsworth, 1973), p. 85.
4.	Frederick Engels, *Principles of Communism* (Beijing, 1977), p. 7.
5.	V. I. Lenin, *The Development of capitalism in Russia* (Moscow, 1956), p. 46.
6.	Lenin, *The Development of capitalism in Russia*, p. 652.
7.	'Revolution in China and in Europe' (14 June 1853), in Dona Torr (ed.), *Marx on China* (London, 1968), p. 3.
8.	Mao Tse-tung [Mao Zedong], 'The Chinese Revolution and the Chinese Communist Party', in *Selected Works of Mao Tse-tung*, vol. 2 (Beijing, 1965), p. 312.
9.	'Manifesto of the Communist Party', in Karl Marx, *The Revolutions of 1848*, p. 71.
10.	V. I. Lenin, *Imperialism, the Highest Stage of Capitalism* (Moscow, 1970), p. 63.
11.	[Editor's note] See Chapter 8 above.
12.	'Yanwu jihe suo nianbao' (1931) in Nankai daxue jingji yanjiu suo jingji shi yanjiu shi (ed.), *Zhongguo jindai yanwu shi ziliao xuanji*, vol. 2 (Tianjin, forthcoming).
13.	'Caizhengbu chong shen feichu zhuanshang yin'an bugao', in the archives of the Yanwu zongju, changchan chu, tongling juan; see Nankai daxue, *Zhongguo jindai yanwu shi ziliao xuanji*, vol. 4.

11 Foreign Trade and China's Economic Modernisation

Ding Richu and Shen Zuwei

Professors Ding Richu and Shen Zuwei are researchers at the Institute of Economics of the Shanghai Academy of Social Sciences. This article is a collaborative effort between a very senior Professor (Ding) and one of China's up-and-coming younger scholars. Ding Richu is one of the leading scholars of the Chinese bourgeoisie and has written widely on their economic and political role in Chinese history. Shen Zuwei has recently published a very influential article summing up changing views on the nature of the Chinese bourgeoisie in the early twentieth century.

The first page or so of this translation (the first three sections of the original article were on the nineteenth century and have been omitted here) outlines the traditional critique of foreign trade by Chinese nationalists. But the key arguments in the rest of the article go on to give considerable detail on the benefits of foreign trade for the Chinese economy.[1]

Because modern China's foreign trade developed against the background of the world capitalist system, while China was a backward and under-developed country which had lost its sovereignty, some of its effects were harmful:

> Because it lacked the right to impose tariff protection, China's foreign trade deficit increased over time. At the same time the price scissors existing between the prices of imported industrial products and those of exported farm and sideline products meant that foreign capitalists made large profits from trade, while China's wealth flowed out of the country. This led to a serious shortfall in the accumulation of money capital, which in turn hindered the progress of industrialisation.
>
> Some foreign imports undermined Chinese indigenous products, thus impoverishing many millions of Chinese farmers and handicraft workers. After its integration into the world economy, Chinese agriculture

often suffered from the vagaries of market competition; the decline in the silk and tea trades increased unrest among the producers and caused greater turbulence in Chinese rural society. After the emergence of Chinese national industry, the continued import of competitive foreign products occupied the markets of Chinese goods. To some extent, this competition suppressed the growth of Chinese industry.

Large-scale smuggling by the Japanese imperialists in order to support their aggressive war against China and the selfish dumping of surplus commodities by the United States after the Second World War caused unexpected losses to China's national industries.

It is natural that many researchers have expressed their indignation over such effects.

From the point of view of long-term trends and development, however, foreign trade played a positive role in modern China's economic development and social progress.

First, foreign trade stimulated the development of the commodity economy and accelerated the disintegration of the natural economy and the emergence of capitalism. Marx said that under certain conditions, 'the sudden expansion of trade and the creation of a new world market had an overwhelming influence on the defeat of the old mode of production and the rise of the capitalist mode'.[2] In talking about the role of foreign capitalism in China's traditional economy, Mao Zedong pointed out that 'on the one hand, it undermined the foundations of her self-sufficient natural economy and wrecked the handicraft industries both in the cities and in the peasants' homes, and on the other, it hastened the growth of a commodity economy in town and country'.[3] Many scholars have made detailed studies of this aspect, which this article will not repeat. What we want to emphasise is that under the stimulus of foreign trade a *new* capitalist commerce gradually emerged, which already represented more than a simple quantitative change within a feudal economy and in fact possessed the characteristics of a capitalist commodity economy.

After the opening of the treaty ports many foreign merchants came to China. By 1876 there were two hundred foreign firms in Shanghai alone.[4] But the whole import and export trade could not be handled just by several hundred foreign firms. It was only through collaboration between foreign firms and Chinese commercial institutions in the form of the foreign trade guilds that the whole process of the circulation of commodities could be completed. In the course of purchasing Chinese products for export and promoting the sale of foreign goods, which accompanied the development of foreign trade, the following two phenomena emerged: (1) The compradors in foreign firms invested in the establishment of commercial institutions in their own names rather than in those of the foreign firms in order to carry on buying and selling businesses in their own right. (2) Chinese merchants without comprador status either established new shops and warehouses or changed the business orientation of existing firms in order to participate in the export trade.

There were many links in the distribution chains from producers of Chinese export goods to foreign firms and from foreign firms to the Chinese consumers of foreign goods, and all those links were composed of Chinese businessmen. This new commerce operated on the basis of foreign industrial capital and, judging things against the background of world capitalism, this commercial capital was one link in the process of the circulation of industrial capital.

Just to take exported consumer goods as an example, through foreign trade, Chinese businessmen came into contact with the world capitalist market and carried out international exchange of commodities. This in turn both stimulated the development of the productive forces and the socialisation of production in the relevant Chinese industries and caused the business operations and mode of management of those commercial enterprises engaged in foreign trade to become increasingly capitalist. This commercial capital was essentially Chinese capital and operated within China. It maintained its independence from foreign capitalism and also developed certain contradictions with foreign interests by attempting to reduce the prices of imports and to increase those of exports. Therefore one can see this as an early manifestation of capitalist commerce in China.[5] After the development of Chinese national industries, it also served national industrial capital as well.

Professor Yen-p'ing Hao, of Tennessee State University, has argued that a kind of 'commercial capitalism' sprung up in the treaty ports; its concrete content included free trade and economic competition, the expansion of money and credit, the opening of new markets, the commercialisation of agriculture and the introduction of western styles of commerce and concepts of value. This 'commercial revolution' greatly promoted China's modernisation.[6] Such an argument is certainly reasonable, as the main difference between the new commerce and traditional commerce lay in its role in providing the necessary market conditions for the development of capitalism. This was a positive factor in China's modernisation.

Second, to some extent the development of the export trade promoted prosperity in the urban and rural economies.

China's farm and sideline exports were produced by making use of surplus labour and therefore offered peasants an opportunity for enhancing their incomes. In the 1930s, one scholar analysed this situation:

China's rural economy has always relied on non-agricultural sidelines in order to get by. If the peasants simply depended on agricultural crops and had no other income, they would make very small profits from a great deal of work. Since the recent importation of machine-made products, peasant consumption has also increased to some extent, so that the extra income from sidelines is all the more necessary. The rural areas of the provinces along the Yellow River do not have flourishing agricultural sidelines and as a result are not as rich as those of Jiangsu or Zhejiang. Silk raising is the most profitable of the sideline occupations and, apart from Jiangsu and Zhejiang, many peasant families in Sichuan, Guangdong and Shandong rely on the profits from the spring cocoons to tide them over. Sometimes they rely completely on silk rearing even for basic clothing needs.[7]

According to Liu Dajun's survey in Wuxing:

Around 1920 was the peak of silk production and sales, at which time silk produced 70 per cent of the income of the Wuxing peasants households, while rice cultivation only contributed 30 per cent.

In Nanxun, at the peak of exports of Jili Lake silk:

As silk prices soared and the industry became more prosperous, the peasants preferred silk-raising to tilling the land. Farmers who raised silkworms could get a bumper harvest within just a month, and by doing so they could support themselves for one year.[8]

Thus it can be seen that the ups and downs of China's rural economy were closely linked to the rise and fall of farm sideline exports.

The growth of the export trade also brought prosperity to cities and towns in the silk producing areas. Nanxun in Huzhou was a famous centre of silk production, with many silk businesses, silk shops, silk brokers, and silk reeling mills. A poem entitled 'A Walk in the Nanxun Silk Market', described the prosperous streets of the town's silk market:

The streets are crowded with people, and hubbub and bustle deafen ones ears;

paper signposts hang above the silk market and in front of every door
of every household;
the hubbub of voices lasts from morning till noon, and one can barely
edge forward even with untiring effort.[9]

Here was a real picture of a bustling bazaar.

In Huzhou, there were many silk fabric shops that purchased the products
of scattered craftsmen and sent them to their sales outlets in Shanghai, from
where they were sold in the domestic or foreign markets. Between 1927 and
1929, with a rapid growth in silk fabric exports, the Huzhou Silk Fabric
Mill was set up:

> At that time there were about ten thousand silk weavers in Huzhou, with
> monthly incomes of 60 yuan. This was the most flourishing period of
> the Huzhou economy.[10]

Later, with the decline of exports, the silk fabric shops, silk fabric mills
and the scattered households of handicraft workers in Huzhou closed down,
the silk textile workers were unemployed and the local economy fell into
depression. This shows the close relationship between economic prosperity
and the export trade.

Starting from the 1850s, the value of Shanghai's import and export
trade accounted for about 50 per cent of that of the whole country and
the city replaced Guangzhou as the national centre for foreign trade. The
concentration of foreign trade commodities in Shanghai stimulated the
development of its trade with its hinterland as well as its own commercial
development and it became the most booming commercial city in China.
The development of trade needed to be accompanied by the development
of transport and communications such as telegraphs. As the import and
export trades developed, Shanghai became by the 1930s the biggest
comprehensive seaport in China and one of the ten biggest ports in the
world. The city was also a pioneer in introducing modern equipment, such
as railways, highways, telegrams and telephones.

With the development of foreign trade, Shanghai also became the
financial centre of China. The foreign banks were based there, while
Chinese banks also centred their activities on the city. By 1933 the total
assets of the member banks of the Shanghai Bankers' Association reached
Ch\$3.3 billion, 89 per cent of the total assets of Chinese banks. Shanghai's
native banks (*qianzhuang*) also played a very important role in financial
transactions all over the country.

Foreign trade also stimulated the development of modern industry and made Shanghai the industrial centre of China, accounting in 1933 for 34 per cent of Chinese factories, 40 per cent of industrial capital, 43 per cent of industrial workers and 50 per cent of industrial output. It is clear that foreign trade was the leading sector in the economic development of Shanghai which, under its stimulus, developed into a multi-functional economic centre.[11]

Third, Chinese merchants made money from the import and export trades and accumulated a great amount of money capital for investment in capitalist industry and other enterprises.

As early as the 1860s, some Chinese businessmen involved in foreign trade invested their money in foreign-owned steamship companies. In the 1870s, some also participated in the Self-strengthening Movement and invested in state capitalist enterprises. Among them those in the silk export industry in particular accumulated money capital and invested it into modern industries. Most of the twelve famous silk merchant families nicknamed the 'four elephants and eight oxen' of Nanxun, after they became rich through silk exports, also tried their hand in modern economic sectors and often invested in industry and communications as well as financial services.

Among them, Liu Yong, leader of the 'four elephants', was already by the early 1860s very wealthy, with a fortune of several hundred thousand taels. Later he became a big salt merchant and operated widely in the pawnshop business; at the same time he bought quite a lot of real estate in Shanghai and Hangzhou and also invested in the Tonghai Farm and Husbandry Company in Nantong, Jiangsu. Because the conditions for investment in modern enterprises were improving, his son, Liu Jinzao, gradually developed his activities in the direction of new economic areas. He invested in the Shanghai-Hangzhou railroad and was himself a director and assistant manager. He also invested in the National Commercial Bank in Hangzhou, established the Dada Steamship Wharf in Shanghai and, together with others, founded the Xunzhen Electric Light Company in Nanxun.

Zhang Songxian, second of the 'four elephants', operated the Tongyun Company and invested in the National Commercial Bank and the Bank of China, Shanghai Branch. Pang Yunceng, the third 'elephant', made a rapid fortune from the Yitai Silk Shop. In Shanghai, his son Pang Laichen invested in the Bank of China and purchased a large number of shares in the foreign-owned Zhengguanghe Soda Water Company. He also set up the Longzhang Paper Company, of which he was general manager. He invested in the National Commercial Bank and the Shanghai-Hangzhou Railway Company in Hangzhou; he established the Dalun Silk Reeling Mill, later renamed as the Chongyu Silk Mill, in Tangqi town in Deqing county; in partnership with others, he established a cotton mill and a dye-printing factory in Suzhou. In an early period, Gu Fuchang, the fourth 'elephant', opened the Fengsheng Silk Shop and became rich exporting thrown silk; later he bought the only freight transport wharf for foreign ships at that time – the Jinliyuan Dock and built a lot of warehouses, which did very good business. Afterwards, because of his high reputation among foreigners, he was invited to be comprador for Jardines.

Among the eight 'oxen', Xing Gangxing, Zhou Changda, Qiu Xiancha, Chen Xuyuan and their descendants also invested in new enterprises. For instance, Zhou Changda 'engaged in commerce in Shanghai, established the Shenchang and Shentai Thrown Silk Shops, which he managed assiduously, and his family property increased rapidly.' His son Zhou Qingyun, in addition to the inherited silk profession, also invested in the Suzhou-Hangzhou Railway and the National Commercial Bank and founded the Tianzhang Silk Weaving Mill in Hangzhou. He also invested in the Hulin Silk Weaving Mill, ran the Model Silk Weaving Mill in Huzhou, established the Xiulun and Housheng Silk Weaving Mills in Jiaxing and invested in the Xunzhen Electric Light Company in Nanxun; he also sponsored the Changxing Coal Mine. He was regarded as a 'relatively far-sighted industrialist in Nanxun'.[12] To cite another example, Chen Xuyuan 'lived away in Shanghai for several score years and was a leader in the silk industry'. He was invited to be a comprador of the American Russell & Co. He also set up the Yuchang Thrown Silk Shop to process Jili Lake Silks and made large amounts of money in the silk export trade.[13]

Businessmen importing and selling foreign goods also accumulated large amounts of capital. The famous industrialist, Ye Chengzhong, started out importing foreign goods. At the beginning, Ye opened a hardware stall and within one or two years accumulated considerable capital. In 1862 he opened the Shunji Foreign Goods Store promoting the sale of foreign hardware. In less than ten years, he became a big businessman with large amounts of money. After 1870, he opened several hardware stores in succession, such as Nanshun ji, Kechi, Xinshun ji and Yichang. From the 1890s he invested in modern industries. In 1890 he provided the total investment of Ch$200 000 for the establishment of the Xiechang Match Company in Shanghai. In 1893 he invested in setting up the Lunhua Silk Reeling Mill. In 1897 he invested Ch$420 000 in a partnership in the Xiechang Match Factory in Hankou.

In some other lines of trade, merchants dealing in imports accumulated a considerable amount of capital and invested in manufacturing products similar to the imports sold in their shops. A very common example was for

pharmacies selling imported Western medicines to invest in the production
of those medicines. Most of Chinese-owned industrial pharmaceutical
enterprises in Shanghai originated as pharmacies.

Fourth, foreign trade stimulated the development of import-substituting
industries in China.

The large-scale import of foreign goods caused a huge trade deficit.
Because production techniques and labour productivity in large-scale
mechanical industries were much more advanced than in handicrafts,
the terms of trade were inevitably unfavourable to China. Taking the
ratio between import and export prices as 100 in 1913, the 1935 ratio
was 122.9, that of 1870 only 76.5.[14] The loss of economic rights caused
by unequal exchange inflicted losses on China but it also was a powerful
stimulus to Chinese officials and civilians and encouraged them to find way
of stopping the losses. In November 1880, Li Hongzhang wrote in his work
'An analysis of the attempt to establish a mechanical cloth weaving bureau
to compete foreign goods':

> Because other countries use machinery in manufacture, they save much
> labour, sell at lower prices and are able to develop wider markets in
> comparison with China's indigenous handicraft products. If we do not
> try to copy them and sell our own products, we will not be able to share
> the profits with foreigners.[15]

Ten years later, many Chinese came to understand that:

> superior will prevail over inferior and the fittest will survive while the
> least fit will be eliminated through natural selection. Foreign needles
> eliminated native needles. Leather shoes and cotton socks eliminated
> cloth shoes and cloth socks; flint-stones have been eliminated by the
> match; tobacco (smoked in a long stemmed Chinese pipe) has been
> eliminated by the cigarette and the cigar. . . . It is most dangerous to
> realise the inferiority of ones own but to fail to improve ones existing
> products or to copy from others.[16]

China's national capitalist industries, such as the cotton textile, flour,
match and tobacco industries, gradually developed during the boycott
movements. We agree with the view of the American scholar, Thomas
G. Rawski:

> the overall course of China's prewar industrial history demonstrates the
> positive impact of foreign trade on industrial progress. The origins of

machinery and chemical manufacture in the private sector illustrate the power of Hirschman's contention that 'imports . . . provide the safest, most incontrovertible proof that the market is there'. Product after product was manufactured domestically only after imports alerted Chinese businessmen to the size and profitability of the local market.[17]

Imports of foreign cotton yarn did damage the hand-spinning sector but they also opened up the market for machine spinning, which promoted the emergence of the Chinese-owned cotton spinning industry, whose products in the end replaced imported yarn. In addition they also stimulated the development of hand-woven cloth: in the mid 1930s, '61 per cent of the cotton cloth produced in China (in square yards; if the unit of measurement were yards the proportion would be 73 per cent) was woven by handicraft methods'.[18] Hand-weaving centres such as Gaoyang and Ding xian using capitalist workshops with manual looms were very prosperous in the early twentieth century; they competed successfully with foreign goods by utilising China's cheap labour and cheap machine-spun yarn. It has been argued that by using improved hand looms the hand-loom industry strengthened its ability to compete with modern industry and in fact hindered its development.[19] Such a viewpoint is not correct. The development of modern industry has to be a process and how can one deny that hand-loom workshops were an intermediate stage in the transition from traditional handicraft to modern industry? If one understands the problem in this way, was not the development of the hand-weaving industry under the stimulus of foreign trade also a positive factor in the progress of China's modernisation?

Fifth, commodity imports enabled the modernisation of production and the improvement of living standards.

Imported producer goods were beneficial to Chinese industry. For instance, cotton yarn imports in the early stages enhanced the quality and competitive strength of indigenous cloth; later, imported dyestuffs allowed China's textile industry to produce coloured cloths which were less likely to fade. Even more clearly, before the emergence of the relevant industries in China, imports of mechanical equipment, iron and metals, timber and automobiles played a useful role in the establishment and operation of China's industry, communications and transport and in the construction of modern cities. As Rawski points out, imports of machinery transferred technology to China. Because imported machinery needed new supplies of raw materials as well as spare parts and maintenance, when the Chinese had become familiar with this equipment, there were able themselves to undertake some relatively simple processing operations and some enterprises emerged to provide a maintenance and repair service. With the increase in their experience and capital, the Chinese engineering industry was able gradually to replace the foreign, and this process of import substitution moved from substituting maintenance services to substituting the production of commodities and the Chinese enterprises managed to gain a comparatively large share of the market. By the 1930s China was already able to produce various kinds of industrial equipment and chemical products.[20]

One study of the issue of China's oil imports has pointed out that petroleum products provided more efficient liquid fuel and stimulated the change from traditional to mechanised industries. Fuel oil imports met the needs of automobiles and stimulated the development of China's highway network. The increase of automobile imports in the 1920s led to the high tide of highway building in 1927. And the use of motor transport was a necessary result of China's industrialisation.[21]

The import of consumer goods such as kerosene, food and clothes, could supplement indigenous supplies of food and clothing and raise the people's standard of living. At the same time, the development of imports and the introduction of western habits led more and more Chinese people, especially among the elite, to become interested in using some fashionable consumer goods, which in turn increased the import of those commodities. In other words, the development of foreign trade had an impact on Chinese social life in the direction of modernisation, while the improvement in living standards in turn promoted the development of foreign trade. Moreover, under suitable conditions, Chinese industry and commerce were able to produce similar products as a substitute for imports, which broadened the scope of China's industrialisation. It has often been argued that imports of producer goods are beneficial to production but imports of consumer goods waste foreign currency and are harmful to capital accumulation and economic development. Of course, to some extent this viewpoint is reasonable but, if it is absolutised without concrete analysis, then it is difficult to avoid a one-sided argument.

After all, modern China was an underdeveloped country with a very low rate of social savings. Where people did have savings, they invested their money in the traditional economic sector, such as land. If imports of consumer goods had been restricted, this might not have stimulated the import of producer goods, but rather the money spent on imported goods would inevitably have been spent on domestic goods or services, having no impact on the structure of the traditional economy, so that social production would remain static. In traditional Chinese society, there existed no autonomous demand for new capitalist technical equipment, so that development economics suggests the money saved from limiting imports of consumer goods 'could not be regarded as funds to form capital':

> It is only with a complementary domestic policy of voluntary or compulsory saving that luxury import restrictions can make a fully effective not contribution to the supply of capital. . . . And even then the contribution will be attributable more properly to the increased saving than to the import restrictions as such.[22]

Although many viewpoints prevailing in development economics are worth deliberation, so far as the problems we touched upon are concerned, it is worth noting those on the relationship between import restrictions and capital formation.

Finally, foreign trade brought China not only capital and foreign currency, but also technology, management knowledge, qualified personnel and entrepreneurs. As pointed out by Professor Yen-p'ing Hao, Sino-American trade was a medium of technology transfer which brought new productive technologies to China. American enterprises brought to Chinese merchants management experience and entrepreneurial spirit. It is beyond doubt that the knowledge of the capitalist economy and industrial technology, which the Chinese acquired in the process of dealing with foreigners, played a positive role in China's modernisation drive.

We have emphasised the positive role played by foreign trade in China's modernisation because this has rarely been discussed by Chinese scholars. However, the problem of China's trade deficit was never solved and the goal of modernisation never achieved. The main reasons for this were various domestic factors, such as political corruption, low efficiency of administration and neglect of foreign trade by the government. Therefore, whether one is talking about foreign trade or about the whole process of national modernisation, it is difficult to achieve success without the guarantee of effective reform of the political system. This is a lesson we should absorb.

Notes

1. [Editor's note] This chapter is a translation of Section 4 of Ding Richu and Shen Zuwei, 'Dui-wai maoyi tong Zhongguo jingji jindaihua de guanxi', *Jindai shi yanjiu* 1987.6 (November 1987): 24–49.
2. Karl Marx, *Capital*, vol. 3 (Harmondsworth, 1981), p. 451.
3. Mao Tse-tung [Mao Zedong], 'The Chinese Revolution and the Chinese Communist Party', in *Selected Works of Mao Tse-tung*, vol. 2 (Beijing, 1965), p. 309.

4.   Ge Yuanxu, *Hu you za ji*, preface.
5.   See Shen Zuwei, 'Shilun wan-Qing Shanghai xinshi shangye de xingcheng yu xingzhi', *Zhongguo jindai jingji shi yanjiu ziliao*, no. 4 (Shanghai, 1986), pp. 32–56.
6.   Yen-p'ing Hao, *The Commercial Revolution in Nineteenth Century China* (Berkeley, 1986), pp. 108–11.
7.   Qian Tianda, *Zhongguo cansi wenti* (Shanghai, 1936), p. 9.
8.   Lin Liyuan, 'Si xiang ba niu – Nanxun sishang shier jiazu', in *Zhejiang ji zibenjia de xingqi* (Hangzhou, 1986), pp. 23–30.
9.   See Lin Liyuan, 'Nanxun shi gao', manuscript copy in the Office of Literature and History, the Zhejiang Committee of the Chinese People's Political Consultative Conference.
10. Ling Qinzai, 'Huzhou hangzhuang diandi', *Huzhou wenshi*, no. 4 (Huzhou, 1986), p. 126.
11. Jin Jisu, 'Jiefang qianhou Shanghai jingji diwei he zuoyong de bianhua', *Shehui kexue*, 1984.10 (October 1984): 14–19.
12. Lin Liyuan, 'Zhejiang ji zibenjia de xingqi', pp. 49–50.
13. Ibid., pp. 51–2.
14. Joseph Esherick, 'Harvard on China: The Apologetics of Imperialism', *Bulletin of Concerned Asian Scholars*, 4.4 (December 1972): 9–16.
15. Quoted in Yan Zhongping, *Zhongguo mianfangzhi shi gao* (Beijing, 1963), p. 88.
16. Hu Xianghan,, *Shanghai xiao zhi*, vol. 10, Miscellanies.
17. Thomas G. Rawski, *China's Transition to Industrialism* (Ann Arbor, 1980), p. 27.
18. Albert Feuerwerker, 'Economic trends in the late Ch'ing empire, 1870–1911', in *The Cambridge History of China*, vol. 11 (Cambridge, UK, 1980), pp. 15–16.
19. Chi-ming Hou, *Foreign Investment and Economic Development in China* (Cambridge, Mass., 1973), pp. 179–86.
20. Rawski, *China's Transition to Industrialism*, p. 2.
21. See Ernest R. May and John K. Fairbank (eds), *America's China Trade in Historical Perspective* (Cambridge, Mass., 1986), pp. 230–3.
22. Ragnar Nurkse, *Problems of Capital Formation in Underdeveloped Countries* (Oxford, 1961), pp. 115–16.

12 British Capital and the Management of the Kailuan Coal Mines

Xiong Xingmei

Professor Xiong Xingmei has been the head of the Institute of Economics and then the Institute of International Economics at Nankai in the 1980s. He is an economic historian and has been involved in the study of the very important archives of the Kailuan Mining Administration, one of China's two largest coal mines, which was dominated by the British from 1900 to 1949. This article makes thorough use of materials from those archives.

The Kailuan Mining Administration was formed in 1912 through the amalgamation of the Chinese-owned Luanzhou Company with the Chinese Engineering and Mining Company, which had been taken over by British interests in somewhat nefarious circumstances in 1900.

This article was originally written in the 1960s and shows that before 1978 there was a wide gap between what historians wrote and what they could publish. Sections II and III of the original article, dealing with the pre-1911 period, have not been translated. The translated sections are important in their concrete analysis of Kailuan's history in economic and political terms, rather than solely in the nationalistic context in which it is usually treated.[1]

The problem of the mining rights of the Kailuan Coal Mines was never simply one of who owned the property and rights. From 1900–1 when the British forcibly occupied the Kaiping Coal Mines up to 1912 when they went on to annex the Luanzhou Coal Mines amd amalgamate them with Kaiping, the Chinese Government never formally recognised British control. Later it was stated in the agreement between the British Chinese Engineering and Mining Company (CEMC), which operated the Kaiping mines, and the Chinese Luanzhou Mining Company that the Kailuan Coal Mines remained 'jointly managed' by the British and the Chinese sides.

TABLE 12.1 *Business and profits of the Kailuan Mining Administration, 1913–1932*

Period	Total output of coal (tons)	Total sales of coal (tons)	Total profit (Ch$)	Profits distributed (Ch$)		
				Total	CEMC	Luanzhou
Average 1912/1913–1916/17	2 583 985	2 453 208	4 829 407	2 968 015	1 755 165	1 212 849
Average 1917/18–1921/22	3 860 738	3 489 545	9 359 040	6 606 398	3 484 562	3 121 837
Average 1922/23–1926/27	3 927 717	3 730 508	8 103 379	5 079 952	2 808 579	2 271 373
Average 1927/28–1931/32	4 997 958	4 616 748	9 984 775	5 964 932	3 347 717	2 617 215

SOURCE: Statistics in the annual reports of the General Manager of the Kailuan Mining Administration.

However, it was an irrefutable fact that British imperialism seized the Kailuan Coal Mines. In essence, with the benefit of the privileges afforded by British imperialism, CEMC was in constant control over the management and administration of the mines; on the other hand, that actual control enabled the British in turn to maintain all their interests.

The fundamental reason why the British were able to take control over the mines was that they enjoyed imperialist privileges in China. That the British imperialists enjoyed privileges and colluded with the Chinese authorities was the prerequisite for their control over Kailuan. This point underlies the author's arguments presented in this article although it is not discussed systematically.

An economic analysis shows that the problem of the Kailuan mining rights centres on the development of an interaction between the British seizure of ownership and their control over management and administration. The author's purpose in writing this article in the early 1960s was to reveal the course of this evolution.

I

The Kailuan Mining Administration [KMA, or Kailuan] was vigorously managed by the British from its foundation and the rapid expansion of its business resulted in large profits as shown in Table 12.1.

It can be seen from Table 12.1 that, within only ten years after the foundation of the KMA, average annual profits increased from Ch$4.80

million to Ch$9.36 million. In the following years, they remained at the level of Ch$8–10 million. Thus total net profit over twenty years reached Ch$161 million. Profits of hundreds of millions of silver dollars continuously flowed into the pockets of the British capitalists and were also shared by the capitalists at Luanzhou. The reasons for these large profits were as follows.

First, the market for Kailuan coal expanded rapidly over the twenty years. During the First World War Chinese-owned industry experienced considerable development and, after the war, direct imperialist investment in China was further strengthened. So the demand for Kailuan coal, especially in the coastal cities, increased rapidly. In addition, large quantities of Kailuan coal were exported to Japan for use as coke in the steel industry. Sales of Kailuan coal in the financial year of 1931/32 were 174 per cent greater than those in 1912/13; sales in the Tianjin area expanded by 112 per cent, whereas those in the Shanghai area expanded by 436 per cent.[2]

Second, the KMA expanded investment and increased their exploitation of workers as a way of improving and expanding production. In order to meet the demands of the developing coal market, they continuously put in additional investment and expanded production facilities. From the time of the amalgamation of the two companies up to 1930, they reinvested Ch$26 million from profits.[3] By the mid-1920s, the mines had a productive capacity of 6 million tons per year.

Although Kailuan continuously increased its investment, this investment was mainly used to expand and improve facilities for power generation, coal washing, underground and railway transport and ports; but the British were quite grudging in investing in the coal cutting process. The mine authorities remained indifferent to the inhuman working conditions in the pits and to the simple and crude coal cutting tools; they did not make any improvements over a long period of time. Under such adverse working conditions the miners were inefficient in their work and shocking accidents often took place underground. The KMA archives reveal that the daily output per coal cutter dropped from 1090 kg in 1912/13 to 930 kg in 1931/32; during those twenty years approximately 3000 miners died in serious accidents. A dead body was left behind with every 25 000 tons of coal plundered by the British. Under the title of 'Savings on the Conditions of Work at the Workers' Expense', Marx pointed out:

Capitalist production . . . is extremely sparing with the realised labour that is objectified in commodities. Yet it squanders human beings, living labour, more readily than does any other mode of production.[4]

Of course, the British had their own smug calculations: to make extensive use of cheap Chinese labour might lead to low productivity and heavy injuries and deaths but, from the viewpoint of profit, it was more beneficial than the extensive use of machinery.

Third, the British at Kailuan colluded with Japanese imperialist coal traders to rig the coal market on the China coast. Japanese coal, Fushun coal and coal from the Japanese-controlled mines in Shandong were Kailuan's main competitors in coastal markets. With the growth in the demand for coal, Kailuan reached an agreement in 1915 with the main Japanese coal traders, in which they divided up the market in the Chinese coastal ports each year and coordinated prices. In some years Kailuan also made agreements with the mines of Jingxing, Lincheng and Yi xian (Zhongxing) to divide up the market. All these agreements enabled Kailuan coal to maintain its sales in coastal cities and keep prices high. Over the twenty years after the foundation of the KMA, the average pithead cost of its coal increased by Ch$2.40 per ton, while the coal price generally increased by over Ch$3. This indicates that, with the expansion of coal sales, the super profit and absolute rent enjoyed by the KMA both increased.

Finally, but by no means unimportantly, the profits made by the Kailuan Mines were inseparable from their reliance upon the privileges provided by British imperialism. The successive years of fighting between warlords in North China caused many coal mines to suffer heavy losses, but the Kailuan Mines were exempt from such war-induced disasters because they operated under the British flag:

> The social upheaval in China has increased the importance of places such as Tianjin, Shanghai and even our mine areas. The residence of foreigners there exempted our mine areas from being looted, and made it possible for industrial production to continue.[5]

In fact, the shelter of British imperialism did not merely bring to Kailuan the 'stable circumstances' under which production could continue smoothly. With the stable circumstances came economic privileges. This was made clear in the comments of P. C. Young, the British General Manager of the KMA, on the payment of taxes:

> It is only the special stipulations concerning the payment of taxes contained in the amalgamation agreement that allow us to be the only one exempted from unlimited exploitation. Once the clauses in this document become a dead letter, and the central government or

any local government is able to levy taxes on us at will, our situation will be no better than other coal mining company in China. As a matter of fact, several of these coal mining companies closed down this year.[6]

To sum up, relying on imperialist privileges, the British strengthened their control over the management of Kailuan and combined the plundering form of management of colonialism and the monopolistic form of management of imperialism. This is the secret of the large profits made by the KMA.

These large profits further consolidated the British rights and interests in the mines. This can easily be seen through an examination of the campaign to 'recover Kaiping on the basis of Luanzhou' in the 1920s.

Article 17 in the 'Preliminary Agreement for the Joint Management of the Kailuan Mining Administration' signed in 1912 stipulated that 'After ten years of the signing of this contract, the Luanzhou Mining Company is entitled to purchase back the whole property of the Chinese Engineering and Mining Company at a fair price agreed after consultation between both sides.' From 1923 on, Chinese public opinion increasingly demanded the recovery of Kaiping. In order to reap some profit, the Zhili (now Hebei) Provincial Parliament, the provincial administrative authorities and the Ministry of Agriculture and Commerce of the central government repeatedly urged the Luanzhou Mining Company to prepare the funds to purchase CEMC from the British. However, those in charge of Luanzhou were slow to take up this clause in the original contract. They preferred to collude with CEMC in dealing with the Chinese authorities.

For example, Major Nathan came to China in 1925 to hold talks with Luanzhou. In his report to the Board of the Kaiping Company he wrote:

I have discussed with the directors of Luanzhou their company's purchase of the property of the Chinese Engineering and Mining Company according to Article 17 of the contract for joint management. Their opinion is that they are neither inclined nor able to go ahead with such a purchase. But outside pressure impels them to hold consultations with us. So they feel compelled to take some actions on the matter. . . . As the present situation in China is constantly changing, we unanimously hold that there is not much possibility for us to take any positive action on it, and hence we consider it appropriate for us to adopt dilatory tactics.[7]

The dilatory tactics, as W. Turner, Chairman of the board, added, were:

. . . to limit the consultations between CEMC and the Luanzhou Mining Company to protracted correspondence, which will not do us the slightest harm, and to shelve and postpone any practical actions.[8]

As a matter of fact, the campaigns to 'recover Kaiping' launched by Luanzhou Mining Company throughout the 1920s were carried out according to these instructions from the British.

It was not at all surprising that the capitalists in Luanzhou should adopt such an attitude. General Manager P. C. Young, who actively participated in the secret activities of both parties, gave a fairly detailed portrayal of the situation and the state of mind of the Luanzhou capitalists:

The avariciousness of the (Hebei) Provincial Government has reached such a degree that a Chinese industrial company finds it very difficult to continue its operations. . . . In order to deal with this situation, they have to adopt various kinds of unusual and expedient measures. They are making use of every dollar of cash they can raise for distribution as dividends and, at the same time, they are distributing to shareholders the proceeds of any property they can sell. With such an administration in power, they are also compelled to try their utmost to express their appreciation of the government's wishes to purchase CEMC As I am writing this letter, I hear that this government [Li Jinglin, a warlord in Hebei] has been forced out of Tianjin by military means. Probably in a few hours this government will no longer exist. A new government may be just as bad, or even worse; nevertheless, the consultations somehow will have to start again from the very beginning. Therefore, the Luanzhou Company has indeed attained its goal of easing its relationship with the government, while at the same time not doing anything in practice.[9]

Obviously the tactics adopted by the Luanzhou Company, in plain terms, reflected their preference for the stable, large profits under British control over the assertion of Chinese rights of management at the risk of decreasing profits. As a consequence, they decided to protect British rights and interests rather than recover Chinese interests and rights. This was a choice made not by the Chinese people but by bureaucratic capital. 'Capital places the safeguarding of the alliance of the capitalists of all countries against the working people above the interests of the fatherland, of the people, or of what you will.'[10] In the final analysis, this was because British capital held sway and accelerated its accumulation.

British capital's victory over Luanzhou opened up a new prospect for the thorough solution of the problem of the mining rights. Now that the interests of the CEMC and Luanzhou companies were further integrated on the basis of protecting the rights and interests of British imperialism, what lay ahead for the British from then on was no longer how to deal with the problem of 'recovering Kaiping on the basis of Luanzhou' but how to collude with the capitalists in Luanzhou and get them to persuade the Chinese Government to legalise British rights and interests in Kailuan.

II

After the promulgation of the Mining Law in October 1931, the Nationalist Government repeatedly urged, in the name of regulating mining affairs, the Luanzhou Company and CEMC to apply for a mining permit and also pressed for the payment of outstanding mine taxes. In the autumn of 1933, in view of the increased pressure from the Government, the Luanzhou Company agreed that Gu Zhen (Assistant Manager of Kailuan) should be sent to Nanjing together with E. J. Nathan (General Manager of Kailuan) for negotiations; but at the same time it wrote to CEMC demanding the revision of the 'Contract for Joint Management' signed in 1912. It called for the properties, profits and rights of management to be equally divided between the two companies while the mine area be shared by the two.

Through negotiations in Nanjing, Nathan and Gu Zhen found that the main demand of the Ministry of Industry was that Kailuan pay in advance Ch$1 million of mine taxes in exchange for mining rights. When Luanzhou's demands were rejected by CEMC, Luanzhou sent Gu Zhen to hold independent negotiations with the Ministry of Industry and made an advance of Ch$500 000 in mine taxes. In return it was granted a mining permit. This independent action by Luanzhou greatly threatened CEMC. Finally, through mediation by Gu Zhen and Nathan, CEMC and Luanzhou came to an agreement that

> the present organisation of the KMA be revised to equalise the share of each company in the ownership of the mines, all interests, and assets, and in the responsibilities and rights of management

and that

> both companies express their desire to transfer all their mine areas to the use and enjoyment of the Kailuan Mining Administration.

On its application to the Ministry of Industry and the payment of Ch$500 000 overdue mine taxes by CEMC, Chen Gongbo, the Minister of Industry, soon agreed to recognise Kailuan. Then, at the end of 1935, on consenting to pay another Ch$134 000 to the Ministry of Industry in the name of a 'deposit for state-owned mine areas', Kailuan finally received its mining permit.

To put it bluntly, for all the interplay of different interests and the frequent negotiations, the real nature of the 'mining case' was simply that, having reached an agreement with Luanzhou, CEMC made only small concessions to the Ministry of Industry and in return the Nanjing Government formally recognised British rights over the mines, which had never been legal since the British seized CEMC in 1900. Based on their convergent interests, the Nationalist reactionary ruling class and the capitalists of the Luanzhou Mines colluded with the British imperialists covertly to sell Chinese coal resources, thus thoroughly giving away to the British the right of mining the Kaiping coalfield. This was the crux of the further loss of the Kailuan mining rights in 1934.

Of course, the complete forfeiture of the mining rights took place because there existed certain political and economic conditions which facilitated its realisation.

The first factor was the political situation in North China. After the Tanggu Truce of 1933, the east Hebei region fell more and more deeply under the direct control of Japanese imperialist forces. In the summer of 1934, while working out the supplementary agreement with Luanzhou on behalf of CEMC, Nathan, on receipt of a telegraphed inquiry from Gu Zhen in Nanjing, reported to London:

> The Minister of Industry (Chen Gongbo) is particularly eager to have this contract signed and put it before the Executive Yuan as soon as he can. I think the reason he is in such a hurry is that he is afraid of possible dispute with the Japanese. . . . I believe you and your colleagues will realise that the most sensible course is to get this contract signed, stamped and issued as soon as possible so that we can rely on the full support of the Chinese and British governments in case the Japanese make an attempt to interfere with our rights.[11]

In other words, the Nationalist Government certainly could not wait to gain some advantage before Kailuan was removed from its control but the British were also anxious to have their rights and interests at the Kailuan coalfield confirmed as protection against possible Japanese encroachment.

Second, the British control over management played an important role in solving and consolidating their rights in the mine. The fact that the British received large profits from the management of Kailuan was an important reason why the Nationalist Government took the opportunity to extort money while discussing the question of mining rights and why they so quickly gave in. This is shown in the secret telegram Gu Zhen sent to the Board of the Luanzhou Mining Company from Nanjing on 7 December 1933:

> If Kailuan can fulfil the following two requirements, the Ministry of Industry can . . . . grant it mining rights for the next forty years and will abandon all claims for outstanding mine taxes: i) Kailuan must write off the money they advanced, amounting to Ch$270,000; ii) It is to pay Ch$1 million as advance payment of the mine area taxes due over the next ten years.

Chen Gongbo as good as informed the British that: On condition that you give us the money, I will present you with the 'mining rights.' Because Chen was so greedy, Kailuan succeeded in purchasing the legal mining rights, which they had wanted for the previous thirty years, at a cost of only Ch$1.4 million altogether (the two items of money advanced plus the above-mentioned Ch$134 000, all of which equalled only 29 per cent of the average annual net profit of Kailuan between 1931/32 and 1934/35). No wonder Nathan was so proud of his receipt of the mining permit and said over and again that it was indeed cheap.

> If we had not been so skilful in dealing with the Minister of Industry who is so shrewd, less than honest and greedy, the cost would have been far more than that.[12]

Moreover, in the course of managing Kailuan over the twenty years after its foundation, the British succeeded in turning the capitalists of Luanzhou practically into compradors, so that the negotiations between the two companies over mining rights became much simpler: any contradictions could be solved on the basis of protecting British interests. For this very reason, at the 'critical moment' of the negotiations over the mining rights in 1934, CEMC put forward the equal division of profits and rights of management as an inducement. Immediately it won the cooperation of leaders of Luanzhou and induced them to pull strings on behalf of CEMC. This resulted in the rapid 'satisfactory solution' of the question of mining rights. True, the British were obliged to give up part of their management rights and profits, but

we particularly rejoice that we have managed to escape following the
stipulation in the Mining Act that the management of the Kailuan
Mining Administration has to be controlled by a Chinese company,
and the clauses (in the supplementary contract) stipulating that if the
establishment of a Chinese company is called for in the future, it can
have only two shareholders (that is, two companies), and the shares must
be divided equally between foreign capital and Chinese capital.[13]

The British knew very clearly that this was certainly a deal worth 'particular
rejoicing' since they not only obtained formal recognition on the part of
the Chinese of their ownership of the Kaiping Mines but also avoided
managerial control by the Luanzhou capitalists.

The reader may ask: After CEMC and Luanzhou signed the 'supplementary contract', which said 'the responsibilities and competence in
management should be divided equally' between both parties, did this
somehow weaken British control over the Kailuan enterprises?

This question can best be answered by examining the appointment in
1934 of Gu Zhen as General Manager of the KMA on equal terms with
Nathan. Now, what kind of person was Gu Zhen in the eyes of the British
and specifically of Nathan?

Gu Zhen turned out to be a 'talented person' constantly advised and
directly promoted by the British. When Gu was appointed associate
manager in 1933, Nathan explained to Turner:

It is strange that when he first joined our business four years ago, none
of the directors of Luanzhou knew of him. . . . His participation in our
business was entirely because P. C. Young knew of his ability . . . Gu
is on extremely familiar terms with the trusted followers of Jiang Jieshi,
and Generalissimo Jiang himself also knows of Gu. Therefore, he will
be very useful in his new post when the problem of mine taxes is brought
forward for serious discussion.[14]

Nathan's estimate was correct, and he greatly appreciated Gu's diligent
cultivation of the power-holders in Nanjing over the Kailuan rights.

The more I have to do with Gu, the more likeable and respected I feel
he is. . . . It is of immeasurable value to me that he is able to carry out
work assigned to him most wisely, under the circumstances when he has
only guidance on principles and not help over details. That we could
finally reach an agreement owes much to him, and to him only. It is by
no means excessive to say so.[15]

Gu Zhen was so resourceful in serving British interests that Turner wrote to Nathan:

> Although Gu works as a representative of the Luanzhou Mining Company, I understand that the relationship between you has reached such a stage that he can be considered as standing completely on your side and therefore being loyal to the interests of the Chinese Engineering and Mining Company.[16]

With such a person as the General Manager of Kailuan, was the British power weakened or consolidated? The answer is clear.

Having received formal approval of their mining rights from the Nationalist authorities, the British immediately went all out to adopt a series of important managerial measures to consolidate the rights and interests they had won and to increase profits.

In April 1934, only two days after Minister Chen Gongbo approved Kailuan's mining rights, Nathan suggested to the Board of CEMC a plan to reorganise the management of the mines, in which the system of the Belgian general mining engineer being in overall charge of the mining operations was replaced by that of a British 'mining manager' being in charge of a unified administration; the Belgian mining engineer was to 'limit the scope of his duties strictly to the area of coal mining'; labour management was entrusted to a Chinese 'mining general affairs manager'. It was by no means fortuitous that the British decided to reorganise the mining administration at this very moment. Outwardly they declared that it was in order to improve productivity and reduce the costs of coal mining but inwardly they had more long-term aims.

After the British and Belgians grabbed the Kaiping Mines, the Belgians for a time enjoyed equal rights in the management. However, after the amalgamation of CEMC and Luanzhou, Belgian influence was weakened, although they still controlled the management of the mines themselves and from time to time resisted British attempts to strengthen their role. The 1930s saw turbulent workers' movements in Kailuan and the Belgians were no longer able to control the situation in the mining areas so that their influence continued to decline, while the relationship between the British and the Nationalist regime was greatly strengthened from 1934. It was under these circumstances that Nathan decided to make an attack on the Belgian mining engineers whom he called 'the iron rulers', forcing them to retreat to the position of being pure technicians. At the same time, he made fuller use of the Chinese administrative personnel employed to deal with the burgeoning workers' struggles. He expressed his ideas in a letter to

Turner: 'Only the British and British methods can successfully deal with the local workers in very difficult situations.'[17] This position was highly praised by Turner:

> The management of the mining areas will be the province of the British whereas the actual mining operations in the mines will that of the Belgians. From the political point of view, the benefits are clear enough.[18]

What were these political benefits? Evidently Turner was referring, first of all, to the fact that, within Kailuan, from the highest level to the grass roots, all the managerial personnel were British. The British on the one hand formally held the Kailuan mining rights and on the other they continued to strengthen their control within the company. But these were mutually dependent on each other.

With the solution of the problem of the mining rights, the British became increasingly close to the Nationalists and so received a series of economic privileges.

In the autumn of 1934 Nathan reported to London another of Gu Zhen's 'contributions':

> The work he has done in Nanjing ever since the (supplementary) contract was signed is enough to prove that his relationship with the ruling group in Nanjing is indeed very valuable to us. . . . Apart from his success in having the contract approved, he has also won the permission of the Ministry of Interior for us to build up mining police ourselves, which the Ministry of Interior at first refused to allow us to do.[19]

Through collusion with the Chinese authorities, the British finally fulfilled their long-cherished ambition to put the armed forces of the mining areas under Kailuan's own direct control so that they were able more easily to command this tool in the bloody suppression of the workers.

In 1935, Kailuan signed a loan contract with the Ministry of Railways in Nanjing, which stipulated that it was to raise Ch$5 million for the completion of the Guangzhou-Hankou Railway project. The British took this opportunity to entice the Ministry of Railways to order the Beijing-Shenyang Railroad to provide them with facilities for coal transport and to reduce freight rates. As a result, the freight charge per ton of Kailuan coal fell from the average of Ch$1.57 between 1927 and 1934 to Ch$1.25 after the new contract was signed in 1935,[20] which greatly strengthened their competitive position in the northern market.

Particularly worth noting are the activities of Kailuan in extending control over the coal markets in North China and Central China during these years.

The world economic crisis of the 1930s affected Chinese industry and commerce and led to a continuous drop in coal prices and the stagnation of coal sales. Apart from concluding agreements on regional markets with the Zhongxing, Jingxing and Liuhegou coal companies in order to preserve its own market, Kailuan tried hard to seek other ways of dealing with the unprecedentedly intense competition and strengthening its own position. Of all these measures, the most important was their collusion with Nationalist bureaucratic capital in establishing a coal cartel to control the market. In the autumn of 1936, with the support of the Zhongfu Bank, Kailuan set up the 'North China Coal Mining Company' in Tianjin, which purchased coal from the Jingxing and Datong coal mines in order to maintain the high prices of coal in the Tianjin-Tanggu area; soon afterwards, Kailuan, together with the Zhongxing coal mine, which was owned by bureaucratic capital, the Jincheng Bank and the National Commercial Bank jointly set up the 'Central China Coal Mining Company', to purchase and resell coal transported into the Shanghai market from coal mines in Shandong and Jiangsu.

The British ambitions extended further and in 1937 they reorganised the 'North China Coal Mining Company' and 'Central China Coal Mining Company' and founded the 'China Industrial and Commercial Company Limited' to control the Shanghai coal market.[21] They also attempted to expand the business by purchasing comparatively important small coal mines in Shandong Province in order

> to prevent the numerous small mining areas from being combined into large mining areas for large-scale mining, for, in our opinion, this is the only way to maintain our position in the market in the Yangzi area.[22]

Nathan wrote:

> I consider this plan extremely satisfactory, for it enables Kailuan to continue to carry out its absolutely necessary aims of control over the Chinese coal market without having to appear in public if possible, as a result of which the competitors who are holding favourable positions will not, with their geographical environment and high-quality coal, be able drive us out of the key areas in the Chinese coal market, while we can maintain our due share of the market in that area at favourable

prices. Such is the indispensable condition for the future prosperity of
Kailuan.[23]

To control the Chinese coal market was Kailuan's 'absolutely necessary
aim'; to protect the key market in the Chinese coal industry was the
'indispensable condition for the future prosperity of Kailuan'! Nathan
talked much bigger than he did before Minister Chen Gongbo formally
approved in 1934 the British ownership of Kailuan and their rights of
management and granted them the mining permit.
    Lenin pointed out:

> The concentration of production; the monopolies arising therefrom; the
> merging or coalescence of the banks with industry – such is the history
> of the rise of finance capital and such is the content of that concept.[24]

The concentration of production in China's coal industry was not carried
out on the eve of the Anti-Japanese War because capitalism was not yet
fully developed in China. However, since imperialism controlled the coal
industry in pre-Communist China, there was bound to be a special form of
finance capital suited to this situation. In this sense, the establishment of
the 'China Industrial and Commercial Company' was in conformity with
objective laws. For it was an embryonic form of finance capital, being a
combination of the coal mining companies controlled by the British, coal
mines owned and run by Chinese bureaucratic capital and a few banks: its
basis was the recognition by the Chinese regime of the British rights over
the mines and its essential condition for existence and expansion of strength
was collusion with Chinese bureaucratic capital. It can be imagined that,
had it not been for the sudden changes in the political situation, it would
have been further combined with the bureaucratic capital of the four big
monopoly groups in pre-Communist China and would have developed
rapidly.
    After the war broke out, the wishful thinking of the British in expanding
the business came to nothing. This was the turning point at which Kailuan's
management began to decline; it was also a clear indication that the rights
and interests of the British began to be threatened.

CONCLUSION

The historical fact that the British imperialists dominated the Kailuan Coal
Mines for decades illustrates the following points:
    The whole problem of the Kailuan mining rights was the course of

contradictory and interactive development between the British seizure of ownership and their control over the rights of management and administration. Generally speaking, the rights and interests of the British underwent a process of gradual development, consolidation and then, after the outbreak of the Anti-Japanese War, gradual decline. The British at first established their control over the Kaiping Coal Mine and later, in the form of a joint venture, they made large profits from their control over the management and administration of the Kailuan mines. This played an important role in the further solution and protection of their ownership of the mine; and then the further solution of the ownership problem, in turn, strengthened the British control over the whole of Kailuan and promoted the development of their business activities.

The British management and control over the Kailuan mines was an all-round control. The Board of the CEMC was the policy maker and decider of important issues. It was also supported by certain West European consortia.

To train and bring into being a number of compradors was an important feature of the managerial activities of Kailuan under the control of the British. The gradual compradorisation of the people in authority in Luanzhou created important conditions for the British gradually to strengthen their control over the Kailuan mines and further to solve the problem of mining rights.

The enjoyment of imperialist privileges was the precondition for British control over the management of the mines. Relying on political and economic privileges, the British were able to collude with the reactionary ruling class of pre-Communist China for the further consolidation of their rights and interests; once they lost their privileged position, they found it difficult to maintain their managerial rule and, finally, even lost their entire rights and interests in Kailuan. Consequently, it could be predicted that it was inevitable that the entire British rights and interests in the mines would be weakened when the Chinese people stood up and would be abolished when the rule of the Nationalist reactionaries collapsed.

Notes

1. [Editor's note] This chapter is a translation of parts of Xiong Xingmei, 'Lun Yingguo ziben dui Kailuan meikuang jingying de kongzhi – Kailuan kuangquan sangshi de yuanyin fenxi zhi yi', *Nankai jingji yanjiu suo jikan* 1986.2 (June 1986): 49–63.
2. Annual report of the General Manager of the KMA, 1931/32.
3. Balance sheet of the KMA, 1929/30.

4. Karl Marx, *Capital*, vol. 3 (Harmondsworth, 1981), p. 182.
5. Annual report of the General Manager of KMA, 1921/22.
6. Annual report of the General Manager of KMA, 1927/28.
7. An official letter from Major Nathan to the secretary of CEMC in London, 6 June 1925.
8. Turner to P C Young, 27 November 1925.
9. P C Young to Turner, 24 December 1925.
10. A report by Lenin on foreign policy delivered at a joint meeting on the all-Russian Central Executive Committee and the Moscow Soviet, 14 May 1918, in V. I. Lenin, *Collected Works*, vol. 27 (Moscow, 1965), p. 366.
11. Nathan to Turner, 20 July 1934.
12. Nathan to Turner, 31 December 1935.
13. Turner to Nathan, 30 June 1934.
14. Nathan to Turner, 11 June 1933
15. Nathan to Turner, 10 February 1934.
16. Turner to Nathan, 22 December 1933.
17. Nathan to Turner, 27 April 1934.
18. Turner to Nathan, 8 June 1934.
19. Nathan to Turner, 22 September 1934.
20. Annual report of the General Manager of KMA, 1935/36.
21. The 'China Industrial and Commercial Co. Ltd.' drew its capital from the KMA, the Zhongxing Coal Mine and the Zhongfu, National Commercial, Jincheng and Salt Banks, with the total capital stock being 2 million yuan. The two mines each accounted for 20 per cent of the stocks, the four banks for 15 per cent each. Moreover, it was financially supported by the Nationalist Central Bank and the Bank of China. But because the Anti-Japanese War broke out soon afterwards, this company had practically no time to engage in actual operations.
22. Gu Zhen's memorandum relating to the 'China Industrial and Commercial Co. Ltd.'
23. Nathan to Turner, 10 March 1937.
24. Lenin, 'Imperialism, the Highest Stage of Capitalism', in *Collected Works*, Vol. 22 (Moscow, 1964), p. 226.

13 On the Consequences of the 1935 Currency Reform

Ci Hongfei

Ci Hongfei is a young scholar at the Nankai Institute of Economics, who has worked on the salt industry as well as on the Nationalist state.

This is one of several articles published in the mid and late 1980s which began a process of re-evaluation of key aspects of Nationalist economic policy. Important features of the article include its attempts to provide macroeconomic estimates of the money supply (though these differ from those produced by Thomas Rawski)[1] and its depiction of the chaos of China's monetary system before 1935.[2]

Most scholars (including those writing recently) have argued that the main historical consequences of the 1935 Nationalist currency reform were inflation and the formation of the bureaucratic monopoly capital of the Four Great Families. As shown below, the author believes such an analysis to be incorrect.

DID THE CURRENCY REFORM CAUSE INFLATION?

Some scholars believe that there were only currency disorders but no inflation prior to the reform of the currency system in 1935; and it was this reform that 'started the inflation of old China'.[3] Therefore, if we wish to get a clear idea of any harmful consequences of the reform, we need to know whether the prewar inflation was caused by the reform or by the previous situation.

Those who hold that there was no inflation before the reform base their arguments on two grounds: first, in spite of the very disordered nature of the issue of paper money before the reform, all 'the paper money (except that issued by some local warlords) was of the nature of fiduciary money';[4] second, 'despite their wide issue of paper currencies, the fact that at the time China was on a silver standard set a limit to the ability of the warlords to loot the people's wealth'.[5]

It is my opinion that serious inflation did exist before the reform. Those arguing against the existence of inflation on the first ground are obviously more concerned with the big banks, both official and private, in the coastal cities but their banknotes alone did not represent the total circulation of paper currency. Up to the end of 1933 the total amount of currency issued by the ten big banks in China (the Bank of China, the Central Bank of China, the Commercial Bank of China, the National Commercial Bank, the Bank of Communications, the Ningpo Commercial and Savings Bank, The Agricultural and Industrial Bank of China, The National Industrial Bank of China, the Land Bank of China and The-Four-Bank-Preparation-Club) amounted to less than Ch$500 million (see the Notes for how the Ch$ is defined). But in April 1934 the paper currency in circulation in Shanghai alone reached Ch$323 million, 99 per cent of which was issued by Chinese-owned banks.[6] That is to say, the value of the notes issued by these ten major ten banks which circulated in the other thirty-odd provinces and cities of China was less than that of those circulating in Shanghai. What a striking contrast! Such a situation was well in line with the uneven economic development of the then semi-feudal semi-colonial China. The more developed capitalist economy was mainly concentrated in the coastal areas while the vast interior was still mostly a natural economy, with little commercialisation.

The case was the same with silver currency. According to Zhang Jiaao in 1932, 'more than half of the silver currency circulating was in Shanghai'. Therefore, a clear understanding of any possible serious inflation (or currency devaluation) in China before the reform requires a close examination not only of Shanghai, but of the whole country. The following figures may illustrate the serious depreciation of the various local banknotes as well as metal currencies.

In Sichuan, a total of $71.1 million of paper currency was issued from 1911 to 1935 and the losses from failure to redeem the currency or from redemption at a discount amounted to $22.93 million.[7] In Yunnan, $92 million was issued by the Fudian Bank, which was later redeemed at a discount of 80 per cent. The loss suffered by the people amounted to as much as $73 600 000.[8]

In Guangxi the various note issues by the local warlords from 1912 to 1931 amounted to more than $60 million, of which some was devalued to one-fiftieth of its face value, some simply became waste paper, and some was redeemed at a great discount. The people suffered a heavy loss of at least $63 million.[9]

In Guangdong, from June 1937 onwards, the exchange rate of the local currency to 'the national *fabi*' was set at 1.44 to 1. Up to that time a total of $329 289 000 of local paper currency had been issued and so the people incurred a loss of at least $80–90 million.[10] In Shantou alone, more than $10 million of paper currency was issued, only to be redeemed later at a discount of 75 per cent.

In Jilin and Heilongjiang, 5.5 billion 'strings' of government notes were issued between 1914 and 1928. During those fourteen years, the currencies in the two provinces depreciated to one thirty-sixth and one fourteenth of their face value respectively so that the people lost at least 5 billion.[11] In Liaoning, from July 1927 onward $992 million of local *'fengpiao'* were issued ($3 billion according to the *Manchuria and Mongolia Year Book*). From 1924 to 1929, the money depreciated to one thirty-second of its face value, and the people were robbed of about $1 billion.[12]

In Xinjiang, in 1933, 1.2 billion taels (a 'tael' was an ounce of silver in the old monetary system.) of paper money were issued and by 1939 as much as 4000 taels of local notes were required to exchange for one dollar *'fabi'*. The plundering was simply beyond any measurement.[13] In Suiyuan, there were about $6 million of local paper notes by 1931. In Baotou alone, there were eleven types of notes based on copper to a total of 8 million dollars but they circulated only at a discount of 60–90 per cent.[14]

In Shanxi, 1930 alone saw an issue of more than $75 million. From 1932, however, $20 could only be exchanged for 1 *'fabi'*. The people in the province were robbed of nearly $75 million. In Shandong, at least $7–8 million issued in 1926 by Zhang Zongchang in the form of the New Army currency became waste paper. At the same time, the Shandong Bank issued $23 million, all of which were inconvertible after Zhang's downfall. By 1925 the Hubei Provincial Bank had already issued $80–90 million worth of official notes to the value of 1000 cash or 100 copper coins. These were depreciated by 14.5 times in comparison with their value three years earlier and by forty times in comparison with that twenty years before.[15]

The available figures for other provinces are: the Hebei Provincial Bank issued $16 million in 1928, all of which became waste paper after the downfall of Zhang Zuolin. The $20 million issue by the Henan Provincial Bank in 1925 was all inconvertible. After the war between Sun Dianyin and Ma Hongkui, $1.1 million of currency became inconvertible in Ningxia.

Even such big and famous banks as the Bank of China and the Bank of Communications could not avoid depreciation as exemplified by the dispute in 1916 in Beijing over their failure to redeem their notes. In 1927, those two banks stopped converting $30 million 'Hanchao' notes, and later converted $7.8 million at a discount of 80 per cent. There were also innumerable other small scale incidents nation-wide where currency was depreciated or made inconvertible. The present writer's research covering sixteen provinces shows that the devaluation of banknotes all over the country prior to the reform was a widespread and serious phenomenon rather than, as believed by the above authors, limited to the paper currency issued by a few warlords.

Therefore, in most places and during most of the period, those banknotes were by no means fiduciary money. Given that, in the view of Western economists, an annual inflation rate of 10 per cent amounts to serious inflation, the rates in the above sixteen provinces were all above that figure. In Shanxi, Guangxi, Hubei, Yunnan and particularly Liaoning, Jilin and Heilongjiang, inflation had already reached the stage of 'hyper-inflation'. It was only because of the absence of a large-scale and prolonged war at the time that this inflation was outpaced by depreciation of the German Mark and later of the Guomindang '*fabi*'.

The same was the case with metal currencies. The issue of copper coins from the end of the Qing Dynasty to the early 1930s was so enormous that by 1923 the aggregate was already over 40 billion.[16] At the beginning of the century, about 80–90 coins each representing ten cash could be exchanged for a silver dollar, that is the exchange rate was 1:80–90 . But by the early 1930s, in Shanghai, Jiangsu and Zhejiang, the exchange rate dropped to 1:300; in Beijing and Tianjin, 1:400–500; in Hankou, 1:600–odd.[17] This meant that in less than thirty years copper coins in major Chinese cities depreciated by four to five times. The situation was much worse in the interior. For example, in Yunyang the exchange rate dropped to 1:11 000 and in most places in Sichuan to 1:28 000 and a maximum of 1:130 000. The depreciation of copper coins had a devastating effect on the people's livelihood, for the great masses of workers, peasants and ordinary city-dwellers used copper coins as the medium of exchange in their everyday business transactions. The farmers were hit most of all by the depreciation. While being paid in copper coins for their products, they had to pay their debts and taxes with silver dollars.

The situation was much the same with subsidiary silver coins. By the late 1920s at least 2 billion such coins circulated in the market. An investigation carried out in the winter of 1926 showed that among the thirty types of subsidiary silver coins circulating in Shanghai the lowest exchange rate (for privately minted coins) was 24–5 ten-cent-pieces to one silver dollar. Low-quality coins minted in various factories exchanged at 20:1, good quality coins at 12:1. In other words the subsidiary silver coins were depreciated by 20 to 150 per cent in relation to the silver dollar.[18] The situation in the interior was naturally much worse than in Shanghai. One important reason for such a depreciation was the rampant private and bogus mintages, which are extremely difficult to investigate and quantify.

Some bogus mintages had only 27–31 per cent silver as against 60 per cent copper.

On the surface depreciation of silver dollars was not large but they still depreciated for two main reasons. The first was the world-wide fall in silver prices. From 1873 to 1933, the world price of silver dropped to one quarter its original value. This means that the value of the Chinese silver dollars declined by four times as against the value of the gold-standard currencies. The falling price of world silver was in step with the growth of China's foreign trade deficit. Previous scholars used to attribute this trade deficit only to the dumping of foreign goods. But as a matter of fact, the depreciation of the Chinese silver currency was also a very important cause.

Second, depreciation of the silver dollar resulted from the lack of regional integration of the feudal economy on the one hand and private and bogus mintage on the other. Most importantly 'false silver dollars' appeared from time to time in various places. The depreciation of the silver dollar itself had, however, only a minor detrimental effect as compared with the fact that most of the silver dollars in circulation were concentrated in Shanghai and a few other coastal cities, resulting in a shortage of silver in the interior and a serious depreciation of various currencies in the interior relative to the silver dollar. This in turn resulted in a decrease in the share of silver standard currency in the total currency in circulation. Because of the great shortage of ready silver in the interior, the reserves possessed by the various banks in the interior when making new note issues were extremely low. For instance, the cash reserve of the Sichuan Local Bank was only 4 per cent in the early 1930s; and that for the note issues by the old Guangxi clique in the early 1920s was only 0.7 per cent, a world of difference from the 60 per cent norm. Such being the case, whenever a war broke out, banks were closed and the people suffered a great deal from the fact that currencies were inconvertible. As a consequence, from the first day of issue, the local currencies were doomed to circulated at a discount. The depreciation of copper coinage relative to silver dollars was also for similar reasons, especially that there was more copper than silver.

One thing to make clear is that metal currencies are by no means immune from depreciation. As a matter of fact, metal currencies have always been liable to depreciation. Paper currency, in fact, came into being only after there had been a depreciation of metal currencies. Karl Marx put it clearly:

Thus the pound sterling denotes less than one-third of its original weight, the 'pound Scots' before the union, only one 36th; the French livre one

74th, the Spanish maravedi, less than one 1000th, and the Portuguese rei a still smaller fraction.'[19]

The depreciation of metal currencies was even more obvious in China's history, as elaborated by Peng Xinwei in his book, *The History of China's Currencies*. In a word, the statement by previous authors that the silver standard system prior to the reform could set a limit to the warlords' ability to plunder and could give protection to the people is not only contrary to the historical facts but arises from a theoretical misunderstanding.

Scholars generally agree on the monetary chaos rampant prior to the currency reform but what is controversial is whether that chaos itself contained within itself an inflationary nature. The currency disorders caused regional inconvertibility between the various local currencies and consequently serious depreciation. This naturally hampered the development of commodity circulation and led to a break in the process of exchange. Marx once said:

> Exchange consists of buying and selling; if one can just buy without selling (that is, hoard goods), or sell without buying (that is accumulate currency), this divorce leads to the possibility of speculation. . . . When currency clearly shows itself as only a means of exchange, currency depreciation occurs.[20]

What, then, about the situation after currency reform? Was there any inflation after the reform? Some writers, in light of the increase in the issue of '*fabi*' after the reform, concluded that inflation broke out from the very beginning of the reform. But my own calculation shows that the aggregate amount of currency in circulation between November 1935 and July 1937 decreased by Ch$1 billion compared to that before the reform.

The total currency in circulation in the two years prior to November 1935 was about Ch$3.2 billion. The details of this estimate are as follows. The amount of silver dollars was very large but there have been many different estimates: according to Dai Mingli there were at least 1.2 billion silver dollars circulating before 1929 (excluding private and bogus mintages);[21] Eduard Kann's estimate was 2.2 billion (in 1930); that of the Inspectorate General of Customs, 1.7 billion (in 1931).[22] Ma Yinchu estimated that 2 billion silver dollars were circulating before the reform.[23] Recently, Qian Jiaju has estimated that there were a total of 1.4 billion silver dollars in China before the currency reform. I believe that the figure was at most 1.7 billion, because Dai's estimate was based on the research by the Kemmerer Commission and included the major components of silver currency. Taking into account the fact that there was a limit to the private and bogus mintages, the total of the Kemmerer figure and the 100 million new dollars minted after 1933 should not be over 1.7 billion.

As for note issue, the sixteen major banks[24] had issued an aggregate of Ch$681 498 943.92 of paper currency by October, 1935;[25] the total issue of various local banks up to 1935 was generally estimated at between Ch$100 and Ch$150 million.[26] Twenty other banks of issue issued 88 million. The issue by the foreign-owned banks was sharply reduced in the 1930s and estimates range between 5 million and 300 million.[27] But the note issue of the foreign banks was still important, as the 1936 *Chinese Banking Yearbook* stated: 'The Banque de l'Indochine notes in Yunnan and those of the Hong Kong and Shanghai Banking Cooperation in Guangdong . . . outnumbered Chinese banknotes in those two provinces'. Therefore, I estimate the amount of foreign bank notes at approximately Ch$100 million.

The aggregate of the sundry privately issued currencies is generally estimated at several tens of millions of dollars.

Thus the total of these note issues was about Ch$1 billion. In addition, there were about 40 billion copper coins and 2 billion subsidiary silver coins. These would amount to about Ch$500 million according to the exchange rate at the time. Thus the total amount of currency in circulation was about Ch$3.2 billion.

We will now consider the aggregate after the reform. Up to the end of June 1936, the four banks – Bank of China, Central Bank of China, Bank of Communications and Farmers Bank of China – issued an aggregate of Ch$1 407 202 334 and the other banks in the country about Ch$400 million.

The Nationalist government had intended to convert the old metal fractional currencies but up to the outbreak of the Anti-Japanese War only 880 million new nickel and copper coins were minted, worth Ch$25 660 300.85.[28] Thus only a limited amount of the old silver and copper fractional currencies were converted. But taking into account the issue of local currencies in Guangdong, Guangxi and Yunnan, in fact a considerable portion of the subsidiary coins were converted. Therefore, I estimate the subsidiary coins in circulation after the reform at about Ch$300 million, including the new mintage of some Ch$20 million.

The issue of notes by foreign banks was even more reduced after the reform and is difficult to estimate exactly; the author provisionally estimates it at Ch$50 million.

Thus, the total of the above figures for currency in circulation after the reform approximates 2.2 billion, a sharp reduction of 1 billion compared to that before the reform. Even if before the reform a considerable proportion of the silver currency was hoarded or withdrawn from circulation for various reasons, the aggregate of currency in circulation after the reform was still less than that before the reform, or at least not more. And this was only a comparison with the aggregate of currencies in circulation during the two years before the reform, not with that of the 1920s or early 1930s when the various warlords were fighting among themselves.

Therefore, the argument that the monetary reform was 'an inflationary policy converting an expanded issue into a wanton issue'[29] is completely unfounded. The price indexes in the big coastal cities did rise after the reform but only up to the 1931 level. To take Shanghai for example, the wholesale price index was 100 in 1926, 126.7 in 1931, 104.3 in January 1936, and 123 in March 1937, still below the 1931 level. This was mainly due to the fall in the foreign currency value of the '*fabi*': before the reform Ch$1 was worth 18.5 pence sterling but after the reform only 14.25–14.5 pence, a level that was held constant from November 1935 to March 1938.[30] This put the Chinese currency in a favourable position in a time of competitive devaluation.

The recovery of price indexes in some cities was brought about by increased velocity of circulation as a result of the gradual coordination of the currency issue and the consequent reduction in the blockage of circulation. The prosperity of industry and commerce in 1936 shows that the greater velocity of currency circulation and the actual expansion of currency supplies were well in accord with the needs of economic development. The inflation, if any, was appropriate to the situation and within the normal range.

This stimulation to the economy was, however, only apparent in the major coastal cities where the capitalist economy was quite developed, and was much less apparent in the interior. Nevertheless, on the whole 1936 saw the economic high-point of the Nationalist period.

A distinction must be made between the '*fabi*' in the first years after the reform and that during the galloping inflation in the years to come. The cause of any kind of inflation should be sought in the social, economic and political contradictions of the time, rather than in the form of currency itself. The argument that because the '*fabi*' was paper currency it was doomed to inflation is in fact a misunderstanding. As a matter of fact, metal currency is not immune from inflation and paper currency is not necessarily inflationary. The inflation of any currency depends on the social, economic and political situation. What is more, the '*fabi*' was not at the outset a pure paper currency. Therefore, there is no reason whatsoever to believe that the issue of the '*fabi*' based on a foreign exchange standard would inevitably give rise to inflation. But this is by no means to say that the Nationalist government could never practise an inflationary policy. All I mean to say is that the use of the *'fabi'* as a form and system of currency, that is the abolition of the silver standard and the unified issue of currency throughout the country, should not in itself be viewed as an inflationary policy. Unified national currencies have long been the norm throughout the world. Can we judge all such practices as inflationary? The later runaway inflation of the *'fabi'* was mainly due to the exercise of an inflationary policy by the Nationalist government under the exigencies of its war effort. The authority of unified issue it gained in the currency reform – a freedom to practise inflation – only played a minor role.

DID THE CURRENCY REFORM PROMOTE THE FORMATION OF BUREAUCRATIC MONOPOLY CAPITALISM?

Many scholars have held that the currency reform helped the Nationalist Government to bring about financial monopoly and then go on to monopolise industry. Thus the currency reform and the so-called financial monopoly were often described as 'the major symbol of the formation of the bureaucratic monopoly capital of the Four Great Families' before the Anti-Japanese War.[31] This view exaggerates the role of finance. The author does not consider the currency reform to be of any special significance in the formation of bureaucratic monopoly capital. In fact, even after the reform was carried out, the bureaucratic monopoly capital of the Four Great Families did not really come into existence before the Anti-Japanese War. Instead, it took advantage of the war to establish itself. This can be proved by the following facts.

First, in industry, the total capital of industrial enterprises owned by the Nationalist Government up to December 1935 amounted to Ch$30.3 million (another estimate was Ch$26.6 million) – about 11 per cent of total Chinese industrial capital as registered at the Ministry of Industry. Up to 1936, total Chinese industrial capital amounted to Ch$8210 million, of which Ch$6434 million was accounted for by foreign capital. But the foreign capital included that, mainly Japanese, in North-east China. Excluding North-east China, foreign industrial capital in China reached some Ch$2843 million. Even according to this figure, the bureaucratic capital owned by the Nationalist Government accounted for only about 9.5 per cent of productive capital in China and 24.8 per cent of Chinese capital, the remaining 75.2 per cent being private capital (see Table 2.4).

Up to the 1920s imperialism had controlled mainly Chinese trade and finance, with little investment in industry. But by the 1930s it also came to hold monopoly status in Chinese industry. By 1936 in the whole of China foreign capital roughly controlled 95 per cent of the output of pig iron, 83 per cent of steel output, 66 per cent of mechanised coal-mining and 55 per cent of electric energy production. It had virtually gained control over China's main natural and energy resources. In the textile industry, foreign capital also possessed 46 per cent of the spindles and 56 per cent of the looms. It is clear that before the Anti-Japanese War in 1937 Nationalist bureaucratic capital did not occupy an important position in industry. It was foreign capital that really monopolised Chinese industry!

Second, in finance, the total paid-up capital of the Central Bank, Bank of China, Bank of Communications and Farmers' Bank of China, the four major banks of the Nationalist Government, was still less than that of the private banking and finance sector in China. In 1936, the total capital of 164 banks in China amounted to Ch\$400 496 027, while that of the four major banks (including the Central Trust of China) was Ch\$166 915 750, less than 45 per cent of the total.[32] Even with the addition of the Ch\$10 586 390 invested in the spring of 1937 by the Ministry of Finance in the 'three minor banks', including the Commercial Bank of China, the total bank capital of the Nationalist Government was only just over Ch\$170 million, whereas the paid up capital of the more than one hundred purely private banks was about Ch\$150 million. If one includes the total capital of Ch\$77 848 881 of all the 1269 Chinese native banks and the total capital of Ch\$42 221 210 of the 35 basically privately-owned insurance companies in China, the total capital of the Chinese private financial sector amounted to about 160 per cent of the total capital of the four major banks. Only by relying on political privilege and the state's power to create credit did the four major banks succeed in occupying a relatively dominant position in China's banking and finance sector.

The assets of the four major banks were greater than those of the foreign banks, at least on the surface. The Japanese East Asian Research Institute estimated that total foreign investment in China's banking and financial sectors in 1936 amounted to US \$727 440 000. This figure refers to the total value of assets, that is the total banking and financial assets, including loans, negotiable notes, foreign exchange, real estate and cash. At 1936 exchange rates this equated to Ch\$2.5 billion. In the same year, the total assets of the four major banks were approximately Ch\$4.2 billion. Despite this, however, a large proportion of the assets of the four major banks was property held under trust and much of it was reserve deposits from private commercial banks. Hence many of the assets of the four major banks were only paper assets. For example, the assets of the Central Bank in 1935 included the money deposited by Chinese banks and native banks, amounting to Ch$176 063 992.03. On the other hand, the foreign commercial banks redeposited abroad a considerable proportion of Chinese deposits, the exact amount of which outsiders have no way to know. And those redeposits were usually not included in the assets of the foreign commercial banks in China.

The actual financial strength of the foreign commercial banks was far greater than their asset figures. For example, the volume of import and export trade in China before 1937 was approximately Ch$2 billion and about 80 per cent of the export and nearly 100 per cent of the import trade was run by foreign merchants. As another example, the British Hong Kong and Shanghai Banking Corporation in Shanghai was established with 160 000 shares, the denomination of each share being HK$125, but the market value of each share in Shanghai in 1931 was Ch$2300.[33] The market price of the shares was 16 to 17 times their face value. That was due to the substantial profits made by the Bank, for there was a dividend of £7–8 per share each year, and this situation remained unchanged until 1936. This fact alone can prove the financial strength of the foreign banks.

Therefore, the actual financial strength of the four major banks might not necessarily have been greater than that of the foreign commercial banks. Moreover, the imperialist governments were much more powerful than the backstage boss of the four major banks. In addition, with contradictions existing between directors representing the government shares and private shares respectively, the four major banks were not internally united, mainly because the Nationalist Government could not exert its absolute control over the Bank of China and the Bank of Communications before the Anti-Japanese War. When the Bank of China was reorganised with increased capital, the directors representing the private shares rejected the plan drawn by the Ministry of Finance, which stipulated that government capital should control 60 per cent of the bank capital, private capital only 40 per cent, and that there should be more directors representing the government than the private shareholders. Instead they stipulated that the government and private capital each should make up 50 per cent of the total capital of the bank, whose paid-in capital was Ch$40 million in all, and that the board should consist of 12 private directors and 9 government directors. The Bank of Communications followed suit except in that government capital accounted for 55 per cent of the total.[34] This situation lasted till 1937. It has been said that in 1937 Song Ziwen and Kong Xiangxi were in fact officials while acting as directors representing private shares but in fact there were also others, like Rong Zongjing and Qian Xinzhi, who were private businessmen acting as directors representing government shares.

The Central Bank failed to function as 'the bank of banks' and the Bank of China was in fact more important than the Central Bank. For example, the deposits and loans from financial interests to the Bank of China increased by Ch$90 million in 1935, while the Central Bank was compelled to make a huge deposit of Ch$176 063 992.03 in various banks in order to earn interest. Thus the financial strength of the four major banks was limited. Under intense competition from the foreign commercial banks and the domestic private financial community, therefore, it was impossible for the four major banks really to hold a monopoly position in China's financial community. As far as the actual resources were concerned, it was the foreign commercial banks that occupied the monopoly status.

All in all, the currency reform did not help Nationalist bureaucratic capital to gain a monopoly in China. It was in fact foreign capital that really held monopoly status in the entire Chinese economy.

Some experts mistakenly believe that the currency reform brought about the formation of bureaucratic monopoly capitalism, mainly because they regard the capital of the Four Great Families as a combination of banking and industrial capital, evidently influenced by Chen Boda's mechanical application of Lenin's concept of finance capital.[35] In fact, as Lenin said, monopoly takes place first in the realm of production rather than in that of finance. The concept of 'finance capital' does not suggest that finance has any specific role *vis-à-vis* industry; it merely points out that the interpenetration of bank capital and industrial capital will only occur on the premise of the concentration of production and under such specific circumstances as exist in imperialist countries.[36]

This can be proved by the histories of various countries in the world. Long before the formation of state monopoly capitalism, the main capitalist countries had their state banks, especially state or semi-state central banks, such as the Bank of England which, as Karl Marx pointed out in *Capital*, had the status of 'a semi-state institution'.[37] Another example is the Bank of Japan in which, as early as the end of the nineteenth century, over 50 per cent of the shares were owned by the government.

Moreover, the main capitalist countries began to adopt the system of unified issue of currency as early as the beginning of the nineteenth century. However, no scholars have come to the conclusion that state monopoly capitalism therefore emerged at that time in the West. This is because a unified currency is closely connected with the unification and consolidation of a country. So money is called 'a king without a crown' and banking is considered a special sort of enterprise. Its resources cannot be judged merely by the volume of its capital.

In fact, the formation of state monopoly capitalism in some capitalist countries and semi-colonial countries started with the governments directly controlling a few principal industrial sectors rather than with the so-called 'financial monopoly'. For instance, Mexico proclaimed laws on the 'nationalisation of railways' and the 'nationalisation of oil' in 1937 and 1938 respectively and took over many foreign enterprises. Therefore, we cannot, on any account, hold that the Nationalist Government constituted bureaucratic monopoly capital just because it controlled the four major banks. To be more practical, it was not so much financial monopoly as a kind of financial control.

In fact, after the currency reform, of the four major banks only the Bank of China played a vigorous role in industry. Apart from increasing its loans to industrial and communications enterprises, the Bank of China bought half the shares in the Nanyang Brothers' Tobacco Company for Ch$1 million in March 1937 and, taking advantage of their inability to pay back loans, temporarily took control of the administration of some textile mills. But these investments were of no consequence when compared with the industry of the whole country. Besides, up to the eve of the Anti-Japanese War in 1937, China did not have a real industrial stock market. Clearly, the capital of the four major banks had not been really combined with industrial capital, which means that they had not enabled bureaucratic capital to monopolise industry. Because currency reform did not bring about the formation of monopoly capital, bureaucratic capital in turn did not yet seriously oppress private capital.

Currency reform was beneficial not only to the development of the Nationalist Government's state capital but also to the development of enterprises run by national capital. For example, after the currency reform was carried out, with a bumper cotton harvest and a general increase in prices, the Rongs' cotton spinning and weaving enterprises transformed their deficits into surpluses. Within only one year, they moved from a deficit of Ch$1 271 510 in 1935 to a profit of Ch$3 084 990.[38] As far as the general situation of national industry in 1936 was concerned, production increased substantially. Taking July 1935 as 100, in June 1936 the production index of cotton yarn was 171.26, cigarettes 175.73, matches 263.76, cement 96.16, and wheat flour 76.87.[39] This can also be illustrated by many other examples. Needless to say, currency reform was but one of the causes which contributed to economic development in 1936.

To sum up, we cannot on any account regard the inflation and the formation of the monopoly capital of the Four Great Families as inevitable consequences of currency reform. These situations arose mainly because the Nationalist Government took advantage of the Anti-Japanese War in 1937 and they reached their peak in the Civil War soon after the victory over Japan. The fact that the Nationalist Government carried out currency reform does not suggest that its counter-revolutionary nature had completely or fundamentally changed: its main intention was to escape its own economic crisis. But objective results in history often transcend the subjective motive of the rulers. This is certainly not against the logic of history.

Notes

*In this article 'Ch$' refers to the standard silver dollar or to the managed *'fabi'* after 1935; '$' refers to the various dollars issued by local governments, whose nominal value was initially similar to the national dollar.

1. [Editor's note] Thomas G. Rawski, *Economic Growth in Prewar China* (Berkeley and Los Angeles, 1989), ch. 3 and Appendix C.
2. [Editor's note] This chapter is a translation of Ci Hongfei, 'Guanyu 1935 nian Guomindang zhengfu bizhi gaige de lishi houguo wenti bianxi', *Nankai jingji kexue* 1985.5 (October 1935): 28–35.
3. Wu Gang, *Jiu Zhongguo tonghuo pengzhang shiliao* (Shanghai, 1958), p. 2.
4. Qian Jiaju et al, *Zhongguo huobi fazhan jianshi he biaojie* (Beijing, 1982), p. 51.
5. Wu Gang, *Jiu Zhongguo tonghuo pengzhang*, p. 2.
6. Xiang Jinsheng, 'Zhongguo zhibi de xianzhuang', *Zhongguo jingji* 3.12 (December 1935).
7. Sichuan wenshi guan, *Sichuan junfa shiliao*, vol. 2 (Chengdu, 1983), p. 517.
8. Zhongguo renmin yinhang Yunnan sheng fenhang jinrong yanjiu shi, *Yunnan jindai huobi shi ziliao huibian*, vol. 1.
9. Zheng Jiadu, *Guangxi jin bai nian huobi shi* (Guangxi, 1981), p. 121.
10. Zhongguo kexue yuan lishi di san suo, *Zhongguo xiandai zhengzhi shi ziliao huibian*, 2nd collection, vol. 20.
11. Eduard Kann, 'Zhongguo zhi qianpiao', *Yinhang zhoubao*, 30.29 (July 1929).
12. 'Dongbei zhi huobi wenti', *Xin beifang yuekan* 1.5 (May 1931).
13. Zou Qipan, 'Xinjiang zhibi de zhengli', *Bianshi yanjiu* 9.6 (1939).
14. 'Guanyu Suiyuan Baotou zhibi faxing de sanze ziliao', *Zhonghang yuekan* 2.9–10.
15. Kann, 'Zhongguo zhi qianpiao'.
16. Dai Mingli, *Zhongguo huobi shi*, p. 162.
17. Arthur N. Young. *China's Nation-Building Effort, 1927–1937: The Financial and Economic Record* (Stanford, 1971), p. 165.
18. Dai Mingli, *Zhongguo huobi shi*, p. 158.

19. Karl Marx, *Capital*, vol. 1 (Harmondsworth, 1976), p. 194.
20. *Makesi Engesi quanji*, vol. 46, Part I (Beijing, 1979), p. 148.
21. Dai Mingli, *Zhongguo huobi shi*, p. 152.
22. Young, *China's Nation-Building Effort*, p. 198; the above estimates do not take into account the 147 442 329 'Chuanyang' minted by the Nationalist government up to 1937.
23. Ma Yinchu, *Zhongguo zhi xin jinrong zhengce* (Shanghai, 1936), p. 63.
24. The China & South Sea Bank, The National Industrial Bank of China, The Ningpo Commercial and Saving Bank, The Commercial Bank of China, The National Commercial Bank, The Reclamation Bank of China, the Central Bank of China, Bank of Agriculture and Commerce, Bank of Zhili, Dazhong Bank, Bianye Bank, The Agricultural and Industrial Bank of China, The Zhejiang Provincial Bank, together with the Bank of China, The Central Bank of China, The Bank of Communications and The Farmers Bank of China.
25. 'Guomindang zhengfu de fabi zhengce', *Lishi dang'an*, 1982.1 (February 1982): 66.
26. Xiang Jinsheng, 'Zhongguo zhibi de xianzhuang'.
27. Xian Ke, *Jin bai nian lai diguozhuyi zai-Hua yinhang faxing zhibi gaikuang* (Shanghai, 1958), p. 36.
28. Ma Yinchu, *Zhongguo zhi xin jinrong zhengce*, p. 63.
29. Zhongguo renmin yinhang zonghang, *Jindai Zhongguo jinrong shi gao*.
30. *Guomin jingji yuekan* 1.1 (1937): appendix, tables.
31. Zhongguo renmin daxue zhengzhi jingjixue xi, *Zhongguo jindai jingji shi* (Beijing, 1978), vol. 2, pp. 29–31.
32. *Quanguo yinhang nianjian, 1937*, Zhongguo yinhang jingji yanjiu shi (Shanghai, 1937).
33. C. F. Remer, *Foreign Investments in China* (New York, 1968), p. 400.
34. See documents in *Zhongguo xiandai zhengzhi shi ziliao huibian*.
35. This view is still held by some experts. See 'Si da jiazu guanliao ziben' in *Xue dian Minguo shi*, Renmin ribao lilun bu (Beijing, 1984), pp. 250–7.
36. See V. I. Lenin, *Imperialism, the Highest Stage of Capitalism* (Beijing, 1970), pp. 44–5.
37. Karl Marx, *Capital*, vol. 3 (Harmondsworth, 1981), p. 675.
38. *Rong jia qiye shiliao*, Shanghai shehui kexue yuan, jingji yanjiu suo, comp, 2 vols (Shanghai, 1980), p. 644.
39. Shiyebu, tongji chu, *Minguo ershiwu nian quanguo shiye gaikuang* (Nanjing, 1937), p. 59.

Index